Elegant Glassware
of the
Depression Era

EIGHTH EDITION

IDENTIFICATION AND VALUE GUIDE

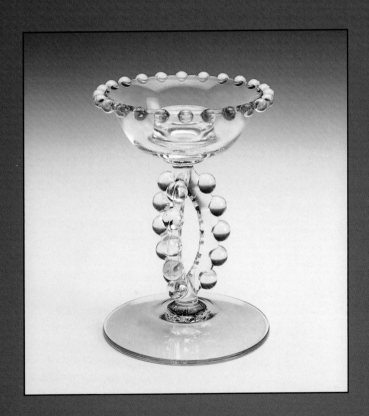

Gene Florence

The current values in this book should be used only as a guide. They are not intended to set prices, which vary from one section of the country to another. Auction prices as well as dealer prices vary greatly and are affected by condition as well as demand. Neither the Author nor the Publisher assumes responsibility for any losses that might be incurred as a result of consulting this guide.

Searching For A Publisher?

We are always looking for knowledgeable people considered to be experts within their fields. If you feel that there is a real need for a book on your collectible subject and have a large, comprehensive collection, contact Collector Books.

On the Cover

Front:
Heisey, Gascony, tangerine decanter, $4,000.00.
Cambridge, Elaine, goblet, $150.00.
Candlewick amethyst, footed pitcher, $1,000.00.

Back:
Cambridge, Portia, gold encrusted ruby high sherbet, $150.00.
Cambridge, Everglade, double candle, $175.00.

Title page:
Imperial, Candlewick candleholder, 400/264, $125.00.

Cover design by Beth Summers
Book design by Beth Ray

COLLECTOR BOOKS
P.O. Box 3009
Paducah, KY 42002-3009

Gene Florence

P.O. Box 22186   P.O. Box 64
Lexington, KY 40522   Astatula, FL 34705

ABOUT THE AUTHOR

Gene M. Florence, Jr., a native Kentuckian, graduated from the University of Kentucky in 1967. He held a double major in mathematics and English which he immediately put to use in industry and subsequently, in teaching junior and senior high school. He taught one year at the Lincoln Institute for gifted, but disadvantaged, students — a wonderful teaching experience, but a 160 mile daily commute!

A collector since childhood, Mr. Florence progressed from baseball cards, comic books, coins, and bottles to glassware. His buying and selling glassware "hobby" began to usurp his nine-year teaching career. During a teaching hiatus in the summer of 1972, he wrote a book on Depression glassware that was well received by collectors in the field, ultimately persuading him to leave teaching and pursue the glass business full time. This freed him to travel to glass shows throughout the country, where he diligently studied both the glass being marketed and the prices the ware commanded. This, also, allowed him to devote more time to research on glass.

Books written by Mr. Florence include the following titles: *The Collector's Encyclopedia of Depression Glass, Stemware Identification, The Collector's Encyclopedia of Akro Agate, The Pocket Guide to Depression Glass, Kitchen Glassware of the Depression Years, Collectible Glassware from the 40s, 50s, 60s..., Standard Baseball Card Price Guide,* and six editions of *Very Rare Glassware of the Depression Years.* He has also written five volumes of *The Collector's Encyclopedia of Occupied Japan* and a book on Degenhart Glassware for that museum. His most recent books are *Anchor Hocking's Fire-King and More* and *Glassware Pattern Identification Guide.* Mr. Florence has now authored 66 books on collectibles.

FOREWORD

"Elegant" glassware, as defined in this book, refers to the handmade and acid etched glassware that was sold by department and jewelry stores during the Depression era through the 1950s, differentiating it from the dime store and give-away glass that has become known as Depression glass. The word "Elegant" has become "official" nomenclature among today's dealers for designating handmade glassware.

The evolution of collecting "Elegant" glassware has been extraordinary and many dealers who would not dare stock that crystal glass a few years ago are buying as much "Elegant" as basic Depression glass today. Glass shows used to be inventoried with 15% to 20% "Elegant" glass, but now there is more than 50% at many shows.

I hope you enjoy this book, and I hope you will feel my years of endeavoring to furnish you the best books possible on "Elegant" glassware were well spent.

PRICING

All prices in this book are retail for mint condition glassware. This book is only intended as **a guide to prices**. There remains a regional price difference that cannot adequately be dealt with herein.

You may expect dealers to pay approximately 30 to 60 percent less than the prices listed if selling to them. My personal knowledge of prices comes from my experience of buying and selling glass for 30 years and from traveling to and selling at shows in various parts of the United States. I am working even harder at markets and shows to remain in contact with the ever-changing prices since the closing of my Grannie Bear Antique Shop. You can also find me on the always changing Internet at http://www.geneflorence.com. I readily admit that I solicit price information from persons known to be experts in these various fields to provide you with the latest, most accurate pricing information possible. However, final pricing judgments are mine!

MEASUREMENTS AND TERMS

All measurements and terms in this book are from factory catalogs or actual measurements from the piece. It has been my experience that actual measurements vary slightly from those listed in most factory catalogs; so do not get unduly concerned over slight variations. For example, Fostoria always measured plates to the nearest inch, but I have found that most Fostoria plates are never exact inches in measurement.

ACKNOWLEDGMENTS

Photography sessions for this book were spread over a two-year period with one session lasting longer than a week. A special note of appreciation is due Dick and Pat Spencer for lending their glass, gathering up other collector's treasures to transport, working at the photography sessions, and rendering their information and pricing help on Heisey patterns in this book.

There are numerous people behind the scenes in the production of this book! Some lent glass, some, their time; others lent their talents and expertise. These people somehow have remained friends even after exhausting hours of packing, unpacking, arranging, sorting, and repacking glass! Some traveled hundreds of miles to bring their valuable glass to share with you. Others spent hours discussing and listing their prices, often late at night after long show hours. Without these unbelievable people, this book would not be a reality. Those special people include Dan Tucker and Lorrie Kitchen, Charles Larson, Gary and Sue Clark, Bill and Lottie Porter, Quinten Keech, Leroy and Susan Allen, Jane White, Lisa Stroup, Della Maze, Beth Summers, Zibby Walker, and numerous unnamed readers from throughout the U.S. and Canada who shared pictures and information about their collections and findings. Richard Walker and Charley Lynch did all the photography for this book. (Richard and Zibby travel from New York each October to "enjoy" long studio hours, ending after dark!)

Family provides the single most important assistance in my work. Charles, Cathy's dad, helped sort glass, cart boxes, and redesigned more shelves for storage, while Sibyl, her mom, spent days helping Cathy sort glass into various patterns and boxes. Chad and Marc have both helped loading and unloading van loads of glass for each photography session. Marc attended to shipping book orders and managing my web page.

Cathy has worked even harder than normal on my new books this last year. With blood sugar and other old age problems attacking me head on last summer, she jumped in even deeper than ever, dragging out of bed at three in the morning (no easy task for a night owl) to travel with me to several "shop by flashlight" antique shows and flea markets when my body was facing some major energy dilemmas. She has always worked long hours as chief editor, critic, and proofreader. (Her job is to transform words and paragraphs so you are able to decipher what I thought I said in the first place!) This particular book has been accomplished via e-mail and long conversations by phone late at night, because she spent the entire writing time in Kentucky helping Chad and Rebecca move, and paint and fix up their two houses, their new as well as their old one for the market!

Thanks, also, to Beth Ray of Collector Books for transcribing all my Microsoft words into Quark and my scribbled prices into existence! I understand she's handling even more books than I am in this time frame!

Thanks to you readers whose generous response to my books have made this career possible. Too, many pieces have been added to lists over the years via your efforts, and collectors as a whole have benefited. If you are one of those who have sent a postcard with prices or shared your expertise, give yourself a well deserved pat on the back!

CONTENTS

CONTENTS BY COMPANY

Colors: crystal; some amber, blue, green, yellow, pink tinting to purple in late 1920s; white, red in 1980s; and being newly made in red and crystal for Lancaster Colony by Dalzell Viking.

If Fostoria American calls to you as a collector, then by all means buy it for yourself! I've always believed you never go wrong by buying what gives your spirit a lift when you look at it! However, from an investment standpoint you need to know that Fostoria American, manufactured for years and adored by collectors for decades, has begun to pall with collectors of late. The reason, of course, is due to its continuing manufacture by Lancaster Colony who bought out Fostoria. None of the current American or look-alike American pieces are marked in any way. Recently made American can be found in all the Fostoria outlet stores throughout the Midwest. I have not seen these outlet stores in the South, but they may have escaped my eye. American pieces currently being remade or pieces that have been fabricated in recent years are marked with an asterisk (*) in the price listing. Even before the closing of the original Fostoria factory in 1986, Lancaster Colony marketed its "Whitehall" glassware line that is similar to American, and made by Indiana Glass at Dunkirk, Indiana. Often I have seen the red trimmed or plain "Whitehall" punch set being passed off as American. The punch cups to this set are footed and are not the same clarity as American.

You will find an abundance of "Whitehall" in colors of pink, avocado green, and several shades of blue. Peruse the glassware section of your local discount store for new colors and items being made. Numerous specialty catalogs insinuate this colored glassware to be Depression glass. "Whitehall's" pink colored ware is commonly confused by novice collectors with Jeannette's Depression era Cube pattern. There is no footed pitcher or tumbler in Cube.

Red is still being sold at the Fostoria outlet stores in an abundance of pieces. American was never made in red until the 1980s and then it was made by Viking Glass for Fostoria. Dalzell Viking has now taken over the manufacturing of red for Lancaster Colony. Other colored pieces of older American are still in demand.

The major price adjustments in American pieces concern those being found in England which I mentioned last time. Many of those pieces are selling for less than half of their former prices. You will still find some dealers pricing these items quite high; but if you shop around, you'll probably find a better price! British antique dealers have become cognizant of our glass collecting proclivities. Those formerly hard-to-find Fostoria American pieces (from England) are no longer hard to find here — since so many have been shipped back! Dealers who had been asking elevated prices for these items, especially the wash bowl and pitcher sets, have been slowly setting their sights a little lower. My opinion is that the collectors willing to spend thousands of dollars to get these sets, already possess them. Once glass items reach prices in the four digit area, modest collectors willingly do without!

That blue dresser set pictured on page 9 was bought from the granddaughter of the original owner. This set entered the market due to a divorce and not a death as is often the case. I might also point out the banana split pictured on the bottom right on that page. It was found in the Houston area a couple of years ago. Rarely found glass can turn up almost anywhere.

Reissued cookie jars continue to pose a problem for collectors! A majority of the new issues have wavy lines in the pattern itself and crooked knobs on the top. Old cookie jars do not. (A telling point that works 80% of the time is to try to turn the lid around while it rests inside the cookie jar. The new lids seem to hang up and stop somewhere along the inside making the whole cookie jar turn. The old jars will allow you to turn the lid completely around without catching on the sides!) That old axiom "let the buyer beware" continues to follow Fostoria American!

	*Crystal			*Crystal
Appetizer, tray, 10½", w/6 inserts	250.00		Bowl, finger, 4½" diam., smooth edge	40.00
Appetizer, insert, 3¼"	30.00		Bowl, 3½", rose	20.00
Ash tray, 2⅞", sq.	7.50		Bowl, 3¾", almond, oval	18.00
Ash tray, 3⅞", oval	9.00		Bowl, 4¼", jelly, 4¼" h.	15.00
Ash tray, 5", sq.	42.50	*	Bowl, 4½", 1 hdld.	10.00
Ash tray, 5½", oval	20.00		Bowl, 4½", 1 hdld., sq.	11.00
Basket, w/reed handle, 7" x 9"	95.00		Bowl, 4½", jelly, w/cover, 6¾" h.	25.00
Basket, 10", new in 1988	35.00	*	Bowl, 4½", nappy	12.00
Bell	395.00		Bowl, 4½", oval	15.00
Bottle, bitters, w/tube, 5¾", 4½ oz.	72.50		Bowl, 4¾", fruit, flared	15.00
Bottle, condiment/ketchup w/stopper	135.00		Bowl, 5", cream soup, 2 hdld.	45.00
Bottle, cologne, w/stopper, 6 oz., 5¾"	72.50		Bowl, 5", 1 hdld., tri-corner	12.00
Bottle, cologne, w/stopper, 7¼", 8 oz.	80.00	*	Bowl, 5", nappy	10.00
Bottle, cordial, w/stopper, 7¼", 9 oz.	90.00		Bowl, 5", nappy, w/cover	30.00
Bottle, water, 44 oz., 9¼"	595.00		Bowl, 5", rose	25.00
Bowl, banana split, 9" x 3½"	395.00		Bowl, 5½", lemon, w/cover	45.00

	*Crystal
Bowl, 5½", preserve, 2 hdld., w/cover .	90.00
Bowl, 6", bonbon, 3 ftd......................	15.00
* Bowl, 6", nappy	15.00
Bowl, 6", olive, oblong	12.00
Bowl, 6½", wedding,	
w/cover, sq., ped.ft., 8" h.	100.00
Bowl, 6½", wedding, sq., ped. ft., 5¼" h.	60.00
Bowl, 7", bonbon, 3 ftd......................	12.50
Bowl, 7", cupped, 4½" h......................	55.00
* Bowl, 7", nappy	25.00
Bowl, 8", bonbon, 3 ftd......................	17.50
Bowl, 8", deep...................................	60.00
Bowl, 8", ftd.....................................	60.00
Bowl, 8", ftd., 2 hdld., "trophy" cup ...	120.00
* Bowl, 8", nappy	22.00
* Bowl, 8", pickle, oblong	13.00
Bowl, 8½", 2 hdld.............................	45.00
* Bowl, 8½", boat..............................	16.00
Bowl, 9", boat, 2 pt.	12.50
* Bowl, 9", oval veg.	25.00
Bowl, 9½", centerpiece......................	42.50
Bowl, 9½", 3 pt., 6" w.	37.50
Bowl, 10", celery, oblong....................	20.00
* Bowl, 10", deep...............................	35.00
Bowl, 10", float	45.00
Bowl, 10", oval, float	32.50
Bowl, 10", oval, veg., 2 pt.	35.00
Bowl, 10½", fruit, 3 ftd......................	40.00
Bowl, 11", centerpiece.......................	40.00
Bowl, 11", centerpiece, tri-corner	45.00
Bowl, 11", relish/celery, 3 pt.............	30.00
Bowl, 11½", float	55.00
Bowl, 11½", fruit, rolled edge, 2¾" h. .	42.50
Bowl, 11½", oval, float	45.00
Bowl, 11½", rolled edge	45.00
Bowl, 11¾", oval, deep......................	42.50
Bowl, 12", boat.................................	17.50
* Bowl, 12", fruit/sm. punch, ped. ft.,	
(Tom & Jerry)	175.00
Bowl, 12", lily pond	65.00
Bowl, 12", relish "boat," 2 pt.	20.00
Bowl, 13", fruit, shallow	65.00
Bowl, 14", punch, w/high ft. base (2 gal.).	275.00
Bowl, 14", punch, w/low ft. base........	250.00
Bowl, 15", centerpiece, "hat" shape	175.00
Bowl, 16", flat, fruit, ped. ft.	185.00
Bowl, 18", punch, w/low ft. base (3¾ gal.).	350.00
Box, pomade, 2" square......................	275.00
* Box, w/cover, puff, 3⅛" x 2¾"	185.00
Box, w/cover, 4½" x 4½"...................	185.00
Box, w/cover, handkerchief, 5⅝" x 4⅝".	265.00
Box, w/cover, hairpin, 3½" x 1¾"	295.00
Box, w/cover, jewel, 5¼" x 2¼"	295.00
Box, w/cover, jewel, 2 drawer, 4¼" x 3¼" .	2,500.00
* Box, w/cover, glove, 9½" x 3½"...........	275.00
* Butter, w/cover, rnd. plate, 7¼"	120.00

	*Crystal
* Butter, w/cover, ¼ lb.	25.00
Cake stand, (see salver)	
Candelabrum, 6½", 2-lite, bell base	
w/bobeche & prisms......................	115.00
Candle lamp, 8½", w/chimney, candle	
part, 3½"	135.00
Candlestick, twin, 4⅛" h., 8½" spread.	60.00
Candlestick, 2", chamber with finger-	
hold	45.00
* Candlestick, 3", rnd. ft......................	15.00
Candlestick, 4⅜", 2-lite, rnd. ft.	35.00
Candlestick, 6", octagon ft.	25.00
Candlestick, 6½", 2-lite, bell base........	100.00
Candlestick, 6¼", round ft.	175.00
* Candlestick, 7", sq. column................	100.00
Candlestick, 7¼", "Eiffel" tower	135.00
Candy box, w/cover, 3 pt., triangular ..	85.00
Candy, w/cover, ped. ft.	37.50
Cheese (5¾" compote) & cracker	
(11½" plate)	60.00
Cigarette box, w/cover, 4¾"	37.50
Coaster, 3¾"	9.00
Comport, 4½", jelly............................	15.00
* Comport, 5", jelly, flared	15.00
* Comport, 6¾", jelly, w/cover	35.00
Comport, 8½", 4" high	45.00
Comport, 9½", 5¼" high......................	65.00
Comport, w/cover, 5"...........................	25.00
* Cookie jar, w/cover, 8⅞" h.	275.00
Creamer, tea, 3 oz., 2⅜" (#2056½)........	9.00
Creamer, individual, 4¾ oz.................	9.00
Creamer, 9½ oz.	12.50
Crushed fruit, w/cover & spoon, 10" ...	1,500.00
Cup, flat	7.50
Cup, ftd., 7 oz.	8.00
Cup, punch, flared rim........................	11.00
Cup, punch, straight edge	10.00
Decanter, w/stopper, 24 oz., 9¼" h.	105.00
Dresser set: powder boxes w/covers	
& tray	425.00
Flower pot, w/perforated cover, 9½"	
diam.; 5½" h.	1,500.00
Goblet, #2056, 2½ oz., wine, hex ft.,	
4⅜" h..	12.00
Goblet, #2056, 4½ oz., oyster cocktail,	
3½" h.	17.50
Goblet, #2056, 4½ oz., sherbet, flared,	
4⅜" h.	9.00
Goblet, #2056, 4½ oz., fruit, hex ft.,	
4¾" h.	9.00
Goblet, #2056, 5 oz., low ft., sherbet,	
flared, 3¼" h.	9.00
Goblet, #2056, 6 oz., low ft., sundae,	
3⅛" h..	9.00
Goblet, #2056, 7 oz., claret, 4⅞" h.	55.00
* Goblet, #2056, 9 oz., low ft., 4⅜" h......	11.00

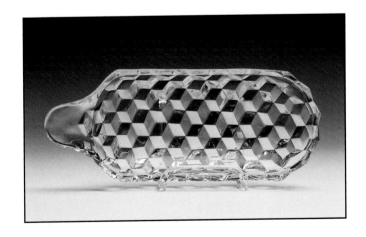

AMERICAN

	*Crystal
Goblet, #2056, 10 oz., hex ft., water, 6⅞" h.	13.00
Goblet, #2056, 12 oz., low ft., tea, 5¾" h..	14.00
Goblet, #2056½, 4½ oz., sherbet, 4½" h. ..	10.00
Goblet, #2056½, 5 oz., low sherbet, 3½" h.	10.00
Goblet, #5056, 1 oz., cordial, 3⅛", w/plain bowl	30.00
Goblet, #5056, 3½ oz., claret, 4⅝", w/plain bowl	13.50
Goblet, #5056, 3½ oz., cocktail, 4", w/plain bowl	11.00
Goblet, #5056, 4 oz., oyster cocktail, 3½", w/plain bowl	10.00
Goblet, #5056, 5½ oz., sherbet, 4⅛", w/plain bowl	10.00
Goblet, #5056, 10 oz., water, 6⅛", w/plain bowl	12.00
Hair receiver, 3" x 3"	300.00
Hat, 2⅛", (sm. ash tray)	16.00
Hat, 3" tall	27.50
Hat, 4" tall	50.00
Hat, western style	295.00
Hotel washbowl and pitcher	3,500.00
Hurricane lamp, 12" complete	175.00
Hurricane lamp base	55.00
Ice bucket, w/tongs	60.00
Ice cream saucer (2 styles)	55.00
Ice dish for 4 oz. crab or 5 oz. tomato liner	32.50
Ice dish insert	10.00
Ice tub, w/liner, 5⅝"	90.00
Ice tub, w/liner, 6½"	95.00
Jam pot, w/cover	60.00
Jar, pickle, w/pointed cover, 6" h.	325.00
Marmalade, w/cover & chrome spoon...	50.00
* Mayonnaise, div.	15.00
Mayonnaise, w/ladle, ped. ft.	50.00
Mayonnaise, w/liner & ladle	32.50
Molasses can, 11 oz., 6¾" h., 1 hdld....	375.00
* Mug, 5½ oz., "Tom & Jerry," 3¼" h.	40.00
* Mug, 12 oz., beer, 4½" h.	65.00
Mustard, w/cover	30.00
Napkin ring	12.50
Oil, 5 oz.	35.00
Oil, 7 oz.	35.00
Picture frame	15.00
Pitcher, ½ gal. w/ice lip, 8¼", flat bottom .	85.00
Pitcher, ½ gal., w/o ice lip	275.00
Pitcher, ½ gal., 8", ftd.	70.00
Pitcher, 1 pt., 5⅜", flat	27.50
Pitcher, 2 pt., 7¼", ftd.	65.00
Pitcher, 3 pt., 8", ftd.	70.00
Pitcher, 3 pt., w/ice lip, 6½", ftd., "fat"...	60.00
* Pitcher, 1 qt., flat	30.00

	*Crystal
Plate, cream soup liner	12.00
Plate, 6", bread & butter	12.00
Plate, 7", salad	10.00
Plate, 7½" x 4⅜", crescent salad	47.50
Plate, 8", sauce liner, oval	25.00
Plate, 8½", salad	12.00
Plate, 9", sandwich (sm. center)	14.00
Plate, 9½", dinner	22.50
Plate, 10", cake, 2 hdld.	27.50
Plate, 10½", sandwich (sm. center)	20.00
Plate, 11½", sandwich (sm. center)	20.00
Plate, 12", cake, 3 ftd.	25.00
Plate, 13½", oval torte	45.00
Plate, 14", torte	55.00
Plate, 18", torte	125.00
Plate, 20", torte	165.00
Plate 24", torte	225.00
* Platter, 10½", oval	40.00
Platter, 12", oval	55.00
Ring holder	200.00
Salad set: 10" bowl, 14" torte, wood fork & spoon	67.50
Salt, individual	9.00
Salver, 10", sq., ped. ft. (cake stand)	125.00
Salver, 10", rnd., ped. ft. (cake stand)...	100.00
* Salver, 11", rnd., ped. ft. (cake stand)..	30.00
Sauce boat & liner	50.00
Saucer	3.00
Set: 2 jam pots w/tray	145.00
Set: decanter, 6 – 2 oz. whiskeys on 10½" tray	215.00
Set: toddler, w/baby tumbler & bowl...	90.00
Set: youth, w/bowl, hdld. mug, 6" plate.	90.00
Set: condiment, 2 oils, 2 shakers, mustard w/cover & spoon w/tray ..	295.00
Shaker, 3", ea.	10.00
* Shaker, 3½", ea.	7.00
Shaker, 3¼", ea.	10.00
Shakers w/tray, individual, 2"	22.00
Sherbet, handled, 3½" high, 4½ oz.	85.00
Shrimp bowl, 12¼"	355.00
Spooner, 3¾"	35.00
**Strawholder, 10", w/cover	235.00
Sugar, tea, 2¼" (#2056½)	13.00
Sugar, hdld., 3¼" h.	12.00
Sugar shaker	55.00
Sugar, w/o cover	10.00
Sugar, w/cover, no hdl., 6¼" (cover fits strawholder)	60.00
Sugar, w/cover, 2 hdld.	20.00
Syrup, 6½ oz., #2056½, Sani-cut server .	80.00
Syrup, 6 oz., non pour screw top, 5¼" h..	225.00
Syrup, 10 oz., w/glass cover & 6" liner plate	155.00
Syrup, w/drip proof top	35.00

** Bottom only

	*Crystal
Toothpick	25.00
Tray, cloverleaf for condiment set	165.00
Tray, tid bit, w/question mark metal handle	40.00
Tray, 5" x 2½", rect.	80.00
Tray, 6" oval, hdld.	35.00
Tray, pin, oval, 5½" x 4½"	130.00
Tray, 6½" x 9" relish, 4 part	45.00
Tray, 9½", service, 2 hdld.	35.00
Tray, 10", muffin (2 upturned sides)	30.00
Tray, 10", square, 4 part	85.00
Tray, 10", square	115.00
Tray, 10½", cake, w/question mark metal hdl.	32.00
Tray, 10½" x 7½", rect.	70.00
Tray, 10½" x 5", oval hdld.	45.00
Tray, 10¾", square, 4 part	130.00
Tray, 12", sand. w/ctr. handle	35.00
Tray, 12", round	140.00
Tray, 13½", oval, ice cream	165.00
Tray for sugar & creamer, tab. hdld., 6¾".	12.00
Tumbler, hdld. iced tea	250.00
Tumbler, #2056, 2 oz., whiskey, 2½" h..	11.00
Tumbler, #2056, 3 oz., ftd. cone, cocktail, 2⅞" h.	14.00
Tumbler, #2056, 5 oz., ftd., juice, 4¾".	12.00
Tumbler, #2056, 6 oz., flat, old-fashioned, 3⅜" h.	14.00
Tumbler, #2056, 8 oz. flat, water, flared, 4⅛" h.	14.00
* Tumbler, #2056, 9 oz. ftd., water, 4⅞" h..	14.00
Tumbler, #2056, 12 oz., flat, tea, flared, 5¼" h.	16.00

	*Crystal
Tumbler, #2056½, 5 oz., straight side, juice	12.00
Tumbler, #2056½, 8 oz., straight side, water, 3⅞" h	12.00
Tumbler, #2056½, 12 oz., straight side, tea, 5" h.	17.50
Tumbler, #5056, 5 oz., ftd., juice, 4⅛" w/plain bowl	12.00
Tumbler, #5056, 12 oz., ftd., tea, 5½" w/plain bowl	12.00
Urn, 6", sq., ped. ft	30.00
Urn, 7½", sq. ped. ft.	35.00
Vase, 4½", sweet pea	75.00
Vase, 6", bud, ftd.	18.00
* Vase, 6", bud, flared	18.00
Vase, 6", straight side	35.00
Vase, 6½", flared rim	15.00
Vase, 7", flared	75.00
* Vase, 8", straight side	40.00
* Vase, 8", flared	80.00
Vase, 8", porch, 5" diam.	395.00
Vase, 8½", bud, flared	25.00
Vase, 8½", bud, cupped	25.00
Vase, 9", w/sq. ped. ft.	45.00
Vase, 9½", flared	125.00
Vase, 10", cupped in top	195.00
Vase, 10", porch, 8" diam.	395.00
* Vase, 10", straight side	90.00
Vase, 10", swung	200.00
Vase, 10", flared	90.00
Vase, 12", straight side	145.00
Vase, 12", swung	200.00
Vase, 14", swung	235.00
Vase, 20", swung	365.00

Colors: amber, blue, crystal, light and dark green, Heatherbloom, pink, yellow

Yellow and crystal are the easiest Apple Blossom sets to gather. You will have to search much harder for other colors, but it will be worth the work! A setting for eight of Heatherbloom Apple Blossom was offered at the February show in Houston.

Few pitchers and even fewer butter dishes are seen in any color other than yellow or crystal. Several collections of yellow were brought onto the market all at once a few years ago. Recently, financial considerations have been significant motivation for relinquishing collections, to be relinquished and have caused assembled elegant glass sets to return to the collecting world. In marketing terms, collectors have been profit taking!

Apple Blossom is found on several Cambridge stemware lines, but the #3130 line is most often seen. Serving pieces, dinner plates, and unusual items are elusive in any color; buy them when you have the chance!

	Crystal	Yellow Amber	Pink *Green
Ash tray, 6", heavy	50.00	125.00	
Bowl, #3025, ftd., finger, w/plate	25.00	40.00	45.00
Bowl, #3130, finger, w/plate	30.00	40.00	45.00
Bowl, 3", indiv. nut, 4 ftd	50.00	65.00	70.00
Bowl, 5¼", 2 hdld., bonbon	12.50	25.00	25.00
Bowl, 5½", 2 hdld., bonbon	12.50	25.00	25.00
Bowl, 5½", fruit "saucer"	10.00	18.00	20.00
Bowl, 6", 2 hdld., "basket" (sides up)	20.00	30.00	35.00
Bowl, 6", cereal	18.00	28.00	32.00
Bowl, 9", pickle	17.00	35.00	40.00
Bowl, 10", 2 hdld.	35.00	70.00	85.00
Bowl, 10", baker	35.00	70.00	85.00
Bowl, 11", fruit, tab hdld.	35.00	75.00	80.00
Bowl, 11", low ftd.	30.00	75.00	90.00
Bowl, 12", relish, 4 pt.	30.00	50.00	65.00
Bowl, 12", 4 ftd.	40.00	70.00	85.00
Bowl, 12", flat	35.00	60.00	65.00
Bowl, 12", oval, 4 ftd.	40.00	60.00	85.00
Bowl, 12½", console	35.00	50.00	55.00
Bowl, 13"	35.00	60.00	65.00
Bowl, cream soup, w/liner plate	20.00	35.00	45.00
Butter w/cover, 5½"	125.00	250.00	395.00
Candelabrum, 3-lite, keyhole	27.50	45.00	55.00
Candlestick, 1-lite, keyhole	17.50	25.00	27.50
Candlestick, 2-lite, keyhole	22.50	32.50	37.50
Candy box w/cover, 4 ftd. "bowl"	70.00	90.00	130.00
Cheese (compote) & cracker (11½" plate)	40.00	65.00	85.00
Comport, 4", fruit cocktail	12.50	20.00	25.00
Comport, 7", tall	35.00	60.00	80.00
Creamer, ftd.	12.50	17.50	22.50
Creamer, tall ftd.	12.50	20.00	25.00
Cup	15.00	22.00	26.00
Cup, A.D.	40.00	50.00	85.00
Fruit/oyster cocktail, #3025, 4½ oz.	12.50	18.00	22.00
Mayonnaise, w/liner & ladle (4 ftd. bowl)	35.00	55.00	70.00
Pitcher, 50 oz., ftd., flattened sides	125.00	210.00	275.00
Pitcher, 64 oz., #3130	135.00	250.00	300.00
Pitcher, 64 oz., #3025	135.00	250.00	300.00
Pitcher, 67 oz., squeezed middle, loop hdld.	135.00	275.00	325.00
Pitcher, 76 oz.	145.00	250.00	325.00
Pitcher, 80 oz., ball	130.00	175.00	300.00
Pitcher w/cover, 76 oz., ftd., #3135	195.00	375.00	495.00
Plate, 6", bread/butter	6.00	7.00	8.00
Plate, 6", sq., 2 hdld.	8.00	9.00	10.00
Plate, 7½", tea	9.00	12.00	13.00

* Blue prices 25% to 30% more.

	Crystal	Yellow Amber	Pink *Green
Plate, 8½"	14.00	20.00	22.00
Plate, 9½", dinner	45.00	65.00	77.50
Plate, 10", grill	25.00	45.00	55.00
Plate, sandwich, 11½", tab hdld.	22.00	32.50	35.00
Plate, sandwich, 12½", 2 hdld.	25.00	37.50	40.00
Plate, sq., bread/butter	5.00	7.00	8.00
Plate, sq., dinner	45.00	65.00	75.00
Plate, sq., salad	10.00	12.00	13.00
Plate, sq., service	17.50	20.00	22.00
Platter, 11½	37.50	65.00	95.00
Platter, 13½" rect., w/tab handle	40.00	90.00	125.00
Salt & pepper, pr.	37.50	75.00	95.00
Saucer	4.00	5.00	5.00
Saucer, A.D.	12.00	15.00	17.50
Stem, #1066, parfait	65.00	100.00	150.00
Stem, #3025, 7 oz., low fancy ft., sherbet	11.00	15.00	16.00
Stem, #3025, 7 oz., high sherbet	12.00	18.00	20.00
Stem, #3025, 10 oz.	18.00	22.00	25.00
Stem, #3130, 1 oz., cordial	60.00	100.00	155.00
Stem, #3130, 3 oz., cocktail	15.00	24.00	27.50
Stem, #3130, 6 oz., low sherbet	10.00	15.00	16.00
Stem, #3130, 6 oz., tall sherbet	10.00	18.00	20.00
Stem, #3130, 8 oz., water	15.00	25.00	32.50
Stem, #3135, 3 oz., cocktail	13.00	24.00	27.50
Stem, #3135, 6 oz., low sherbet	10.00	15.00	16.00
Stem, #3135, 6 oz., tall sherbet	10.00	18.00	20.00
Stem, #3135, 8 oz., water	14.00	22.00	30.00
Stem, #3400, 6 oz., ftd., sherbet	9.00	15.00	16.00
Stem, #3400, 9 oz., water	12.50	22.00	30.00
Sugar, ftd.	12.00	16.00	20.00
Sugar, tall ftd.	12.00	18.00	22.50
Tray, 7", hdld. relish	15.00	25.00	30.00
Tray, 11", ctr. hdld. sand.	25.00	40.00	47.50
Tumbler, #3025, 4 oz.	12.00	18.00	20.00
Tumbler, #3025, 10 oz.	15.00	22.00	24.00
Tumbler, #3025, 12 oz.	18.00	32.50	40.00
Tumbler, #3130, 5 oz., ftd.	11.00	22.00	28.00
Tumbler, #3130, 8 oz., ftd.	12.00	25.00	27.50
Tumbler, #3130, 10 oz., ftd.	13.00	25.00	27.50
Tumbler, #3130, 12 oz., ftd.	17.50	35.00	42.50
Tumbler, #3135, 5 oz., ftd.	10.00	22.00	28.00
Tumbler, #3135, 8 oz., ftd.	12.00	25.00	27.50
Tumbler, #3135, 10 oz., ftd.	13.00	25.00	27.50
Tumbler, #3135, 12 oz., ftd.	17.50	35.00	42.50
Tumbler, #3400, 2½ oz., ftd.	20.00	50.00	65.00
Tumbler, #3400, 9 oz., ftd.	12.00	25.00	27.50
Tumbler, #3400, 12 oz., ftd.	17.50	35.00	42.50
Tumbler, 12 oz., flat (2 styles) – 1 mid indent to match 67 oz. pitcher	20.00	35.00	40.00
Tumbler, 6"	15.00	30.00	35.00
Vase, 5"	25.00	45.00	50.00
Vase, 6", rippled sides	30.00	80.00	95.00
Vase, 8", 2 styles	40.00	90.00	125.00
Vase, 12", keyhole base w/neck indent	45.00	150.00	225.00

* Blue prices 25% to 30% more.

Note: See pages 228 – 229 for stem identification. 14

Colors: crystal, Azure blue, Topaz yellow, amber, green, pink, red, cobalt blue, black amethyst

Be aware that Indiana made a few pieces of Baroque in a color similar to Wisteria for Tiara. I have had reports of bowls, vases, and even one of candlesticks which I have not confirmed as yet. These are a purple/pink tint; do not pay a high price for Baroque pieces in this color. Baroque was never originally made in that color.

Triple candlesticks have been found in all the colors listed above, but matching console bowls have not been found in red, cobalt blue, or amethyst to match them. You may find pieces of blue Baroque that appear to be light green (bad batches of blue that were released anyway). As with Jeannette's Ultramarine, a few collectors seek color variances; but you will probably not find enough pieces of this hue to complete a set.

Candlesticks are obtainable in a variety of styles. You will find both 4" and 5½" single lite candles and a 4½" double candle. The 6", 3-lite candlesticks were discussed above. It is the candelabra with the prisms that drive many collectors to distraction. Not only are these candles elusive, but it is a pain to keep the prism wires attached. Many collectors are replacing the old rusty wires with new ones. If you have the time or inclination for tedious work, by all means use new wires!

Many pieces of Baroque are evasive. Cream soups and individual shakers are most exasperating in all colors; blue pitchers and punch bowls have never been plentiful. They, at least, have always been expensive; the other items were merely costly, but affordable, if they could be located!

Sweetmeats are 9" tall covered dishes; the covered jelly stands 7½" tall. Sweetmeats are more expensive; be sure you buy the right piece for your money. Shakers came with both metal and glass tops, although most collectors today prefer glass lids. Glass lids were easily broken by dropping or **over tightening** them; so the company was changing to metal before Baroque was discontinued. Metal lids are most often found on crystal and etched crystal patterns on Baroque mould blank #2496 (Navarre, Chintz, and Meadow Rose).

Pitchers with a lip seem to be more desirable to collectors (and therefore are more expensive) than those without a lip.

Straight tumblers are more difficult to find than footed ones, but are preferred to cone-shaped, footed pieces. Price concerns may enter into that decision!

	Crystal	Blue	Yellow
Ash tray	7.50	16.00	14.00
Bowl, cream soup	35.00	75.00	75.00
Bowl, ftd., punch	400.00	1,250.00	
Bowl, 3¾", rose	25.00	55.00	45.00
Bowl, 4", hdld. (4 styles)	11.00	22.50	20.00
Bowl, 5", fruit	15.00	30.00	25.00
Bowl, 6", cereal	20.00	42.00	35.00
Bowl, 6", sq.	8.00	20.00	22.00
Bowl, 6½", 2 pt.	9.00	25.00	20.00
Bowl, 7", 3 ftd.	12.50	25.00	25.00
Bowl, 7½", jelly, w/cover	30.00	100.00	65.00
Bowl, 8", pickle	8.50	27.50	22.50
Bowl, 8½", hdld.	14.00	35.00	30.00
Bowl, 9½", veg., oval	25.00	65.00	50.00
Bowl, 10", hdld.	15.00	60.00	40.00
Bowl, 10½", hdld., 4 ftd.	17.50	47.50	37.50
Bowl, 10" x 7½"	25.00		
Bowl, 10", relish, 3 pt.	20.00	30.00	22.50
Bowl, 11", celery	12.00	45.00	25.00
Bowl, 11", rolled edge	20.00	50.00	37.50
* Bowl, 12", flared	21.50	40.00	32.50
Candelabrum, 8¼", 2-lite, 16 lustre	95.00	140.00	110.00
Candelabrum, 9½", 3-lite, 24 lustre	125.00	195.00	165.00
Candle, 7¾", 8 lustre	50.00	90.00	80.00
Candlestick, 4"	12.50	35.00	30.00
Candlestick, 4½", 2-lite	15.00	55.00	50.00

*Pink just discovered.

16

	Crystal	Blue	Yellow
Candlestick, 5½"....................................	9.00	40.00	35.00
* Candlestick, 6", 3-lite	17.50	75.00	60.00
Candy, 3 part w/cover	30.00	125.00	85.00
Comport, 4¾"...	15.00	30.00	25.00
Comport, 6½"...	17.50	35.00	30.00
Creamer, 3¼", indiv.	9.00	30.00	25.00
Creamer, 3¾", ftd.	8.00	14.00	14.00
Cup...	9.00	30.00	20.00
Cup, 6 oz., punch	12.00	30.00	
Ice bucket...	35.00	125.00	80.00
Mayonnaise, 5½", w/liner	15.00	55.00	40.00
Mustard, w/cover	22.00	65.00	50.00
Oil, w/stopper, 5½"	85.00	400.00	225.00
Pitcher, 6½"...	110.00	800.00	450.00
Pitcher, 7", ice lip	110.00	750.00	400.00
Plate, 6"..	3.00	10.00	8.00
Plate, 7½"...	4.00	12.50	10.00
Plate, 8½"...	6.00	20.00	17.50
Plate, 9½"...	15.00	60.00	47.50
Plate, 10", cake..	20.00	35.00	30.00
Plate, 11", ctr. hdld., sand	25.00		
Plate, 14", torte	13.00	40.00	25.00
Platter, 12", oval......................................	22.00	65.00	45.00
Salt & pepper, pr.......................................	45.00	120.00	100.00
Salt & pepper, indiv., pr.	50.00	250.00	150.00
Saucer	2.00	5.00	4.00
Sherbet, 3¾", 5 oz....................................	10.00	27.50	17.50
Stem, 6¾", 9 oz., water............................	12.00	27.50	22.50
Sugar, 3", indiv.	5.00	27.50	22.50
Sugar, 3½", ftd.	6.00	15.00	11.00
Sweetmeat, covered, 9"	75.00	200.00	150.00
Tray, 11", oval	15.00	47.50	37.50
Tray, 6¼" for indiv. cream/sugar..................	15.00	25.00	20.00
Tumbler, 3½", 6½ oz., old-fashioned............	22.50	95.00	60.00
Tumbler, 3", 3½ oz., ftd., cocktail	10.00	20.00	15.00
Tumbler, 6", 12 oz., ftd., tea	20.00	40.00	30.00
Tumbler, 3¾", 5 oz., juice..........................	12.00	42.00	25.00
Tumbler, 5½", 9 oz., ftd., water...................	12.00	30.00	25.00
Tumbler, 4¼", 9 oz., water	25.00	50.00	25.00
Tumbler, 5¾", 14 oz., tea...........................	27.50	80.00	55.00
Vase, 6½"...	45.00	125.00	100.00
Vase, 7"...	40.00	125.00	85.00

* Red $150.00
  Green $120.00
  Black Amethyst $140.00
  Cobalt Blue $140.00
  Amber $75.00

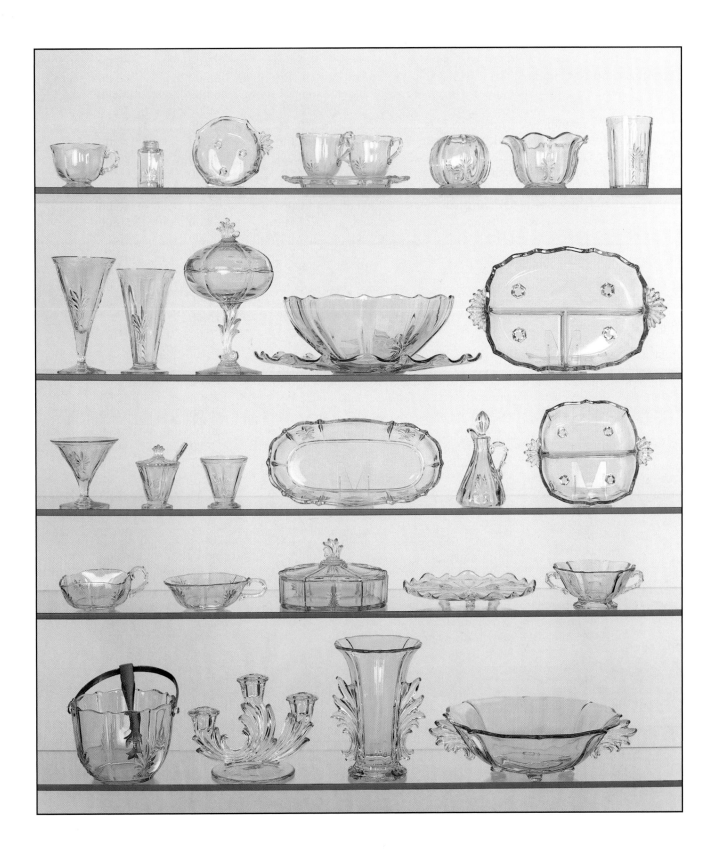

BLACK FOREST, Possibly Paden City for Van Deman & Son, late 1920s – early 1930s

Colors: amber, black, ice blue, crystal, green, pink, red, cobalt

Prices for Black Forest have risen dramatically over those of two years ago. The influx of new collectors has caused a shortfall for those now seeking it. Recently, several 10" black gold encrusted dinner plates and a pair of perfumes were found!

Black Forest is often confused with the U.S. Glass Deerwood pattern. Some pieces etched Deerwood (made by Tiffin) have been found on Paden City blanks which adds to the confusion. You can see a pink Deerwood candy on page 77 which is a typical, flat, divided blank of Paden City. Black Forest shows moose and trees, while deer and trees are dominant on Deerwood.

The night set (pitcher and tumbler) commonly called a tumble-up is found in pink and green. That hard-to-find, unetched tumbler has an extra large band that will only allow it to drop down as far as the neck of the pitcher when inverted.

I am constantly asked about those heavy Black Forest goblets that were made in the 1970s in amber, dark green, blue, crystal, and red (reportedly by L.E. Smith). They are selling in the $24.00 to $33.00 range with red and blue on the upper side of that price. Newer goblets have a heavy, predominant "Daisy and Button" stem.

	Amber	*Black	Crystal	Green	Pink	Red
Batter jug			150.00			
Bowl, 4½", finger				20.00		
Bowl, 9¼", center hdld.				85.00	85.00	
Bowl, 11", console	50.00	60.00	40.00	50.00	50.00	
Bowl, 11", fruit		50.00		35.00	35.00	
Bowl, 13", console			100.00			
Bowl, 3 ftd.			60.00			
Cake plate, 2" pedestal	40.00	65.00		45.00	40.00	
Candlestick, mushroom style	30.00	40.00	18.00	35.00	35.00	
Candlestick double			40.00			
Candy dish, w/cover, several styles	90.00	150.00		125.00	125.00	
Creamer, 2 styles		40.00	20.00	35.00	35.00	65.00
Comport, 4", low ftd.				35.00	35.00	
Comport, 5½", high ftd.		40.00		30.00	28.00	
Cup and saucer, 3 styles		90.00		85.00	85.00	110.00
Decanter, w/stopper, 8½", 28 oz., bulbous				195.00	195.00	
Decanter w/stopper, 8¾", 24 oz., straight			85.00	175.00	175.00	
Ice bucket		110.00			85.00	85.00
Ice pail, 6", 3" high	75.00					
Ice tub, 2 styles (ice blue $195.00)	80.00	85.00		85.00	75.00	
Mayonnaise, with liner		70.00		60.00	60.00	
Night set: pitcher, 6½", 42 oz. & tumbler				450.00	450.00	
Pitcher, 8", 40 oz., (cobalt $900.00)						
Pitcher, 8", 62 oz.			175.00			
Pitcher, 9", 80 oz.					400.00	
Pitcher, 10½", 72 oz.				500.00	500.00	
Plate, 6½", bread/butter		22.00		22.00		30.00
Plate, 8", luncheon		25.00			25.00	30.00
Plate, 10", dinner		175.00				
Plate, 11", 2 hdld.		45.00		25.00	25.00	
Plate, 13¾", 2 hdld.				75.00	75.00	
Relish, 10½", 5 pt. covered				195.00	195.00	
Salt and pepper, pr.			125.00		175.00	
Server, center hdld.	50.00	40.00	35.00	35.00	35.00	
Shot Glass, 2 oz., 2½"	40.00					
Stem, 2 oz., wine, 4¼"			17.50	50.00		
Stem, 6 oz., champagne, 4¾"			17.50		30.00	
Stem, 9 oz., water, 6"			22.50			
Sugar, 2 styles		35.00	20.00	35.00	35.00	65.00
Tumbler, 3 oz., juice, flat or footed, 3½"			25.00	40.00	40.00	
Tumbler, 8 oz., old fashioned, 3⅞"					40.00	
Tumbler, 9 oz., ftd., 5½"	30.00					
Tumbler, 12 oz., tea, 5½"				45.00	45.00	
Vase, 6½" (Cobalt $150.00)		55.00	45.00	50.00	50.00	
Vase, 10", 2 styles in black		110.00		75.00	75.00	
Whipped cream pail	75.00					

*Add 20% for gold decorated.

20

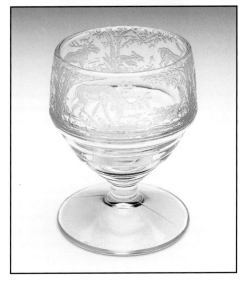

Colors: crystal, yellow; some pink

 Cadena is one of Tiffin's patterns where collectors have little trouble finding stemware. Finding serving pieces becomes quite another story. Did buyers purchase only the stemware to compliment their china and leave the glass serving pieces on the store shelves, a theory recently propounded by a reader? You will note the lack of serving pieces in my photograph! Even if you are willing to pay the price for serving pieces, they are rarely available! A recent discovery of Cadena included grapefruits and liners.

 Pink Cadena is rarely seen; I have been unable to find a piece to photograph! Cadena is seldom seen at Depression glass shows and that also leads to fewer collectors. Occasionally, you will find a piece or two. The days of yesteryear when finding a large set was the norm have mostly disappeared. Apparently, Tiffin did not advertise this pattern as extensively as they did their Cherokee Rose, June Knight, and Flanders patterns, all of which are sought by today's collectors!

 Pitchers were sold both with and without a lid. If you try to put a lid on one of the pitchers originally sold without one, you may find that the lid will not fit. Pitchers sold without lids were often curved in so much that a lid will not fit inside the top rim. Bear in mind that the pitcher cover is plain; no pattern is etched on it.

 One of the reasons I have been adding catalog pages is to help identify some individual pieces since I am repeatedly asked why I can't show each item and identify them piece by piece. Actually, the major reason is economics. I couldn't afford to buy every piece in every pattern even if I could find them; and you couldn't afford the book (or would have to employ a magnifying glass) if I did. I try to show you as much glass as possible to whet your collecting appetite. Where apropos, a close-up shot has been included to embellish pattern identification. Colors and items are modified in every other edition, and major patterns are changed every edition as new items are discovered. Believe me, we keep trying to improve information and photos with each new edition!

	Crystal	Pink/ Yellow
Bowl, cream soup	20.00	30.00
Bowl, finger, ftd.	15.00	25.00
Bowl, grapefruit, ftd.	25.00	55.00
Bowl, 6", hdld.	10.00	22.00
Bowl, 10", pickle	15.00	27.50
Bowl, 12", console	25.00	47.50
Candlestick	20.00	35.00
Creamer	15.00	25.00
Cup	30.00	75.00
Mayonnaise, ftd., w/liner	30.00	50.00
Oyster cocktail	15.00	25.00
Pitcher, ftd.	175.00	250.00
Pitcher, ftd., w/cover	235.00	350.00
Plate, 6"	5.00	8.00
Plate, 7¾"	7.00	12.00
Plate, 9¼"	30.00	45.00
Saucer	10.00	12.50
Stem, 4¾", sherbet	15.00	22.00
Stem, 5¼", cocktail	17.50	25.00
Stem, 5¼", ¾ oz., cordial	60.00	95.00
Stem, 6", wine	25.00	40.00
Stem, 6⁵⁄₁₆", 8 oz., parfait	25.00	35.00
Stem, 6½", champagne	17.00	30.00
Stem, 7½", water	20.00	35.00
Sugar	15.00	23.00
Tumbler, 4¼", ftd., juice	17.50	27.50
Tumbler, 5¼", ftd., water	20.00	30.00
Vase, 9"	45.00	90.00

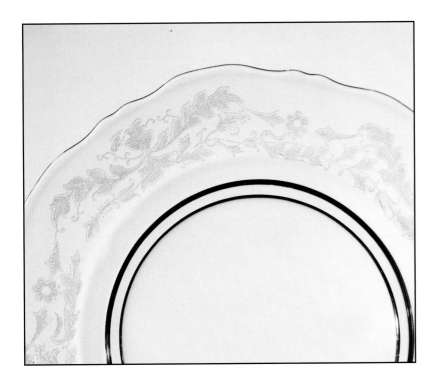

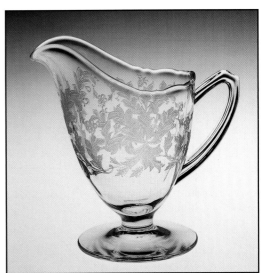

Colors: crystal, crystal and Crown Tuscan with gold decoration

Candlelight prices continue to rise due both to scarcity and new collecting interest. Candlelight was manufactured in two different ways. The pattern was cut into some pieces, but was acid etched on others. The cut items are rarer, but there are fewer collectors searching for it. The bowl pictured at the bottom of page 25 exhibits the cut style while most of the other pieces shown are etched. There are two icers and liners in the photograph, one etched, the other cut. The pattern is harder to see on the cut! Etching was accomplished by covering the glass with wax except where the design was desired and then dipping the glass into acid.

Candlelight stemware items are the easiest to find, except for cordials and wines. You will look long and hard for shakers, basic serving pieces, and lamps. I have been unable to find a cup and saucer. Even one or two pieces of Candlelight can improve modern day decor when used for accent, something many collectors do!

That 1951 Candlelight brochure pictured on page 25 was typically given to people registering for a pattern, valuable to researchers like myself!

	Crystal		Crystal
Bonbon, 7", ftd., 2 hdld., #3900/130	35.00	Plate, 13½", cake, 2 hdld., #3900/35	75.00
Bowl, 10", 4 toed, flared, #3900/54	60.00	Plate, 13½", cracker, #3900/135	65.00
Bowl, 11", 2 hdld., #3900/34	70.00	Plate, 14", rolled edge, #3900/166	70.00
Bowl, 11", 4 ftd., fancy edge, #3400/48	65.00	Relish, 7", 2 hdld., #3900/123	35.00
Bowl, 11½", ftd., 2 hdld., #3900/28	75.00	Relish, 7", div., 2 hdld., #3900/124	40.00
Bowl, 12", 4 ftd., flared, #3400/4	70.00	Relish, 8", 3 part, #3400/91	45.00
Bowl, 12", 4 ftd., oblong, #3400/160	75.00	Relish, 9", 3 pt., #3900/125	47.50
Bowl, 12", 4 toed, flared, #3900/62	75.00	Relish, 12", 3 pt., #3900/126	55.00
Bowl, 12", 4 toed, oval, hdld., #3900/65	95.00	Relish, 12", 5 pt., #3900/120	65.00
Butter dish, 5", #3400/52	250.00	Salt & pepper, pr., #3900/1177	125.00
Candle, 5", #3900/67	40.00	Saucer, #3900/17	5.00
Candle, 6", 2-lite, #3900/72	45.00	Stem, 1 oz., cordial, #3776	75.00
Candle, 6", 3-lite, #3900/74	55.00	Stem, 2 oz., sherry, #7966	75.00
Candlestick, 5", #646	40.00	Stem, 2½ oz., wine, #3111	60.00
Candlestick, 6", 2-lite, #647	50.00	Stem, 3 oz., cocktail, #3111	35.00
Candlestick, 6", 3-lite, #1338	65.00	Stem, 3 oz., cocktail, #3776	30.00
Candy box and cover, 3-part, #3500/57	110.00	Stem, 3½ oz., wine, #3776	55.00
Candy w/lid, rnd. #3900/165	125.00	Stem, 4 oz., cocktail, #7801	30.00
Cocktail shaker, 36 oz., #P101	175.00	Stem, 4½ oz., claret, #3776	65.00
Comport, 5", cheese, #3900/135	35.00	Stem, 4½ oz., oyster cocktail, #3111	30.00
Comport, 5⅜", blown, #3121	60.00	Stem, 4½ oz., oyster cocktail, #3776	25.00
Comport, 5½", #3900/136	52.50	Stem, 7 oz., low sherbet, #3111	17.50
Creamer, #3900/41	20.00	Stem, 7 oz., low sherbet, #3776	16.50
Creamer, indiv., #3900/40	22.50	Stem, 7 oz., tall sherbet, #3111	22.50
Cruet, 6 oz., w/stopper, #3900/100	125.00	Stem, 7 oz., tall sherbet, #3776	20.00
Cup, #3900/17	30.00	Stem, 9 oz., water, #3776	35.00
Decanter, 28 oz., ftd., #1321	175.00	Stem, 10 oz., water, #3111	35.00
Ice bucket, #3900/671	150.00	Sugar, #3900/41	20.00
Icer, 2 pc., cocktail, #968	90.00	Sugar, indiv., #3900/40	20.00
Lamp, hurricane, #1617	165.00	Tumbler, 5 oz., ftd., juice, #3111	25.00
Lamp, hurricane, keyhole, w/bobeche, #1603	200.00	Tumbler, 5 oz., juice, #3776	22.00
Lamp, hurricane, w/bobeche, #1613	295.00	Tumbler, 12 oz., ftd., iced tea., #3111	32.50
Mayonnaise, 3 pc., #3900/129	57.50	Tumbler, 12 oz., iced tea, #3776	30.00
Mayonnaise, div., 4 pc., #3900/111	65.00	Tumbler, 13 oz., #3900/115	40.00
Mayonnaise, ftd., 2 pc., #3900/19	47.50	Vase, 5", ftd., bud, #6004	40.00
Nut cup, 3", 4 ftd., #3400/71	65.00	Vase, 5", globe, #1309	55.00
Oil, 6 oz., #3900/100	75.00	Vase, 6", ftd., #6004	45.00
Pitcher, Doulton, #3400/141	350.00	Vase, 8", ftd., #6004	55.00
Plate, 6½", #3900/20	12.50	Vase, 9", ftd., keyhole, #1237	65.00
Plate, 8", 2 hdld., #3900/131	25.00	Vase, 10", bud, #274	50.00
Plate, 8", salad, #3900/22	17.00	Vase, 11", ftd. pedestal, #1299	125.00
Plate, 10½", dinner, #3900/24	70.00	Vase, 11", ftd., #278	85.00
Plate, 12", 4 toed, #3900/26	60.00	Vase, 12", ftd., keyhole, #1238	100.00
Plate, 13", torte, 4 toed, #3900/33	60.00	Vase, 13", ftd, #279	135.00

CANDLEWICK, Line #400, Imperial Glass Company, 1936 – 1984

Colors: crystal, blue, pink, yellow, black, red, cobalt blue, green, carmel slag

When the table outside the studio was covered with Mallard cut candlewick, my publisher walked by, took one look and told me to figure up how much I wanted for it. Since he bought this, he may now be officially classified a glass "hunter"! You can see this Mallard cut on pages 34 and 35.

Candlewick stemware and tumbler identification is a major concern of new collectors until they learn all the different lines. In the bottom photo on page 29 are two different stem lines on which ruby and cobalt Candlewick is found. The round stems and tumblers are 3800 while the flared rim style is 3400 line. If your red or cobalt stemware has some other shape, then it is not Candlewick and could be Bryce. Another stemware line is 400/190 and is found with a hollow stem. These can easily be seen in the picture at the bottom of page 27. The tumblers shown on the bottom left of page 33 have the designation 400/19. The bases on these tumblers are flat as opposed to 400/18 which has a domed foot on page 31. The 400/... was Imperial's factory listing for each piece. If you can find a copy of my first *Elegant Glassware of the Depression Era* book, there is a 15 page reprint of Imperial's Catalog B showing Candlewick listings.

Viennese blue pieces of Candlewick (light blue shown below) are selling well, but sales of higher priced red and black items have moderated. In the past, prices on colored Candlewick increased very swiftly; now, those prices have diminished, a characteristic of a too rapid price rise. Ruby and black fancy bowls have steadied in the ball park of $200.00 – 235.00 with the Viennese blue pieces bringing 50 to 60 percent of that. Ruby stems continue to be found in the 3400 and 3800 lines with most of these selling in the $50.00 to $85.00 range. However, cordials are selling in Ruby and Ritz blue (cobalt) from $110.00 to $150.00. Other Ritz blue stems are fetching $80.00 to $110.00. All of these colored pieces of Candlewick except black were made before 1940.

The family punch bowl (400/139/2) is shown at the top of page 27. Note the notched lid for the ladle. That bottom with an unnotched lid is the snack jar (400/139/1) pictured on the top of page 31. Everyone seeks the 14" birthday cake plate (400/160) shown (top of page 27) with fewer candles than its 72 potential. Scratches from years of cake cutting devalue these cake plates.

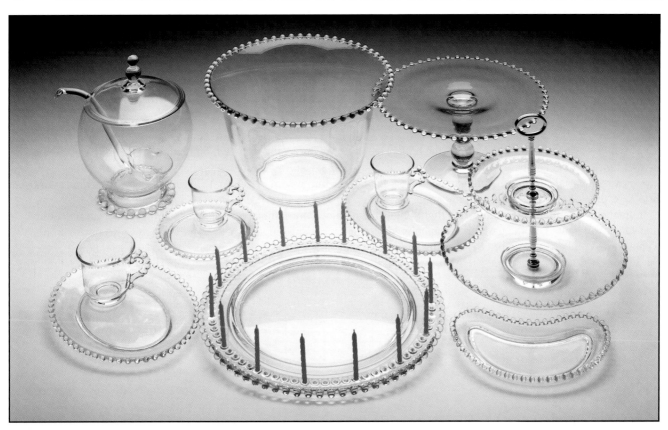

	Crystal
Ash tray, eagle, 6½", 1776/1	55.00
Ash tray, heart, 4½", 400/172	10.00
Ash tray, heart, 5½", 400/173	12.00
Ash tray, heart, 6½", 400/174	15.00
Ash tray, indiv., 400/64.	8.00
Ash tray, oblong, 4½", 400/134/1	6.00
Ash tray, round, 2¾", 400/19	9.00
Ash tray, round, 4", 400/33	11.00
Ash tray, round, 5", 400/133	8.00
Ash tray, square, 3¼", 400/651	37.50
Ash tray, square, 4½", 400/652	37.50
Ash tray, square, 5¾", 400/653	45.00
Ash tray, 6", matchbook holder center, 400/60	110.00
Ash tray set, 3 pc. rnd. nest. (crys. or colors), 400/550	30.00
Ash tray set, 3 pc. sq. nesting, 400/650	110.00
Ash tray set, 4 pc. bridge (cig. hold at side), 400/118	40.00
Basket, 5", beaded hdld., 400/273	225.00
Basket, 6½", hdld., 400/40/0	30.00
Basket, 11", hdld., 400/73/0	225.00
Bell, 4", 400/179	65.00
Bell, 5", 400/108	75.00
Bottle, bitters, w/tube, 4 oz., 400/117	60.00
Bowl, bouillon, 2 hdld., 400/126	45.00
Bowl, #3400, finger, ftd.	30.00
Bowl, #3800, finger	30.00
Bowl, 4½", nappy, 3 ftd., 400/206	70.00
Bowl, 4¾", round, 2 hdld., 400/42B	12.00
Bowl, 5", cream soup, 400/50	42.50
Bowl, 5", fruit, 400/1F	12.00
Bowl, 5", heart w/hand., 400/49H	20.00
Bowl, 5", square, 400/231	95.00
Bowl, 5½", heart, 400/53H	22.00
Bowl, 5½", jelly, w/cover, 400/59	60.00
Bowl, 5½", sauce, deep, 400/243	40.00
Bowl, 6", baked apple, rolled edge, 400/53X	30.00
Bowl, 6", cottage cheese, 400/85	25.00
Bowl, 6", fruit, 400/3F	12.00
Bowl, 6", heart w/hand., 400/51H	25.00
Bowl, 6", mint w/hand., 400/51F	20.00
Bowl, 6", round, div., 2 hdld., 400/52	25.00
Bowl, 6", 2 hdld., 400/52B	15.00
Bowl, 6", 3 ftd., 400/183	60.00
Bowl, 6", sq., 400/232	120.00
Bowl, 6½", relish, 2 pt., 400/84	25.00
Bowl, 6½", 2 hdld., 400/181	30.00
Bowl, 7", round, 400/5F	25.00
Bowl, 7", round, 2 hdld., 400/62B	17.50
Bowl, 7", relish, sq., div., 400/234	135.00
Bowl, 7", ivy, high, bead ft., 400/188	195.00
Bowl, 7", lily, 4 ft., 400/74J	65.00
Bowl, 7", relish, 400/60	25.00
Bowl, 7", sq., 400/233	145.00
Bowl, 7¼", rose, ftd. w/crimp edge, 400/132C	425.00
Bowl, 7½", pickle/celery, 400/57	27.50
Bowl, 7½", lily, bead rim, ftd., 400/75N	295.00
Bowl, 7½", belled (console base), 400/127B	85.00

	Crystal
Bowl, 8", round, 400/7F	37.50
Bowl, 8", relish, 2 pt., 400/268	20.00
Bowl, 8", cov. veg., 400/65/1	295.00
Bowl, 8½", rnd., 400/69B	35.00
Bowl, 8½", nappy, 4 ftd., 400/74B	70.00
Bowl, 8½", 3 ftd., 400/182	120.00
Bowl, 8½", 2 hdld., 400/72B	22.00
Bowl, 8½", pickle/celery, 400/58	20.00
Bowl, 8½", relish, 4 pt., 400/55	22.00
Bowl, 9", round, 400/10F	45.00
Bowl, 9", crimp, ftd., 400/67C	145.00
Bowl, 9", sq., fancy crimp edge, 4 ft., 400/74SC.	75.00
Bowl, 9", heart, 400/49H	120.00
Bowl, 9", heart w/hand., 400/73H	145.00
Bowl, 10", 400/13F	45.00
Bowl, 10", banana, 400/103E	1,350.00
Bowl, 10", 3 toed, 400/205	150.00
Bowl, 10", belled (punch base), 400/128B	70.00
Bowl, 10", cupped edge, 400/75F	45.00
Bowl, 10", deep, 2 hdld., 400/113A	125.00
Bowl, 10", divided, deep, 2 hdld., 400/114A	145.00
Bowl, 10", fruit, bead stem (like compote), 400/103F	195.00
Bowl, 10", relish, oval, 2 hdld., 400/217	40.00
Bowl, 10", relish, 3 pt., 3 ft., 400/208	90.00
Bowl, 10", 3 pt., w/cover, 400/216	325.00
Bowl, 10½", belled, 400/63B	60.00
Bowl, 10½", butter/jam, 3 pt., 400/262	145.00
Bowl, 10½", salad, 400/75B	40.00
Bowl, 10½", relish, 3 section, 400/256	30.00
Bowl, 11", celery boat, oval, 400/46	60.00
Bowl, 11", centerpiece, flared, 400/13B	55.00
Bowl, 11", float, inward rim, ftd., 400/75F	40.00
Bowl, 11", oval, 400/124A	240.00
Bowl, 11", oval w/partition, 400/125A	285.00
Bowl, 12", round, 400/92B	40.00
Bowl, 12", belled, 400/106B	90.00
Bowl, 12", float, 400/92F	40.00
Bowl, 12", hdld., 400/113B	165.00
Bowl, 12", shallow, 400/17F	47.50
Bowl, 12", relish, oblong, 4 sect., 400/215	115.00
Bowl, 13", centerpiece, mushroom, 400/92L	55.00
Bowl, 13", float, 1½" deep, 400/101	65.00
Bowl, 13½", relish, 5 pt., 400/209	77.50
Bowl, 14", belled, 400/104B	90.00
Bowl, 14", oval, flared, 400/131B	225.00
Butter and jam set, 5 piece, 400/204	350.00
Butter, w/ cover, rnd., 5½", 400/144	32.50
Butter, w/ cover, no beads, California, 400/276.	135.00
Butter, w/ bead top, ¼ lb., 400/161	30.00
Cake stand, 10", low foot, 400/67D	55.00
Cake stand, 11", high foot, 400/103D	70.00
Calendar, 1947, desk	195.00
Candleholder, 3 way, beaded base, 400/115	125.00
Candleholder, 2-lite, 400/100	20.00
Candleholder, flat, 3½", 400/280	50.00
Candleholder, 3½", rolled edge, 400/79R	12.00
Candleholder, 3½", w/fingerhold, 400/81	50.00
Candleholder, flower, 4", 2 bead stem, 400/66F.	50.00
Candleholder, flower, 4½", 2 bead stem, 400/66C	60.00

	Crystal		Crystal
Candleholder, 4½", 3 toed, 400/207	75.00	Fork & spoon, set, 400/75	35.00
Candleholder, 3-lite on cir. bead. ctr., 400/147	35.00	Hurricane lamp, 2 pc. candle base, 400/79	120.00
Candleholder, 5", hdld./bowled up base, 400/90	50.00	Hurricane lamp, 2 pc., hdld. candle base, 400/76	175.00
Candleholder, 5", heart shape, 400/40HC	75.00	Hurricane lamp, 3 pc. flared & crimped edge globe, 400/152	150.00
Candleholder, 5½", 3 bead stems, 400/224	90.00	Ice tub, 5½" deep, 8" diam., 400/63	100.00
Candleholder, flower, 5" (epergne inset), 400/40CV	125.00	Ice tub, 7", 2 hdld., 400/168	195.00
Candleholder, 5", flower, 400/40C	35.00	Icer, 2 pc., seafood/fruit cocktail, 400/53/3	95.00
Candleholder, 6½", tall, 3 bead stems, 400/175	95.00	Icer, 2 pc., seafood/fruit cocktail #3800 line, one bead stem	70.00
Candleholder, flower, 6", round, 400/40F	25.00	Jam set, 5 pc., oval tray w/2 marmalade jars w/ladles, 400/1589	115.00
Candleholder, urn, 6", holders on cir. ctr. bead, 400/129R	135.00	Jar tower, 3 sect., 400/655	375.00
Candleholder, flower, 6½", square, 400/40S	40.00	Knife, butter, 4000	325.00
Candleholder, mushroom, 400/86	35.00	Ladle, marmalade, 3 bead stem, 400/130	12.00
Candleholder, flower, 9", centerpiece, 400/196FC	175.00	Ladle, mayonnaise, 6¼", 400/135	12.00
Candy box, round, 5½", 400/59	45.00	Marmalade set, 3 pc., beaded ft. w/cover & spoon, 400/1989	40.00
Candy box, sq., 6½", rnd. lid, 400/245	225.00	Marmalade set, 3 pc. tall jar, domed bead ft., lid, spoon, 400/8918	65.00
Candy box, w/ cover, 7", 400/259	150.00	Marmalade set, 4 pc., liner saucer, jar, lid, spoon, 400/89	42.50
Candy box, w/ cover, 7" partitioned, 400/110	75.00	Mayonnaise set, 2 pc. scoop side bowl, spoon, 400/23	37.50
Candy box, w/ cover, round, 7", 3 sect., 400/158	165.00	Mayonnaise set, 3 pc. hdld. tray/hdld. bowl/ladle, 400/52/3	45.00
Candy box, w/ cover, beaded, ft., 400/140	350.00	Mayonnaise set, 3 pc. plate, heart bowl, spoon, 400/49	33.00
Cigarette box w/cover, 400/134	35.00	Mayonnaise set, 3 pc. scoop side bowl, spoon, tray, 400/496	40.00
Cigarette holder, 3", bead ft., 400/44	35.00	Mayonnaise 4 pc., plate, divided bowl, 2 ladles, 400/84	40.00
Cigarette set: 6 pc. (cigarette box & 4 rect. ash trays), 400/134/6	67.50	Mirror, 4½", rnd., standing	115.00
Clock, 4", round	275.00	Mustard jar, w/spoon, 400/156	30.00
Coaster, 4", 400/78	7.00	Oil, 4 oz., bead base, 400/164	55.00
Coaster, w/spoon rest, 400/226	16.00	Oil, 6 oz., bead base, 400/166	65.00
Cocktail, seafood w/bead ft., 400/190	60.00	Oil, 4 oz., bulbous bottom, 400/274	45.00
Cocktail set: 2 pc., plate w/indent; cocktail, 400/97	35.00	Oil, 4 oz., hdld., bulbous bottom, 400/278	65.00
Compote, 4½", 400/63B	40.00	Oil, 6 oz., hdld., bulbous bottom, 400/279	85.00
Compote, 5", 3 bead stems, 400/220	75.00	Oil, 6 oz., bulbous bottom, 400/275	55.00
Compote, 5½", 4 bead stem, 400/45	25.00	Oil, w/stopper, etched "Oil," 400/121	60.00
Compote, 5½, low, plain stem, 400/66B	22.00	Oil, w/stopper, etched "Vinegar," 400/121	60.00
Compote, 5½", 2 bead stem, 400/66B	22.00	Party set, 2 pc., oval plate w/indent for cup, 400/98	27.50
Compote, 8", bead stem, 400/48F	80.00	Pitcher, 14 oz., short rnd., 400/330	185.00
Compote, 10", ftd. fruit, crimped, 40/103C	165.00	Pitcher, 16 oz., low ft., 400/19	210.00
Compote, ft. oval, 400/137	1,075.00	Pitcher, 16 oz., no ft., 400/16	175.00
Condiment set: 4 pc. (2 squat bead ft. shakers, marmalade), 400/1786	67.50	Pitcher, 20 oz., plain, 400/416	40.00
Console sets: 3 pc. (14" oval bowl, two 3-lite candles), 400/1531B	295.00	Pitcher, 40 oz., juice/cocktail, 400/19	175.00
3 pc. (mushroom bowl, w/mushroom candles), 400/8692L	105.00	Pitcher, 40 oz., manhattan, 400/18	225.00
Creamer, domed foot, 400/18	125.00	Pitcher, 40 oz., plain, 400/419	40.00
Creamer, 6 oz., bead handle, 400/30	8.00	Pitcher, 64 oz., plain, 400/424	50.00
Creamer, indiv. bridge, 400/122	7.50	Pitcher, 80 oz., plain, 400/424	55.00
Creamer, plain ft., 400/31	9.00	Pitcher, 80 oz., 400/24	130.00
Creamer, flat, bead handle, 400/126	32.50	Pitcher, 80 oz., beaded ft., 400/18	225.00
Cup, after dinner, 400/77	17.50	Plate, 4½", 400/34	6.00
Cup, coffee, 400/37	7.50	Plate, 5½", 2 hdld., 400/42D	10.00
Cup, punch, 400/211	7.50	Plate, 6", bread/butter, 400/1D	8.00
Cup, tea, 400/35	8.00	Plate, 6", canape w/off ctr. indent, 400/36	14.00
Decanter, w/stopper, 15 oz. cordial, 400/82/2	295.00	Plate, 6¾", 2 hdld. crimped, 400/52C	25.00
Decanter, w/stopper, 18 oz., 400/18	395.00	Plate, 7", salad, 400/3D	8.00
Decanter, w/stopper, 26 oz., 400/163	295.00		
Deviled egg server, 12", ctr. hdld., 400/154	110.00		
Egg cup, bead. ft., 400/19	47.50		

CANDLEWICK

	Crystal
Plate, 7½", 2 hdld., 400/52D	10.00
Plate, 7½", triangular, 400/266	85.00
Plate, 8", oval, 400/169	22.50
Plate, 8", salad, 400/5D	9.00
Plate, 8", w/indent, 400/50	11.00
Plate, 8¼", crescent salad, 400/120	50.00
Plate, 8½", 2 hdld., crimped, 400/62C	20.00
Plate, 8½", 2 hdld., 400/62D	12.00
Plate, 8½", salad, 400/5D	10.00
Plate, 8½", 2 hdld. (sides upturned), 400/62E	25.00
Plate, 9", luncheon, 400/7D	13.50
Plate, 9", oval, salad, 400/38	40.00
Plate, 9", w/indent, oval, 400/98	15.00
Plate, 10", 2 hdld., sides upturned, 400/72E	22.50
Plate, 10", 2 hdld. crimped, 400/72C	30.00
Plate, 10", 2 hdld., 400/72D	17.50
Plate, 10½", dinner, 400/10D	37.50
Plate, 12", 2 hdld., 400/145D	27.50
Plate, 12", 2 hdld. crimp., 400/145C	32.50
Plate, 12", service, 400/13D	30.00
Plate, 12½", cupped edge, torte, 400/75V	27.50
Plate, 12½", oval, 400/124	85.00
Plate, 13½", cupped edge, serving, 400/92V	40.00
Plate, 14" birthday cake (holes for 72 candles), 400/160	495.00
Plate, 14", 2 hdld., sides upturned, 400/113E	35.00
Plate, 14", 2 hdld., torte, 400/113D	30.00
Plate, 14", service, 400/92D	30.00
Plate, 14", torte, 400/17D	42.50
Plate, 17", cupped edge, 400/20V	50.00
Plate, 17", torte, 400/20D	50.00
Platter, 13", 400/124D	90.00
Platter, 16", 400/131D	195.00
Punch ladle, 400/91	30.00
Punch set, family, 8 demi cups, ladle, lid, 400/139/77	600.00
Punch set, 15 pc. bowl on base, 12 cups, ladle, 400/20	245.00
Relish & dressing set, 4 pc. (10½" 4 pt. relish w/marmalade), 400/1112	90.00
Salad set, 4 pc. (buffet; lg. rnd. tray, div. bowl, 2 spoons), 400/17	120.00
Salad set, 4 pc. (rnd. plate, flared bowl, fork, spoon), 400/75B	85.00
Salt & pepper pr., bead ft., straight side, chrome top, 400/247	16.00
Salt & pepper pr., bead ft., bulbous, chrome top, 400/96	15.00
Salt & pepper pr., bulbous w/bead stem, plastic top, 400/116	75.00
Salt & pepper, pr., indiv., 400/109	11.00
Salt & pepper, pr., ftd. bead base, 400/190	47.50
Salt dip, 2", 400/61	11.00
Salt dip, 2¼", 400/19	11.00
Salt spoon, 3, 400/616	11.00
Salt spoon, w/ribbed bowl, 4000	11.00
Sauce boat, 400/169	110.00
Sauce boat liner, 400/169	40.00
Saucer, after dinner, 400/77AD	5.00
Saucer, tea or coffee, 400/35 or 400/37	2.50

	Crystal
Set: 2 pc. hdld. cracker w/cheese compote, 400/88	37.50
Set: 2 pc. rnd. cracker plate w/indent; cheese compote, 400/145	45.00
Snack jar w/cover, bead ft., 400/139/1	450.00
Stem, 1 oz., cordial, 400/190	70.00
Stem, 4 oz., cocktail, 400/190	18.00
Stem, 5 oz., tall sherbet, 400/190	15.00
Stem, 5 oz., wine, 400/190	21.00
Stem, 6 oz., sherbet, 400/190	14.00
Stem, 10 oz., water 400/190	18.00
Stem, #3400, 1 oz., cordial	40.00
Stem, #3400, 4 oz., cocktail	16.00
Stem, #3400, 4 oz., oyster cocktail	14.00
Stem, #3400, 4 oz., wine	25.00
Stem, #3400, 5 oz., claret	55.00
Stem, #3400, 5 oz., low sherbet	10.00
Stem, #3400, 6 oz., parfait	55.00
Stem, #3400, 6 oz., sherbet/saucer champagne	17.50
Stem, #3400, 9 oz., goblet, water	16.00
Stem, #3800, low sherbet	25.00
Stem, #3800, brandy	30.00
Stem, #3800, 1 oz., cordial	45.00
Stem, #3800, 4 oz., cocktail	25.00
Stem, #3800, 4 oz., wine	27.50
Stem, #3800, 6 oz., champagne/sherbet	25.00
Stem, #3800, 9 oz., water goblet	25.00
Stem, #3800, claret	32.00
Stem, #4000, 1¼ oz., cordial	33.00
Stem, #4000, cocktail	22.00
Stem, #4000, 5 oz., wine	25.00
Stem, #4000, 6 oz., tall sherbet	22.00
Stem, #4000, 11 oz., goblet	30.00
Stem, #4000, 12 oz., tea	25.00
Strawberry set, 2 pc. (7" plate/sugar dip bowl), 400/83	50.00
Sugar, domed foot, 400/18	125.00
Sugar, 6 oz., bead hdld., 400/30	7.00
Sugar, flat, bead handle, 400/126	40.00
Sugar, indiv. bridge, 400/122	6.00
Sugar, plain ft., 400/31	6.50
Tete-a-tete 3 pc. brandy, a.d. cup, 6½" oval tray, 400/111	65.00
Tid bit server, 2 tier, cupped, 400/2701	50.00
Tid bit set, 3 pc., 400/18TB	195.00
Toast, w/cover, set, 7¾", 400/123	295.00
Tray, 5½", hdld., upturned handles, 400/42E	18.00
Tray, 5½", lemon, ctr. hdld., 400/221	30.00
Tray, 5¼" x 9¼", condiment, 400/148	45.00
Tray, 6½", 400/29	15.00
Tray, 6", wafer, handle bent to ctr. of dish, 400/51T	22.00
Tray, 10½", ctr. hdld. fruit, 400/68F	110.00
Tray, 11½", ctr. hdld. party, 400/68D	30.00
Tray, 13½", 2 hdld. celery, oval, 400/105	30.00
Tray, 13", relish, 5 sections, 400/102	75.00
Tray, 14", hdld., 400/113E	40.00
Tumbler, 3½ oz., cocktail, 400/18	42.00
Tumbler, 5 oz., juice, 400/18	40.00
Tumbler, 6 oz., sherbet, 400/18	40.00

	Crystal
Tumbler, 7 oz., old-fashioned, 400/18..............	37.50
Tumbler, 7 oz., parfait, 400/18.........................	50.00
Tumbler, 9 oz., water, 400/18	40.00
Tumbler, 12 oz., tea, 400/18	47.50
Tumbler, 3 oz., ftd., cocktail, 400/19................	15.00
Tumbler, 3 oz., ftd., wine, 400/19....................	20.00
Tumbler, 5 oz., low sherbet, 400/19	15.00
Tumbler, 5 oz., juice, 400/19	10.00
Tumbler, 7 oz., old-fashioned, 400/19..............	35.00
Tumbler, 10 oz., 400/19	12.00
Tumbler, 12 oz., 400/19	22.00
Tumbler, 14 oz., 400/19, tea	22.00
Tumbler, #3400, 5 oz., ft., juice	17.50
Tumbler, #3400, 9 oz., ftd.	16.00
Tumbler, #3400, 10 oz., ftd.	15.00
Tumbler, #3400, 12 oz., ftd.	17.00
Tumbler, #3800, 5 oz., juice...........................	25.00
Tumbler, #3800, 9 oz.....................................	25.00
Tumbler, #3800, 12 oz...................................	30.00
Vase, 4", bead ft., sm. neck, ball, 400/25	45.00
Vase, 5¾", bead ft., bud, 400/107	55.00
Vase, 5¾", bead ft., mini bud, 400/107.............	60.00

	Crystal
Vase, 6", flat, crimped edge, 400/287C.............	30.00
Vase, 6", ftd., flared rim, 400/138B...................	110.00
Vase, 6" diam., 400/198.................................	275.00
Vase, 6", fan, 400/287 F.................................	30.00
Vase, 7", ftd., bud, 400/186	225.00
Vase, 7", ftd., bud, 400/187	200.00
Vase, 7", ivy bowl, 400/74J	135.00
Vase, 7", rolled rim w/bead hdld., 400/87 R.....	40.00
Vase, 7", rose bowl, 400/142 K	210.00
Vase, 7¼", ftd., rose bowl, crimped top, 400/132C..	425.00
Vase, 7½", ftd., rose bowl, 400/132	375.00
Vase, 8", fan, w/bead hdld., 400/87F................	35.00
Vase, 8", flat, crimped edge, 400/143C.............	70.00
Vase, 8", fluted rim w/bead hdlds., 400/87C	27.50
Vase, 8½", bead ft., bud, 400/28C....................	75.00
Vase, 8½", bead ft., flared rim, 400/21	185.00
Vase, 8½", bead ft., inward rim, 400/27	185.00
Vase, 8½", hdld. (pitcher shape), 400/227	395.00
Vase, 10", bead ft., straight side, 400/22............	165.00
Vase, 10", ftd., 400/193	175.00

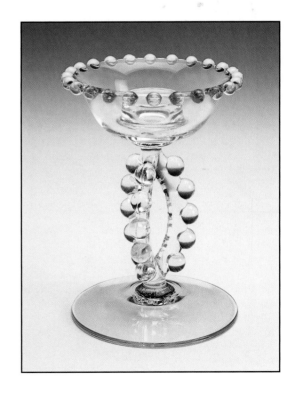

Color: crystal, Sapphire blue, Cape Cod blue, Chartreuse, Ruby, Cranberry pink, Jasmine yellow

Canterbury, or line No. 115, was the blank used for several of Duncan's etched patterns of which First Love is most known. I have had many letters thanking me for including it and a couple chewing me out for exposing it to so many new collectors making it more difficult to buy cheaply. Actually, this is very reasonably priced when compared to patterns made by Cambridge, Heisey, or Fostoria.

Yellow-green color was named Chartreuse and I have now found out that Chartreuse was also a Tiffin color name as well as Duncan. The tumbler and candlestick shown on the bottom of page 37 are most likely Tiffin pieces manufactured from Duncan's moulds. I have amassed several pieces that have the original Tiffin sticker on them which I hope to show in the next edition. Prices for this color seem to be 10% to 20% higher than crystal whether Duncan or Tiffin made. I have not found enough Canterbury in other colors to get a feel for their prices yet. Prices for opalescent seem to at least double those for the crystal.

Duncan's light blue was called Sapphire and the opalescent blue was dubbed Cape Cod blue. The red was Ruby. Although not pictured, you may find opalescent pieces of Canterbury in pink called Cranberry. Jasmine yellow is the name of the opalescent tumbler shown on the bottom of page 37.

The 64 oz. water pitcher seems to be missing from many collections. This was a durable ware, but watch for scratches on the flat pieces. Too, buying early in the morning with dew on the glass can get you in trouble with glass that is cloudy! Look for that especially in areas where well water was predominate. If you know of additional pieces not listed or wish to help in relating prices on colored wares, just drop me a postcard! Computers are making the keeping of this information simpler when I manage to find the time to get it entered!

	Crystal		Crystal
Ash tray, 3"..	6.00	Bowl, 10" x 8½" x 5", oval	27.50
Ash tray, 3", club	8.00	Bowl, 10¾" x 4¾"	27.50
Ash tray, 4½", club	10.00	Bowl, 10½" x 5", crimped.................................	30.00
Ash tray, 5"...	12.00	Bowl, 11½" x 8¼", oval	30.00
Ash tray, 5½", club	15.00	Bowl, 12" x 2¾", gardenia	30.00
Basket, 3" x 3" x 3¼", oval, hdld.	20.00	Bowl, 12" x 3½", flared....................................	30.00
Basket, 3" x 4", crimped, hdld....................	27.50	Bowl, 12" x 3¾", crimped.................................	32.50
Basket, 3½", crimped, hdld	35.00	Bowl, 13" x 8½" x 3¼", oval, flared	35.00
Basket, 3½", oval, hdld.............................	25.00	Bowl, 13" x 10" x 5", crimped, oval	40.00
Basket, 4½" x 4¾" x 4¾", oval, hdld	40.00	Bowl, 15" x 2¾", shallow salad.........................	42.00
Basket, 4½" x 5" x 5", crimped, hdld.	45.00	Candle, 3", low...	12.50
Basket, 9¼" x 10" x 7¼"	55.00	Candle, 3½"..	12.50
Basket, 10" x 4¼" x 7", oval, hdld.	70.00	Candlestick, 6", 3-lite	25.00
Basket, 10" x 4½" x 8", oval, hdld.	75.00	Candlestick, 6"...	22.50
Basket, 11½", oval, hdld.	75.00	Candlestick, 7", w/U prisms.............................	65.00
Bowl, 4¼" x 2", finger...............................	9.00	Candy and cover, 8" x 3½", 3 hdld., 3 part	32.50
Bowl, 5" x 3¼", 2 part, salad dressing	12.50	Candy, 6½", w/5" lid...	32.50
Bowl, 5" x 3¼", salad dressing	12.50	Celery and relish, 10½" x 6¾" x 1¼", 2 hdld.,	
Bowl, 5½" x 1¾", one hdld., heart	9.00	2 part	30.00
Bowl, 5½" x 1¾", one hdld., square..............	9.00	Celery and relish, 10½" x 6¾" x 1¼", 2 hdld.,	
Bowl, 5½" x 1¾", one hdld., star..................	10.00	3 part	32.50
Bowl, 5½" x 1¾", one hdld., fruit	7.00	Celery, 9" x 4" x 1¼", 2 hdld............................	20.00
Bowl, 5½" x 1¾", one hdld., round	7.00	Cheese stand, 5½" x 3½" high	10.00
Bowl, 5", fruit nappy	8.00	Cigarette box w/cover, 3½" x 4½"	18.00
Bowl, 6" x 2", 2 hdld., round......................	10.00	Cigarette jar w/cover, 4"	20.00
Bowl, 6" x 2", 2 hdld.., sweetmeat, star	15.00	Comport, high, 6" x 5½" high	20.00
Bowl, 6" x 3¼", 2 part, salad dressing	14.00	Comport, low, 6" x 4½" high	18.00
Bowl, 6" x 3¼", salad dressing	14.00	Creamer, 2¾", 3 oz., individual........................	9.00
Bowl, 6" x 5¼" x 2¼", oval olive.................	10.00	Creamer, 3¾", 7 oz.	7.50
Bowl, 7½" x 2¼", crimped..........................	15.00	Cup...	10.00
Bowl, 7½" x 2¼", gardenia	15.00	Decanter w/stopper, 12", 32 oz.	55.00
Bowl, 8" x 2¾", crimped............................	20.00	Ice bucket or vase, 7"..	37.50
Bowl, 8" x 2½", flared................................	17.50	Ice bucket or vase, 6"..	32.50
Bowl, 8½" x 4"	22.00	Lamp, hurricane, w/prisms, 15"	75.00
Bowl, 9" x 2", gardenia	25.00	Marmalade, 4½" x 2¾", crimped.......................	12.00
Bowl, 9" x 4¼", crimped............................	27.50	Mayonnaise, 5" x 3¼"	15.00
Bowl, 9" x 6" x 3", oval..............................	30.00	Mayonnaise, 5½" x 3¼", crimped	17.50
Bowl, 10" x 5", salad..................................	30.00	Mayonnaise, 6" x 3¼".......................................	17.50

	Crystal
Pitcher, 9¼", 32 oz., hdld., martini	60.00
Pitcher, 9¼", 32 oz., martini	55.00
Pitcher, 64 oz.	225.00
Plate, 6½", one hdld., fruit	6.00
Plate, 6", finger bowl liner..............................	6.00
Plate, 7½"	9.00
Plate, 7½", 2 hdld., mayonnaise.......................	9.00
Plate, 8½"	10.00
Plate, 11¼", dinner	27.50
Plate, 11", 2 hdld. w/ring, cracker	20.00
Plate, 11", 2 hdld., sandwich	22.00
Plate, 13½", cake, hdld.	25.00
Plate, 14", cake	25.00
Relish, 6" x 2", 2 hdld., 2 part, round	12.00
Relish, 6" x 2", 2 hdld., 2 part, star	12.00
Relish, 7" x 5¼" x 2¼", 2 hdld., 2 part, oval......	15.00
Relish, 8" x 1¾", 3 hdld., 3 part	17.50
Relish, 9" x 1½", 3 hdld., 3 part	20.00
Rose bowl, 5"	20.00
Rose bowl, 6"	22.50
Salt and pepper	22.50
Sandwich tray, 12" x 5¼", center handle...........	35.00
Saucer	3.00
Sherbet, crimped, 4½", 2¾" high	10.00
Sherbet, crimped, 5½", 2¾" high	12.00
Stem, 3¾", 6 oz., ice cream	6.00
Stem, 4", 4½ oz., oyster cocktail	12.50
Stem, 4½", 6 oz., saucer champagne.................	9.00
Stem, 4¼", 1 oz., cordial, #5115......................	25.00
Stem, 4¼", 3½ oz., cocktail	10.00
Stem, 5½", 5 oz., saucer champagne, #5115......	12.00
Stem, 5¼", 3 oz., cocktail, #5115	14.00
Stem, 5", 4 oz., claret or wine	20.00
Stem, 6¾", 5 oz., claret, #5115	27.00
Stem, 6", 3½ oz., wine, #5115	27.50
Stem, 6", 9 oz., water	14.00
Stem, 7¼", 10 oz., water, #5115	17.50
Sugar, 2½", 3 oz., individual...........................	8.00
Sugar, 3", 7 oz.	7.50

	Crystal
Top hat, 3"...	18.00
Tray, 9", individual cr/sug...............................	10.00
Tray, 9" x 4" x 1¼", 2 part, pickle and olive	17.50
Tumbler, 2½", 5 oz., ftd., ice cream, #5115	10.00
Tumbler, 3¼", 4 oz., ftd., oyster cocktail, #5115 .	15.00
Tumbler, 3¾", 5 oz., flat, juice	8.00
Tumbler, 4¼", 5 oz., ftd., juice	7.50
Tumbler, 4¼", 5 oz., ftd., juice, #5115	10.00
Tumbler, 4½", 9 oz., flat, table, straight	12.00
Tumbler, 4½", 10 oz., ftd., water, #5115	12.50
Tumbler, 5½", 9 oz., ftd., luncheon goblet........	12.50
Tumbler, 5¾", 12 oz., ftd., ice tea, #5115.........	14.00
Tumbler, 6¼", 13 oz., flat, ice tea	18.00
Tumbler, 6¼", 13 oz., ftd., ice tea	18.00
Urn, 4½" x 4½"	15.00
Vase, 3", crimped violet.................................	15.00
Vase, 3½", clover leaf...................................	15.00
Vase, 3½", crimped......................................	15.00
Vase, 3½", crimped violet..............................	15.00
Vase, 3½", oval...	15.00
Vase, 4", clover leaf.....................................	17.50
Vase, 4", crimped..	17.50
Vase, 4", flared rim	17.50
Vase, 4", oval...	17.50
Vase, 4½" x 4¾"...	15.00
Vase, 4½", clover leaf...................................	20.00
Vase, 4½", crimped violet...............................	17.50
Vase, 4½", oval...	17.50
Vase, 5" x 5", crimped..................................	17.50
Vase, 5", clover leaf.....................................	25.00
Vase, 5", crimped..	17.50
Vase, 5½", crimped......................................	20.00
Vase, 5½", flower arranger.............................	27.50
Vase, 6½", clover leaf...................................	35.00
Vase, 7", crimped..	32.00
Vase, 7", flower arranger...............................	40.00
Vase, 8½" x 6"	50.00
Vase, 12", flared	75.00

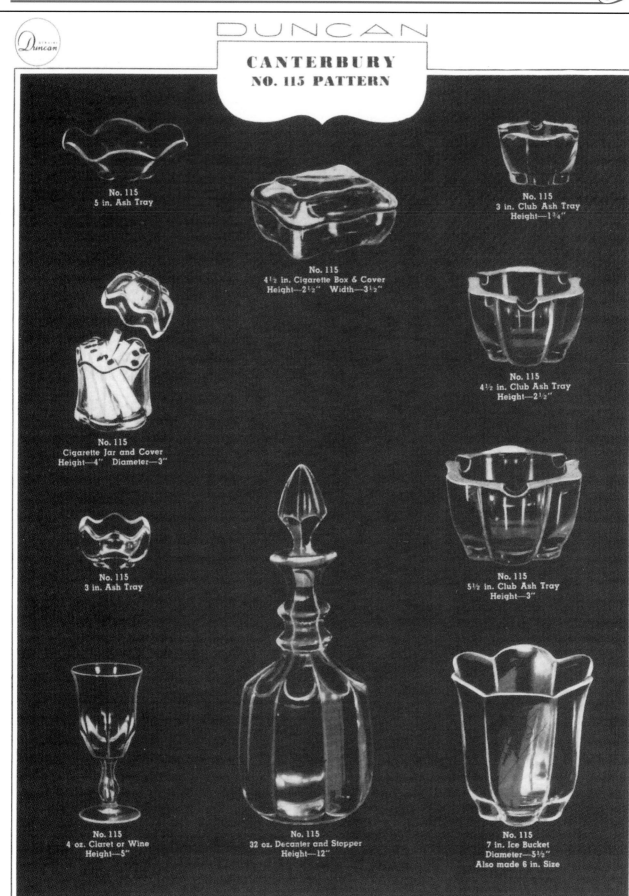

DUNCAN

CANTERBURY
NO. 115 PATTERN

No. 115
5 in. Ash Tray

No. 115
3 in. Club Ash Tray
Height—1¾"

No. 115
4½ in. Cigarette Box & Cover
Height—2½"   Width—3½"

No. 115
Cigarette Jar and Cover
Height—4"   Diameter—3"

No. 115
4½ in. Club Ash Tray
Height—2½"

No. 115
3 in. Ash Tray

No. 115
5½ in. Club Ash Tray
Height—3"

No. 115
4 oz. Claret or Wine
Height—5"

No. 115
32 oz. Decanter and Stopper
Height—12"

No. 115
7 in. Ice Bucket
Diameter—5½"
Also made 6 in. Size

Washington, Pa.   1-1-43

THE DUNCAN & MILLER GLASS CO.

50

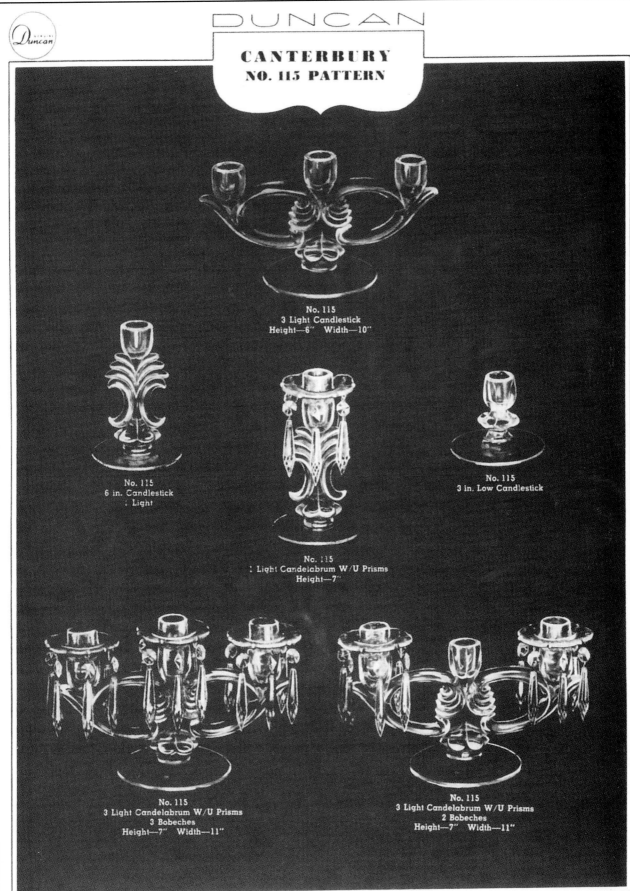

DUNCAN

CANTERBURY
NO. 115 PATTERN

No. 115
3 Light Candlestick
Height—6"   Width—10"

No. 115
6 in. Candlestick
: Light

No. 115
: Light Candelabrum W/U Prisms
Height—7"

No. 115
3 in. Low Candlestick

No. 115
3 Light Candelabrum W/U Prisms
3 Bobeches
Height—7"   Width—11"

No. 115
3 Light Candelabrum W/U Prisms
2 Bobeches
Height—7"   Width—11"

Washington. Pa.   1-1-43

THE DUNCAN & MILLER GLASS CO.

Colors: amber, Antique blue, Azalea, black, crystal, Evergreen, milk glass, Ritz blue, Ruby, Verde

Cape Cod colored pieces, mostly manufactured in the late 1960s and 1970s, have begun to pique the interest of collectors. Most of these colors are shown on page 45. The top two rows show Imperial's green called Verde; the darker green in the top row was known as Evergreen. Amber, black, and milk glass are also shown in row 2. The blue color shown in row 3 was called Antique blue. Row 3 also shows Ruby. Imperial's pink, Azalea, is depicted in the bottom row. Ritz blue (cobalt blue, not pictured) and Ruby are the colors that are most in demand. These two colors are selling 75% to 100% more than crystal, depending upon the piece. Prices for other colors are selling up to 50% more than crystal with most of them selling at reasonable prices. Verde is the slowest seller; but, there is a rising demand for Azalea.

Following the decanter in the bottom row of the next page is (in order) a 1602 cordial, 160 wine, 1602 wine, 1602 juice, 1602 claret, 1602 parfait, 1602 tea, and 1602 water goblet.

I have been seeing a few pieces of red flashed rims on pieces of Cape Cod recently. These were first issued mid-World War II.

	Crystal
Ash tray, 4", 160/134/1	14.00
Ash tray, 5½", 160/150	17.50
Basket, 9", handled, crimped, 160/221/0	195.00
Basket, 11" tall, handled, 160/40	125.00
Bottle, bitters, 4 oz., 160/235	60.00
Bottle, cologne, w/stopper, 1601	60.00
Bottle, condiment, 6 oz., 160/224	65.00
Bottle, cordial, 18 oz., 160/256	115.00
Bottle, decanter, 26 oz., 160/244	115.00
Bottle, ketchup, 14 oz., 160/237	210.00
Bowl, 3", handled mint, 160/183	20.00
Bowl, 3", jelly, 160/33	12.00
Bowl, 4", finger, 1602	12.00
Bowl, 4½", finger, 1604½A	12.00
Bowl, 4½", handled spider, 160/180	22.50
Bowl, 4½", dessert, tab handled, 160/197	23.00
Bowl, 5", dessert, heart shape, 160/49H	18.00
Bowl, 5", flower, 1605N	25.00
Bowl, 5½", fruit, 160/23B	10.00
Bowl, 5½", handled spider, 160/181	25.00
Bowl, 5½", tab handled, soup, 160/198	18.00
Bowl, 6", fruit, 160/3F	10.00
Bowl, 6", baked apple, 160/53X	9.00
Bowl, 6", handled, round mint, 160/51F	22.00
Bowl, 6", handled heart, 160/40H	20.00
Bowl, 6", handled mint, 160/51H	22.00
Bowl, 6", handled tray, 160/51T	20.00
Bowl, 6½", handled portioned spider, 160/187	27.50
Bowl, 6½", handled spider, 160/182	32.50
Bowl, 6½", tab handled, 160/199	25.00
Bowl, 7", nappy, 160/5F	22.00
Bowl, 7½", 160/7F	22.00
Bowl, 7½", 2-handled, 160/62B	27.50
Bowl, 8¾", 160/10F	27.50
Bowl, 9", footed fruit, 160/67F	62.50
Bowl, 9½", 2 handled, 160/145B	37.50
Bowl, 9½", crimped, 160/221C	75.00
Bowl, 9½", float, 160/221F	65.00
Bowl, 10", footed, 160/137B	70.00
Bowl, 10", oval, 160/221	75.00
Bowl, 11", flanged edge, 1608X	135.00
Bowl, 11", oval, 160/124	70.00
Bowl, 11", oval divided, 160/125	80.00
Bowl, 11", round, 1608A	65.00
Bowl, 11", salad, 1608D	40.00
Bowl, 11¼", oval, 1602	75.00
Bowl, 12", 160/75B	40.00

	Crystal
Bowl, 12", oval, 160/131B	70.00
Bowl, 12", oval crimped, 160/131C	90.00
Bowl, 12", punch, 160/20B	60.00
Bowl, 13", console, 160/75L	42.50
Bowl, 15", console, 1601/0L	75.00
Butter, 5", w/cover, handled, 160/144	30.00
Butter, w/cover, ¼ lb., 160/161	45.00
Cake plate, 10", 4 toed, 160/220	95.00
Cake stand, 10½", footed, 160/67D	45.00
Cake stand, 11", 160/103D	80.00
Candleholder, twin, 160/100	65.00
Candleholder, 3", single, 160/170	17.50
Candleholder, 4", 160/81	25.00
Candleholder, 4", Aladdin style, 160/90	135.00
Candleholder, 4½", saucer, 160/175	22.50
Candleholder, 5", 160/80	20.00
Candleholder, 5", flower, 160/45B	60.00
Candleholder, 5½", flower, 160/45N	95.00
Candleholder, 6", centerpiece, 160/48BC	75.00
Candy, w/cover, 160/110	65.00
Carafe, wine, 26 oz., 160/185	195.00
Celery, 8", 160/105	30.00
Celery, 10½", 160/189	55.00
Cigarette box, 4½", 160/134	45.00
Cigarette holder, ftd., 1602	12.50
Cigarette holder, Tom & Jerry mug, 160/200	32.50
Cigarette lighter, 1602	30.00
Coaster, w/spoon rest, 160/76	10.00
Coaster, 3", square, 160/85	12.50
Coaster, 4", round, 160/78	12.50
Coaster, 4½", flat, 160/1R	9.00
Comport, 5¼", 160F	27.50
Comport, 5¾", 160X	30.00
Comport, 6", 160/45	25.00
Comport, 6", w/cover, ftd., 160/140	75.00
Comport, 7", 160/48B	35.00
Comport, 11¼", oval, 1602, 6½" tall	175.00
Creamer, 160/190	30.00
Creamer, 160/30	8.00
Creamer, ftd., 160/31	15.00
Cruet, w/stopper, 4 oz., 160/119	22.50
Cruet, w/stopper, 5 oz., 160/70	25.00
Cruet, w/stopper, 6 oz., 160/241	37.50
Cup, tea, 160/35	7.00
Cup, coffee, 160/37	7.00
Cup, bouillon, 160/250	30.00
Decanter, bourbon, 160/260	80.00

	Crystal
Decanter, rye, 160/260	80.00
Decanter w/stopper, 30 oz., 160/163	65.00
Decanter w/stopper, 24 oz., 160/212	75.00
Egg cup, 160/225	32.50
Epergne, 2 pc., plain center, 160/196	225.00
Fork, 160/701	12.00
Gravy bowl, 18 oz., 160/202	75.00
Horseradish, 5 oz. jar, 160/226	80.00
Ice bucket, 6½", 160/63	175.00
Icer, 3 pc., bowl, 2 inserts, 160/53/3	50.00
Jar, 12 oz., hdld. peanut w/lid, 160/210	65.00
Jar, 10", "Pokal," 160/133	80.00
Jar, 11", "Pokal," 160/128	85.00
Jar, 15", "Pokal," 160/132	135.00
Jar, candy w/lid, wicker hand., 5" h., 160/194	80.00
Jar, cookie, w/lid, wicker hand., 6½" h., 160/195	100.00
Jar, peanut butter w/lid, wicker hand., 4" h., 160/193	75.00
Ladle, marmalade, 160/130	10.00
Ladle, mayonnaise, 160/165	10.00
Ladle, punch	25.00
Lamp, hurricane, 2 pc., 5" base, 160/79	85.00
Lamp, hurricane, 2 pc., bowl-like base, 1604	115.00
Marmalade, 3 pc. set, 160/89/3	32.50
Marmalade, 4 pc. set, 160/89	40.00
Mayonnaise, 3 pc. set, 160/52H	37.50
Mayonnaise, 3 pc., 160/23	27.50
Mayonnaise, 12 oz., hdld., spouted, 160/205	47.50
Mug, 12 oz., handled, 160/188	45.00
Mustard, w/cover & spoon, 160/156	22.50
Nut dish, 3", hdld., 160/183	30.00
Nut dish, 4", hdld., 160/184	30.00
Pepper mill, 160/236	30.00
Pitcher, milk, 1 pt., 160/240	42.50
Pitcher, ice lipped, 40 oz., 160/19	75.00
Pitcher, martini, blown, 40 oz., 160/178	185.00
Pitcher, ice lipped, 2 qt., 160/239	90.00
Pitcher, 2 qt., 160/24	80.00
Pitcher, blown, 5 pt., 160/176	150.00
Plate, 4½" butter, 160/34	8.00
Plate, 6", cupped (liner for 160/208 salad dressing), 160/209	25.00
Plate, 6½", bread & butter, 160/1D	7.00
Plate, 7", 160/3D	8.00
Plate, 7", cupped (liner for 160/205 Mayo), 160/206	35.00
Plate, 8", center handled tray, 160/149D	40.00
Plate, 8", crescent salad, 160/12	50.00
Plate, 8" cupped (liner for gravy), 160/203	40.00
Plate, 8", salad, 160/5D	9.00
Plate, 8½", 2 handled, 160/62D	30.00
Plate, 9", 160/7D	20.00
Plate, 9½", 2 hdld., 160/62D	40.00
Plate, 10", dinner, 160/10D	37.50
Plate, 11½", 2 handled, 160/145D	35.00
Plate, 12½" bread, 160/222	65.00
Plate, 13", birthday, 72 candle holes, 160/72	365.00
Plate, 13", cupped torte, 1608V	35.00
Plate, 13", torte, 1608F	37.50
Plate, 14", cupped, 160/75V	35.00
Plate, 14", flat, 160/75D	35.00
Plate, 16", cupped, 160/20V	60.00
Plate, 17", 2 styles, 160/10D or 20D	55.00
Platter, 13½", oval, 160/124D	55.00

	Crystal
Puff Box, w/cover, 1601	45.00
Relish, 8", hdld., 2 part, 160/223	37.50
Relish, 9½", 4 pt., 160/56	35.00
Relish, 9½", oval, 3 part, 160/55	35.00
Relish, 11", 5 part, 160/102	55.00
Relish, 11¼", 3 part, oval, 1602	70.00
Salad dressing, 6 oz., hdld., spouted, 160/208	60.00
Salad set, 14" plate, 12" bowl, fork & spoon, 160/75	95.00
Salt & pepper, individual, 160/251	15.00
Salt & pepper, pr., ftd., 160/116	20.00
Salt & pepper, pr., ftd., stemmed, 160/243	40.00
Salt & pepper, pr., 160/96	15.00
Salt & pepper, pr. square, 160/109	20.00
Salt dip, 160/61	15.00
Salt spoon, 1600	8.00
Saucer, tea, 160/35	2.00
Saucer, coffee, 160/37	2.00
Server, 12", ftd. or turned over, 160/93	85.00
Spoon, 160/701	12.00
Stem, 1½ oz., cordial, 1602	10.00
Stem, 3 oz., wine, 1602	8.00
Stem, 3½ oz., cocktail, 1602	8.00
Stem, 5 oz., claret, 1602	14.00
Stem, 6 oz., low sundae, 1602	7.00
Stem, 6 oz., parfait, 1602	12.00
Stem, 6 oz., sherbet, 1600	15.00
Stem, 6 oz., tall sherbet, 1602	8.50
Stem, 9 oz., water, 1602	9.50
Stem, 10 oz., water, 1600	20.00
Stem, 11 oz., dinner goblet, 1602	10.00
Stem, 14 oz., goblet, magnum, 160	35.00
Stem, oyster cocktail, 1602	10.00
Sugar, 160/190	30.00
Sugar, 160/30	7.00
Sugar, ftd., 160/31	15.00
Toast, w/cover, 160/123	150.00
Tom & Jerry footed punch bowl, 160/200	350.00
Tray, square covered sugar & creamer, 160/25/26	140.00
Tray, 7", for creamer/sugar, 160/29	15.00
Tray, 11", pastry, center handle, 160/68D	70.00
Tumbler, 2½ oz., whiskey, 160	12.50
Tumbler, 6 oz., ftd., juice, 1602	9.00
Tumbler, 6 oz., juice, 1600	10.00
Tumbler, 7 oz., old-fashioned, 160	12.50
Tumbler, 10 oz., ftd., water, 1602	10.00
Tumbler, 10 oz., water, 160	10.00
Tumbler, 12 oz., ftd., ice tea, 1602	12.00
Tumbler, 12 oz., ftd., tea, 1600	19.00
Tumbler, 12 oz., ice tea, 160	12.50
Tumbler, 14 oz., double old-fashioned, 160	27.50
Tumbler, 16 oz., 160	35.00
Vase, 6¼", ftd., 160/22	35.00
Vase, 6½", ftd., 160/110B	70.00
Vase, 7½", ftd., 160/22	40.00
Vase, 8", fan, 160/87F	195.00
Vase, 8½", flip, 160/143	50.00
Vase, 8½", ftd., 160/28	42.50
Vase, 10", cylinder, 160/192	80.00
Vase, 10½", hdld., urn, 160/186	165.00
Vase, 11", flip, 1603	165.00
Vase, 11½", ftd., 160/21	65.00

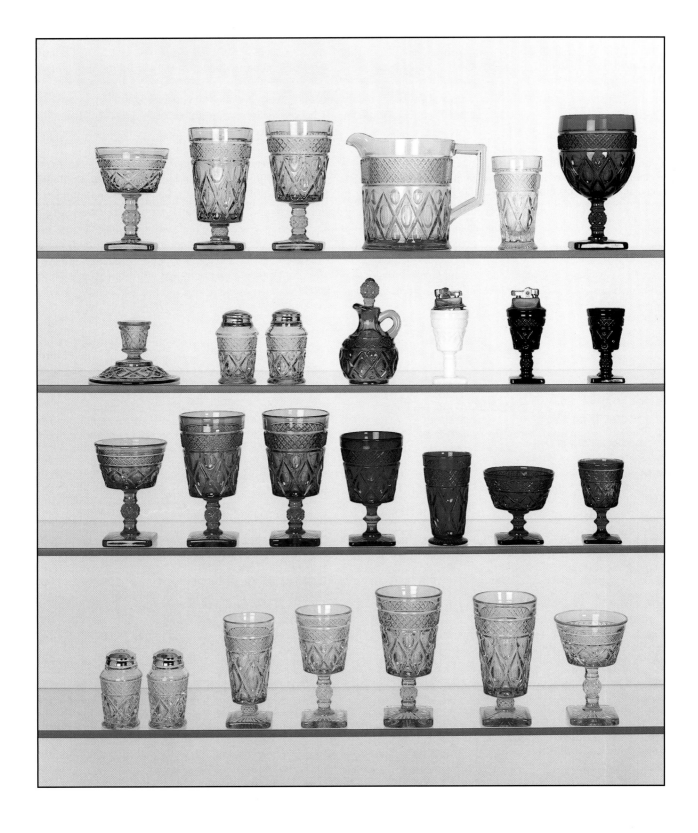

Colors: crystal, Moonlight Blue, white, amber, amethyst, pink, emerald green, pink, cobalt blue, milk glass

A few scarce items of Caprice are on everyone's want list. Clarets, moulded, straight side, nine and twelve ounce tumblers, and footed whiskeys seem to have been swallowed up into long-time collections; most beginners have never had a chance to buy them. Blue bitters bottles and covered cracker jars are only in a few collections although most major collections have the Doulton pitcher. The supply of these has dwindled; the price scares off all but the wealthy.

An Alpine Moonlight Blue Doulton can be seen in my *Very Rare Glassware of the Depression Years — Sixth Edition*. It is the only one confirmed to exist! Alpine pieces have satinized panels or bases (top of page 49). More collectors are soliciting these recently; for a long time they were shunned. You should know that this effect can now be accomplished with materials from a craft shop. The satinized finish on newly adorned pieces is not as smoothly done as it was originally — but it can be done! Crystal Caprice candle reflectors and punch bowls are rarely found; but there is strong demand for them when they do turn up! A punch bowl was recently sold three times at one show in Missouri. Of course, the price went up with each sale!

Many recent collectors who endeavored to collect pink Caprice have already relinquished that task. There just is not enough pink in the market to encourage them to continue. Prices for pink Caprice have equaled those of blue in basic pieces and are zipping by blue in harder-to-find items. Enough pink was made to assemble a basic set; yet a collection of pink will lack many of the interesting pieces found in blue or crystal! As far as I know, colors other than blue, crystal, and pink cannot be collected in anything other than luncheon sets. Prices for infrequently seen colors of Caprice follow those of blue. There are few collectors searching for amber or amethyst, and those particular colored pieces are priced closer to crystal.

A crystal vase shown on page 48 is a factory whimsy as far as we know. If you have or see another like this, please let me know. A whimsy is a piece that was made by workers that was not a factory scheduled piece for the pattern! Usually these were carried home (lunch box) and given as gifts to wives or sweethearts, a souvenir of what the worker was making.

	Crystal	Blue, Pink		Crystal	Blue, Pink
Ash tray, 2¾", 3 ftd., shell, #213	8.00	15.00	* Spade, 6½", #172	30.00	110.00
* Ash tray, 3", #214	6.00	12.00	* Butterdish, ¼ lb., #52	235.00	
* Ash tray, 4", #215	8.00	16.00	Cake plate, 13", ftd., #36	150.00	395.00
* Ash tray, 5", #216	10.00	25.00	Candle reflector, #73	295.00	
Bonbon, 6", oval, ftd., #155	20.00	42.00	Candlestick, 2½", ea., #67	15.00	32.50
Bonbon, 6", sq., 2 hdld., #154	15.00	40.00	Candlestick, 2-lite, keyhole, 5", #647	20.00	65.00
Bonbon, 6", sq., ftd., #133	20.00	50.00	Candlestick, 3-lite, #74	40.00	125.00
Bottle, 7 oz., bitters, #186	195.00	425.00	Candlestick, 3-lite, keyhole, #638	25.00	75.00
Bowl, 2", 4 ftd., almond #95	25.00	65.00	Candlestick, 3-lite, #1338	35.00	75.00
* Bowl, 5", 2 hdld., jelly, #151	15.00	35.00	Candlestick, 5-lite, #1577	155.00	
Bowl, 5", fruit, #18	30.00	75.00	Candlestick, 5", ea., keyhole, #646	20.00	35.00
Bowl, 5", fruit, crimped, #19	30.00	85.00	Candlestick, 6", 2-lite, ea., #72	40.00	95.00
Bowl, 8", 4 ftd., #49	40.00	115.00	Candlestick, 7", ea., w/prism, #70	25.00	75.00
Bowl, 8", sq., 4 ftd., #50	50.00	125.00	Candlestick, 7½", dbl., ea., #69	150.00	525.00
* Bowl, 8", 3 pt., relish, #124	20.00	45.00	Candy, 6", 3 ftd., w/cover, #165	42.50	115.00
Bowl, 9½", crimped, 4 ftd., #52	40.00	115.00	Candy, 6", w/cover (divided), #168	55.00	150.00
Bowl, 9", pickle, #102	25.00	60.00	Celery & relish, 8½", 3 pt., #124	20.00	45.00
Bowl, 10", salad, 4 ftd., #57	40.00	125.00	Cigarette box, w/cover, 3½" x 2¼", #207	20.00	50.00
Bowl, 10", sq., 4 ftd., #58	35.00	115.00	Cigarette box, w/cover, 4½" x 3½", #208	25.00	75.00
Bowl, 10½", belled, 4 ftd., #54	35.00	75.00	Cigarette holder, 2" x 2¼", triangular, #205	20.00	70.00
Bowl, 10½", crimped, 4 ftd., #53	40.00	110.00	Cigarette holder, 3" x 3", triangular, #204	22.00	55.00
Bowl, 11", crimped, 4 ftd., #60	35.00	115.00	Coaster, 3½", #13	15.00	35.00
* Bowl, 11", 2 hdld., oval, 4 ftd., #65	40.00	115.00	Comport, 6", low ftd., #130	22.00	50.00
Bowl, 11½", shallow, 4 ftd., #81	35.00	100.00	Comport, 7", low ftd., #130	24.00	50.00
* Bowl, 12", 4 pt. relish, oval, #126	80.00	235.00	Comport, 7", tall, #136	40.00	100.00
* Bowl, 12", relish, 3 pt., rect., #125	50.00	150.00	Cracker jar & cover, #202	350.00	1,200.00
Bowl, 12½", belled, 4 ftd., #62	35.00	90.00	* Creamer, large, #41	13.00	30.00
Bowl, 12½", crimped, 4 ftd., #61	35.00	100.00	* Creamer, medium, #38	11.00	22.00
Bowl, 13", cupped, salad, #80	75.00	195.00	* Creamer, ind., #40	12.00	27.50
Bowl, 13", crimped, 4 ftd., #66	40.00	125.00	Cup, #17	14.00	35.00
Bowl, 13½", 4 ftd., shallow cupped #82	40.00	110.00	Decanter, w/stopper, 35 oz., #187	150.00	425.00
Bowl, 15", salad, shallow, #84	55.00	175.00	Finger bowl & liner, #16	40.00	110.00
Bridge set:			Finger bowl and liner, blown, #300	45.00	125.00
* Cloverleaf, 6½", #173	30.00	110.00	Ice bucket, #201	60.00	185.00
* Club, 6½", #170	30.00	110.00	Marmalade, w/cover, 6 oz., #89	65.00	210.00
Diamond, 6½", #171	30.00	110.00	* Mayonnaise, 6½", 3 pc. set, #129	42.00	115.00
* Heart, 6½", #169	35.00	125.00			

CAPRICE

	Crystal	Blue, Pink		Crystal	Blue, Pink
* Mayonnaise, 8", 3 pc. set, #106	50.00	120.00	Tumbler, #300, 10 oz., ftd. water	20.00	40.00
Mustard, w/cover, 2 oz., #87	55.00	165.00	Tumbler, #300, 12 oz., ftd. tea	20.00	40.00
Nut Dish, 2½", #93	22.00	55.00	Tumbler, #301, blown, 4½ oz., low		
Nut Dish, 2½", divided, #94	25.00	60.00	oyster cocktail	17.50	
* Oil, 3 oz., w/stopper, #101	30.00	90.00	Tumbler, #301, blown, 5 oz., juice	15.00	
* Oil, 5 oz., w/stopper, #100	70.00	210.00	Tumbler, #301, blown, 12 oz., tea	20.00	
Pitcher, 32 oz., ball shape, #179	135.00	350.00	* Tumbler, 9 oz., straight side, #14	40.00	110.00
Pitcher, 80 oz., ball shape, #183	110.00	335.00	* Tumbler, 10 oz., ftd., #10	20.00	40.00
Pitcher, 90 oz., tall Doulton style, #178	750.00	3,995.00	Tumbler, 12 oz., flat, #184	25.00	50.00
Plate, 5½", bread & butter, #20	12.00	27.50	Tumbler, 12 oz., ftd., #9	22.50	47.50
Plate, 6½", bread & butter, #21	11.00	24.00	* Tumbler, 12 oz., straight side, #15	37.50	95.00
Plate, 6½", hdld., lemon, #152	11.00	20.00	Tumbler, #310, 5 oz., flat, juice	25.00	75.00
Plate, 7½", salad, #23	15.00	27.50	Tumbler, #310, 7 oz., flat, old-		
Plate, 8½", luncheon, #22	14.00	32.50	fashioned	35.00	135.00
* Plate, 9½", dinner, #24	45.00	135.00	Tumbler, #310, 10 oz., flat, table	25.00	65.00
Plate, 11", cabaret, 4 ftd., #32	30.00	70.00	Tumbler, #310, 11 oz., flat, tall, 4¹³⁄₁₆"	25.00	80.00
Plate, 11½", cabaret, #26	30.00	70.00	Tumbler, #310, 12 oz., flat, tea	30.00	135.00
Plate, 14", cabaret, 4 ftd., #33	35.00	85.00	Vase, 3½", #249	70.00	195.00
Plate, 14", 4 ftd., #28	35.00	85.00	Vase, 4", blown, #251, blown	70.00	195.00
Plate, 16", #30	40.00	125.00	Vase, 4¼", #241, ball	45.00	115.00
Punch bowl, ftd., #498	2,500.00		Vase, 4½", #237, ball	60.00	150.00
* Salad dressing, 3 pc., ftd. & hdld.,			Vase, 4½", #252, blown	55.00	160.00
2 spoons, #112	190.00	495.00	Vase, 4½", #337, crimped top	55.00	110.00
Salt & pepper, pr., ball, #91	40.00	115.00	Vase, 4½", #344, crimped top	85.00	185.00
* Salt & pepper, pr., flat, #96	28.00	100.00	Vase, 4½", #244	60.00	150.00
Salt & pepper, indiv., ball, pr., #90	45.00	155.00	Vase, 5", ivy bowl, #232	60.00	225.00
Salt & pepper, indiv., flat, pr., #92	40.00	135.00	Vase, 5½", #245	65.00	165.00
Salver, 13", 2 pc. (cake atop			Vase, 5½", #345, crimped top	65.00	210.00
pedestal), #31	165.00	600.00	Vase, 6", #242, ftd.	35.00	140.00
Saucer, #17	2.50	5.50	Vase, 6", blown, #254	175.00	350.00
Stem, #300, blown, 1 oz., cordial	45.00	140.00	Vase, 6", #342, crimped top	95.00	200.00
Stem, #300, blown, 2½ oz., wine	27.50	62.50	Vase, 6", #235, ftd., rose bowl	75.00	150.00
Stem, #300, blown, 3 oz., cocktail	22.00	45.00	Vase, 6½", #238, ball	65.00	165.00
Stem, #300, blown, 4½ oz., claret	75.00	250.00	Vase, 6½", #338, crimped top	100.00	250.00
Stem, #300, blown, 4½ oz., low			Vase, 7½", #246	65.00	185.00
oyster cocktail	20.00	50.00	Vase, 7½", #346, crimped top	110.00	275.00
Stem, #300, blown, 5 oz., parfait	90.00	215.00	Vase, 8", #236, ftd., rose bowl	100.00	225.00
Stem, #300, blown, 6 oz., low sherbet	11.00	18.00	Vase, 8½", #243	110.00	225.00
Stem, #300, blown, 6 oz., tall sherbet	12.00	27.50	Vase, 8½", #239, ball	95.00	210.00
Stem, #300, blown, 9 oz. water	18.00	38.00	Vase, 8½", #339, crimped top	85.00	225.00
Stem, #301, blown, 1 oz., cordial	40.00		Vase, 8½", #343, crimped top	140.00	325.00
Stem, #301, blown, 2½ oz., wine	27.50		Vase, 9¼", #240, ball	140.00	310.00
Stem, #301, blown, 3 oz., cocktail	20.00		Vase, 9½", #340, crimped top	160.00	395.00
Stem, #301, blown, 4½ oz., claret	50.00				
Stem, #301, blown, 6 oz., sherbet	13.00				
Stem, #301, blown, 9 oz., water	17.50				
* Stem, 3 oz., wine, #6	38.00	135.00			
* Stem, 3½ oz., cocktail, #3	25.00	55.00			
* Stem, 4½ oz., claret, #5	70.00	250.00			
Stem, 4½ oz., fruit cocktail, #7	37.50	110.00			
Stem, 5 oz., low sherbet, #4	25.00	85.00			
* Stem, 7 oz., tall sherbet, #2	17.50	36.00			
Stem, 10 oz., water, #1	27.50	47.50			
* Sugar, large, #41	12.50	25.00			
* Sugar, medium, #38	10.00	22.50			
* Sugar, indiv., #40	12.00	25.00			
* Tray, for sugar & creamer, #37	17.50	40.00			
Tray, 9" oval, #42	22.00	50.00			
* Tumbler, 2 oz., flat, #188	22.00	65.00			
Tumbler, 3 oz., ftd., #12	27.50	75.00			
Tumbler, 5 oz., ftd., #11	20.00	50.00			
Tumbler, 5 oz., flat, #180	22.00	50.00			
Tumbler, #300, 2½ oz., whiskey	40.00	210.00			
Tumbler, #300, 5 oz., ftd., juice	18.00	37.50			

*Moulds owned by Summit Art Glass and many of these pieces
have been reproduced.

48

Colors: blue, crystal, amber, red

Blue Caribbean dinnerware items (dinner plates, cups, and saucers) are creating headaches for collectors searching for them. Add to that the elusive punch bowl and pitchers and blue Caribbean will dig deep into your cash reserves — if you can find these items to buy at all!

A few collectors have begun gathering crystal Caribbean since they are becoming disillusioned in finding blue. Some are combining blue and crystal, the "in" mode of today's collector. In the past, collectors rarely mixed colors or patterns; but today's trend of mixing colors has come about from necessity as much as anything. It's encouraging some wonderfully creative settings!

Notice the amber pieces on page 53. Amber Caribbean is rarely seen except for the cigarette jar and ash trays. The powder jar and candle are unusual. In fact, I had never seen or heard of a three-footed candlestick in Caribbean until this one was brought into a glass show last year. Do you have a mate? I am scheduled to write a candlestick book in 1999, so if you have another color in Caribbean, I'd like to know that!

The crystal punch set with colored handled punch cup and ladle sells for about $75.00 more than the plain crystal set. Red and cobalt blue handled pieces are more desirable than amber! Several collectors have mentioned how they have used a mixture of colored handles on their punch cups.

	Crystal	Blue
Ash tray, 6", 4 indent	15.00	32.50
Bowl, 3¾" x 5", folded side, hdld.	16.00	35.00
Bowl, 4½", finger	16.00	32.00
Bowl, 5", fruit nappy (takes liner), hdld.	12.00	25.00
Bowl, 5" x 7", folded side, hdld.	16.00	37.50
Bowl, 6½", soup (takes liner)	16.00	37.50
Bowl, 7", hdld.	25.00	45.00
Bowl, 7¼", ftd., hdld., grapefruit	20.00	45.00
Bowl, 8½"	27.50	70.00
Bowl, 9", salad	30.00	75.00
Bowl, 9¼", veg., flared edge	30.00	65.00
Bowl, 9¼", veg., hdld.	30.00	75.00
Bowl, 9½", epergne, flared edge	37.50	95.00
Bowl, 10", 6¼ qt., punch	90.00	450.00
Bowl, 10", 6¼ qt. punch, flared top (catalog lists as salad)	90.00	400.00
Bowl, 10¾", oval, flower, hdld.	35.00	80.00
Bowl, 12", console, flared edge	40.00	90.00
Candelabrum, 4¾", 2-lite	40.00	90.00
Candlestick, 7¼", 1-lite, w/bl. prisms	65.00	175.00
Candy dish w/cover, 4" x 7"	40.00	95.00
Cheese/cracker crumbs, 3½" h., plate 11", hdld.	40.00	85.00
Cigarette holder (stack ash tray top)	35.00	80.00
Cocktail shaker, 9", 33 oz.	90.00	195.00
Creamer	14.00	25.00
Cruet	37.50	85.00
Cup, tea	15.00	60.00
Cup, punch	8.00	22.50
Epergne, 4 pt., flower (12" bowl; 9½" bowl; 7¾" vase; 14" plate)	190.00	425.00
Ice bucket, 6½", hdld.	75.00	175.00
Ladle, punch	35.00	100.00
Mayonnaise, w/liner, 5¾", 2 pt., 2 spoons, hdld.	42.50	100.00
Mayonnaise, w/liner, 5¾", hdld., 1 spoon	35.00	80.00
Mustard, 4", w/slotted cover	35.00	65.00
Pitcher, 4¼", 9 oz., syrup	65.00	155.00
Pitcher, 4¾" 16 oz., milk	95.00	250.00

	Crystal	Blue
Pitcher, w/ice lip, 9", 72 oz., water	195.00	595.00
Plate, 6", hdld., fruit nappy liner	4.00	12.00
Plate 6¼", bread/butter	5.00	12.00
Plate, 7¼", rolled edge, soup liner	5.00	12.50
Plate, 7½", salad	10.00	20.00
Plate, 8", hdld., mayonnaise liner	6.00	14.00
Plate, 8½", luncheon	15.00	35.00
Plate, 10½", dinner	55.00	135.00
Plate, 11", hdld., cheese/cracker liner	20.00	42.50
Plate, 12", salad liner, rolled edge	22.00	55.00
Plate, 14"	25.00	70.00
Plate, 16", torte	35.00	85.00
Plate, 18", punch underliner	40.00	95.00
Relish, 6", round, 2 pt.	12.00	25.00
Relish, 9½", 4 pt., oblong	30.00	65.00
Relish, 9½", oblong	27.50	60.00
Relish, 12¾", 5 pt., rnd.	40.00	90.00
Relish, 12¾", 7 pt., rnd.	40.00	90.00
Salt dip, 2½"	11.00	25.00
Salt & pepper, 3", metal tops	32.00	90.00
Salt & pepper, 5", metal tops	37.50	110.00
Saucer	4.00	8.00
Server, 5¾", ctr. hdld.	13.00	45.00
Server, 6½", ctr. hdld.	22.00	50.00
Stem, 3", 1 oz., cordial	70.00	250.00
Stem, 3½", 3½ oz., ftd., ball stem, wine	20.00	40.00
Stem, 3⅝", 2½ oz., wine (egg cup shape)	22.50	35.00
Stem, 4", 6 oz., ftd., ball stem, champagne	14.00	27.50
Stem, 4¼", ftd., sherbet	8.00	17.50
Stem, 4¾", 3 oz., ftd., ball stem, wine	22.00	55.00
Stem, 5¾", 8 oz., ftd., ball stem	18.00	42.50
Sugar	11.00	22.00
Syrup, metal cutoff top	85.00	195.00
Tray, 6¼", hand., mint, div.	14.00	30.00
Tray, 12¾", rnd.	25.00	50.00
Tumbler, 2¼", 2 oz., shot glass	25.00	60.00
Tumbler, 3½", 5 oz., flat	20.00	45.00
Tumbler, 5¼", 11½ oz., flat	20.00	45.00
Tumbler, 5½", 8½ oz., ftd.	22.00	50.00
Tumbler, 6½", 11 oz., ftd., ice tea	27.50	60.00
Vase, 5¾", ftd., ruffled edge	22.00	55.00
Vase, 7¼", ftd., flared edge, ball	27.50	60.00
Vase, 7½", ftd., flared edge, bulbous	32.50	70.00
Vase, 7¾", flared edge, epergne	35.00	110.00
Vase, 8", ftd., straight side	40.00	85.00
Vase, 9", ftd., ruffled top	50.00	195.00
Vase, 10", ftd.	55.00	135.00

Colors: crystal, Ebony (gold encrusted)

A couple of pieces of Chantilly have been highlighted with white powder on the opposite page to give a better view of the pattern.

There is a more extensive listing for Cambridge pieces under Rose Point in this book. Many Chantilly pieces are not listed here. When pricing herein unlisted Chantilly items by the Rose Point list, remember that Rose Point items are a minimum of 30% to 50% higher due to collector demand!

Yes, I know the oil bottle's stopper is missing in the bottom photo. Metal adorned pieces pictured are Faberware or Sterling. Many times these items are more difficult to sell.

Cambridge's Chantilly is most often collected on stemware line #3625. This stem is depicted on page 229.

	Crystal
Bowl, 7", bonbon, 2 hdld., ftd.	17.50
Bowl, 7", relish/pickle, 2 pt.	18.00
Bowl, 7", relish/pickle	20.00
Bowl, 9", celery/relish, 3 pt.	25.00
Bowl, 10", 4 ftd., flared	40.00
Bowl, 11", tab hdld.	35.00
Bowl, 11½", tab hdld. ftd.	35.00
Bowl, 12", celery/relish, 3 pt.	35.00
Bowl, 12", 4 ftd., flared	35.00
Bowl, 12", 4 ftd., oval	40.00
Bowl, 12", celery/relish, 5 pt.	45.00
Butter, w/cover, round	135.00
Butter, ¼ lb.	225.00
Candlestick, 5"	18.00
Candlestick, 6", 2-lite, "fleur-de-lis"	37.50
Candlestick, 6", 3-lite	42.50
Candy box, w/cover, ftd.	145.00
Candy box, w/cover, rnd.	75.00
Cocktail icer, 2 pc.	60.00
Comport, 5½"	30.00
Comport, 5⅜", blown	37.50
Creamer	14.50
Creamer, indiv., #3900, scalloped edge	12.50
Cup	17.50
Decanter, ftd.	165.00
Decanter, ball	195.00
Hat, small	195.00
Hat, large	250.00
Hurricane lamp, candlestick base	120.00
Hurricane lamp, keyhole base w/prisms	185.00
Ice bucket, w/chrome handle	70.00
Marmalade & cover	55.00
Mayonnaise (sherbet type bowl w/ladle)	25.00
Mayonnaise, div. w/liner & 2 ladles	40.00
Mayonnaise, w/liner & ladle	37.50
Mustard & cover	65.00
Oil, 6 oz., hdld., w/stopper	75.00
Pitcher, ball	120.00
Pitcher, Doulton	285.00
Pitcher, upright	185.00
Plate, crescent, salad	125.00
Plate, 6½", bread/butter	6.50
Plate, 8", salad	12.50
Plate, 8", tab hdld., ftd., bonbon	15.00
Plate, 10½", dinner	60.00
Plate, 12", 4 ftd., service	30.00
Plate, 13", 4 ftd.	30.00
Plate, 13½", tab hdld., cake	32.50
Plate, 14", torte	35.00
Salad dressing bottle	110.00
Salt & pepper, pr., flat	27.50
Salt & pepper, footed	30.00
Salt & pepper, handled	30.00
Saucer	3.00

	Crystal
Stem, #3600, 1 oz., cordial	52.50
Stem, #3600, 2½ oz., cocktail	24.00
Stem, #3600, 2½ oz., wine	32.00
Stem, #3600, 4½ oz., claret	42.00
Stem, #3600, 4½ oz., low oyster cocktail	15.00
Stem, #3600, 7 oz., tall sherbet	17.50
Stem, #3600, 7 oz., low sherbet	15.00
Stem, #3600, 10 oz., water	20.00
Stem, #3625, 1 oz., cordial	52.50
Stem, #3625, 3 oz., cocktail	27.50
Stem, #3625, 4½ oz., claret	40.00
Stem, #3625, 4½ oz., low oyster cocktail	16.00
Stem, #3625, 7 oz., low sherbet	16.00
Stem, #3625, 7 oz., tall sherbet	18.00
Stem, #3625, 10 oz., water	25.00
Stem, #3775, 1 oz., cordial	52.50
Stem, #3775, 2½ oz., wine	32.00
Stem, #3775, 3 oz., cocktail	25.00
Stem, #3775, 4½ oz., claret	40.00
Stem, #3775, 4½ oz., oyster cocktail	15.00
Stem, #3775, 6 oz., low sherbet	15.00
Stem, #3775, 6 oz., tall sherbet	17.50
Stem, #3779, 1 oz., cordial	62.50
Stem, #3779, 2½ oz., wine	32.00
Stem, #3779, 3 oz., cocktail	25.00
Stem, #3779, 4½ oz., claret	42.00
Stem, #3779, 4½ oz., low oyster cocktail	15.00
Stem, #3779, 6 oz., tall sherbet	17.50
Stem, #3779, 6 oz., low sherbet	15.00
Stem, #3779, 9 oz., water	20.00
Sugar	13.50
Sugar, indiv., #3900, scalloped edge	11.00
Syrup	150.00
Tumbler, #3600, 5 oz., ftd., juice	17.00
Tumbler, #3600, 12 oz., ftd., tea	22.00
Tumbler, #3625, 5 oz., ftd., juice	15.00
Tumbler, #3625, 10 oz., ftd., water	17.50
Tumbler, #3625, 12 oz., ftd., tea	24.00
Tumbler, #3775, 5 oz., ftd., juice	15.00
Tumbler, #3775, 10 oz., ftd., water	15.00
Tumbler, #3775, 12 oz., ftd., tea	20.00
Tumbler, #3779, 5 oz., ftd., juice	17.00
Tumbler, #3779, 12 oz., ftd., tea	22.00
Tumbler, 13 oz.	24.00
Vase, 5", globe	35.00
Vase, 6", high ftd., flower	30.00
Vase, 8", high ftd., flower	35.00
Vase, 9", keyhole base	40.00
Vase, 10", bud	35.00
Vase, 11", ftd., flower	75.00
Vase, 11", ped. ftd., flower	80.00
Vase, 12", keyhole base	75.00
Vase, 13", ftd., flower	110.00

Note: See pages 228 – 229 for stem identification.

Colors: Crystal, Flamingo, Moongleam, Hawthorne, Marigold

I have been asking for six years for someone to please find a Charter Oak #130 one lite candleholder to photograph. The base is an oak leaf with stem curled up having an acorn for the candle cup! Now that I am beginning a candlestick book, I really need to find one!

I am beginning to see a few pieces of Charter Oak in my travels. Rarely is there more than a piece or two. Stemware is the usual fare, but occasionally other pieces jump out at you! Prices have remained constant over the last few years. The one problem now is that more people recognize this as a Heisey pattern because of its inclusion in my book and mistakes in pricing are not as easily found!

Those acorns are the telltale sign of this pattern. Plantation with its pineapple stems and Charter Oak with acorn stems are hard to miss.

I have only displayed Flamingo (pink), but there are several other colors of Charter Oak that can be collected. I am fond of the Moongleam (green), but I rarely see it for sale! Yeoman cups and saucers are often used with this set since there were no cups and saucers made. A Yeoman set is pictured here, but not priced in the Charter Oak listing. I refer to that since several readers have wanted to know why I did not price a cup and saucer in my listing. These are priced under Yeoman.

Watch for the #4262 Charter Oak lamp that was manufactured from 1928 to 1931. It looks like a blown comport with an acorn in the stem. The lamp has a diamond optic font that was filled with water to magnify the design and to counterbalance the lamp. This is the superlative Charter Oak piece to own!

	Crystal	Flamingo	Moongleam	Hawthorne	Marigold
Bowl, 11", floral, #116 (oak leaf)	30.00	45.00	47.50	75.00	
Bowl, finger, #3362	10.00	17.50	20.00		
Candleholder, 1-lite, #130, "Acorn"	100.00	125.00	135.00		
Candlestick, 3", #116 (oak leaf)	25.00	35.00	45.00	125.00	
Candlestick, 5", 3-lite, #129, "Tricorn"		90.00	110.00	140.00	150.00
Comport, 6", low ft., #3362	45.00	50.00	55.00	70.00	100.00
Comport, 7", ftd., #3362	50.00	55.00	60.00	160.00	175.00
Lamp, #4262 (blown comport/water filled to magnify design & stabilize lamp)	400.00	700.00	850.00		
Pitcher, flat, #3362		160.00	180.00		
Plate, 6", salad, #1246 (Acorn & Leaves)	5.00	10.00	12.50	20.00	
Plate, 7", luncheon/salad, #1246 (Acorn & Leaves)	8.00	12.00	17.50	22.50	
Plate, 8", luncheon, #1246 (Acorn & Leaves)	10.00	15.00	20.00	25.00	
Plate, 10½", dinner, #1246 (Acorn & Leaves)	30.00	45.00	55.00	70.00	
Stem, 3 oz., cocktail, #3362	10.00	25.00	25.00	45.00	40.00
Stem, 3½ oz., low ft., oyster cocktail, #3362	8.00	20.00	20.00	40.00	35.00
Stem, 4½ oz., parfait, #3362	15.00	25.00	35.00	60.00	50.00
Stem, 6 oz., saucer champagne, #3362	10.00	15.00	20.00	50.00	40.00
Stem, 6 oz., sherbet, low ft. #3362	10.00	15.00	20.00	50.00	40.00
Stem, 8 oz., goblet, high ft., #3362	15.00	35.00	35.00	95.00	60.00
Stem, 8 oz., luncheon goblet, low ft., #3362	15.00	40.00	40.00	95.00	60.00
Tumbler, 10 oz., flat, #3362	10.00	15.00	20.00	35.00	30.00
Tumbler, 12 oz., flat, #3362	12.50	17.50	22.50	40.00	35.00

Colors: crystal

Were Cherokee Rose cups and saucers made? I cannot find any collectors who own a set. There are no listings in any of the catalogs I have, but reports of their existence have occurred from time to time. I will try to show you shakers in the next edition; a few pairs have now been found!

I see the stemware line #17399 more than I do #17403, but that might be because of the geographical region I shop. The #17399 is the tear drop style that is shown on most of the stemware in the top picture. The #17403 stem style is represented by the cordial and the wine on the far right in the lower photo. There is little difference in stemware line prices at this time.

My experiences with collectors tell me that most of them have as many stems as they can use, but not serving pieces! Actually, there are more Cherokee Rose serving pieces available than in most other Tiffin patterns. Just be glad you can find some serving pieces! Sugar and creamer sets have turned out to be in greater supply than the demand except for the plain handled style. Those are really scarce. Note that I have not found a sugar with plain handles as yet!

I was happy to find an icer even without a liner for it. It is not as flamboyant as the one in Fuchsia, but it will do as a newly discovered piece of Cherokee Rose. That icer is shown in the bottom photo on the lower right. If you find one with a liner, let me know.

	Crystal
Bowl, 5", finger.	25.00
Bowl, 6", fruit or nut	22.00
Bowl, 7", salad	37.50
Bowl, 10", deep salad	55.00
Bowl, 10½", celery, oblong	35.00
Bowl, 12", crimped	50.00
Bowl, 12½", centerpiece, flared	50.00
Bowl, 13", centerpiece	60.00
Cake plate, 12½", center hdld.	45.00
Candlesticks, pr., double branch	90.00
Comport, 6"	35.00
Creamer	20.00
Icer	90.00
Mayonnaise, liner and ladle	55.00
Pitcher	335.00
Plate, 6", sherbet	6.00
Plate, 8", luncheon	12.50
Plate, 13½", turned-up edge, lily	40.00
Plate, 14", sandwich	40.00
Relish, 6½", 3 pt.	25.00
Relish, 12½", 3 pt.	45.00
Shaker, pr.	65.00

	Crystal
Stem, 1 oz., cordial	50.00
Stem, 2 oz., sherry	35.00
Stem, 3½ oz., cocktail	20.00
Stem, 3½ oz., wine	35.00
Stem, 4 oz., claret	50.00
Stem, 4½ oz., parfait	45.00
Stem, 5½ oz., sherbet/champagne	20.00
Stem, 9 oz., water	25.00
Sugar	20.00
Table bell	75.00
Tumbler, 4½ oz., oyster cocktail	22.00
Tumbler, 5 oz., ftd., juice	22.00
Tumbler, 8 oz., ftd., water	22.50
Tumbler, 10½ oz., ftd., ice tea	35.00
Vase, 6", bud	25.00
Vase, 8", bud	35.00
Vase, 8½", tear drop	70.00
Vase, 9¼", tub	85.00
Vase, 10", bud	40.00
Vase, 11", bud	45.00
Vase, 11", urn	100.00
Vase, 12", flared	125.00

Colors: crystal, Sahara yellow, Moongleam green, Flamingo pink, and Alexandrite orchid

Pieces with encircled flowers are known as "formal" Chintz. All the pieces in the bottom photo are "formal" Chintz while those in top one are Chintz. Notice that I have only found the cream soup in both forms of Chintz. I have never found any stems or tumblers in "formal" Chintz, but maybe I am not looking in the right places. I prefer the more detailed design of "formal" Chintz.

Chintz salt and pepper shakers have been listed! It astounds me how some items slip by for years until someone asks me why an item is not listed. If you have pieces that are not in any pattern's listing, please let me know!

Sahara is the color most collected, but a few collectors latch onto crystal. A set of Alexandrite Chintz appeared at the Heisey show a few years ago. It took only a short while for these beautiful, expensive pieces to disappear into collections.

Do not confuse this pattern with Fostoria's Chintz; and learn that you must also specify the company name when you ask for a pattern named Chintz. It was a popular appelation that was used by many glass companies for their wares.

	Crystal	Sahara
Bowl, cream soup	18.00	35.00
Bowl, finger, #4107	10.00	20.00
Bowl, 5½", ftd., preserve, hdld.	15.00	30.00
Bowl, 6", ftd., mint	20.00	32.00
Bowl, 6", ftd., 2 hdld., jelly	17.00	35.00
Bowl, 7", triplex relish	20.00	40.00
Bowl, 7½", Nasturtium	20.00	40.00
Bowl, 8½", ftd., 2 hdld., floral	35.00	70.00
Bowl, 11", dolphin ft., floral	45.00	110.00
Bowl, 13", 2 pt., pickle & olive	15.00	35.00
Comport, 7", oval	40.00	85.00
Creamer, 3 dolphin ft.	20.00	45.00
Creamer, individual	12.00	28.00
Cup	15.00	25.00
Grapefruit, ftd., #3389, Duquesne	30.00	60.00
Ice bucket, ftd.	85.00	135.00
Mayonnaise, 5½", dolphin ft.	35.00	65.00
Oil, 4 oz.	60.00	135.00
Pitcher, 3 pint, dolphin ft.	125.00	250.00
Plate, 6", square, bread	6.00	15.00
Plate, 7", square, salad	8.00	18.00
Plate, 8", square, luncheon	10.00	22.00
Plate, 10½", square, dinner	40.00	85.00
Plate, 12", two hdld.,	25.00	47.50
Plate, 13", hors d' oeuvre, two hdld.	30.00	65.00
Platter, 14", oval	35.00	85.00
Salt and pepper, pr.	40.00	85.00
Saucer	3.00	5.00
Stem, #3389, Duquesne, 1 oz., cordial	115.00	250.00
Stem, #3389, 2½ oz., wine	25.00	50.00
Stem, #3389, 3 oz., cocktail	17.50	35.00
Stem, #3389, 4 oz., claret	25.00	50.00
Stem, #3389, 4 oz., oyster cocktail	12.50	25.00
Stem, #3389, 5 oz., parfait	17.50	35.00
Stem, #3389, 5 oz., saucer champagne	12.50	25.00
Stem, #3389, 5 oz., sherbet	10.00	17.50
Stem, #3389, 9 oz., water	17.50	35.00
Sugar, 3 dolphin ft.	20.00	45.00
Sugar, individual	12.00	28.00
Tray, 10", celery	15.00	30.00
Tray, 12", sq., ctr. hdld., sandwich	35.00	65.00
Tray, 13", celery	18.00	35.00
Tumbler, #3389, 5 oz., ftd., juice	12.00	22.00
Tumbler, #3389, 8 oz., soda	13.00	24.00
Tumbler, #3389, 10 oz., ftd., water	14.00	27.50
Tumbler, #3389, 12 oz., iced tea	16.00	33.00
Vase, 9", dolphin ft.	95.00	185.00

Colors: crystal, pink

I have enjoyed looking for this pattern. You never know what will turn up. I do know that Classic stems abound. The cup in the top picture was found right before our photography session; but; alas, no saucer. That pink pitcher is a beauty! Note the crystal one at the bottom which is a different style. Watch for scratches on the dinner plates — if you can find any! I, personally, have found few serving pieces save for that lonely two-handled bowl. You will undoubtedly find other pieces of Classic; let me hear what you uncover so I get them in the listing.

Pink Classic stems are found on the #17024 line that is also found with Tiffin's Flanders pattern. I have never seen a pink flat tumbler. Have you? Crystal stemmed items seem to surface on the #14185 line. There are some size inconsistencies within these two stemware lines. We have measured both colors and noted the discrepancies in these price listings.

	Crystal	Pink
Bowl, 2 hdld., 8" x 9¼"	110.00	
Comport, 6" wide, 3¼" tall	60.00	
Creamer, flat	35.00	60.00
Creamer,. ftd.	35.00	
Cup	50.00	
Finger bowl, ftd.	20.00	30.00
Pitcher, 61 oz.	250.00	395.00
Pitcher, 61 oz., w/cover	325.00	495.00
Plate, 6⅜", champagne liner	10.00	
Plate, 8"	12.50	15.00
Plate, 10", dinner	85.00	
Saucer	10.00	
Sherbet, 3⅛", 6½ oz., short	17.50	27.50
Stem, 3⅞", 1 oz., cordial	45.00	
Stem, 4¹⁵⁄₁₆", 3 oz., wine	32.50	47.50
Stem, 4⅞", 3¾ oz., cocktail	40.00	
Stem, 4⅞", 4 oz., cocktail	27.50	
Stem, 6½", 5 oz., parfait	35.00	50.00
Stem, 6", 7½ oz., saucer champagne	22.50	32.50
Stem, 7¼", 9 oz., water	30.00	45.00
Sugar, flat	35.00	60.00
Sugar, ftd.	35.00	
Tumbler, 3½", 5 oz., ftd., juice	17.50	
Tumbler, 4½", 8½ oz., ftd., water	20.00	37.50
Tumbler, 4⅛", 10½ oz., flat, water	25.00	
Tumbler, 5⁹⁄₁₆", 14 oz., ftd., tea	30.00	
Tumbler, 6", 13 oz., ftd., iced tea		47.50
Tumbler, 6¹⁄₁₆", 14 oz., ftd., iced tea	30.00	
Tumbler, 6¼", 6½ oz., ftd., Pilsner	32.50	
Vase, bud, 6½"	27.50	
Vase, bud, 10½"	42.50	

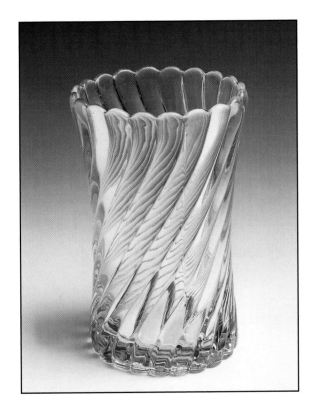

Colors: crystal, Zircon/Limelight, Sahara, and rare in amber

Crystolite is an easily recognized Heisey pattern; and due to the fact that most pieces are marked with the familiar H in a diamond, you will rarely find a bargain. Crystolite prices are creeping upward.

The cocktail shaker is missing from most collections, but you can see one here! The 6" basket, rye bottle, and pressed tumblers have always been difficult to locate. Blown tumblers are found in both photos! You can tell what pieces are elusive by looking at the prices. Many collectors find that the punch set is a practical piece to use or display. The 20" punch liner is harder to find than the punch bowl!

	Crystal
Ash tray, 3½", square	6.00
Ash tray, 4½", square	10.00
Ash tray, 5", w/book match holder	45.00
Ash tray (coaster), 4", rnd.	8.00
Basket, 6", hdld.	550.00
Bonbon, 7", shell	22.00
Bonbon, 7½", 2 hdld.	15.00
Bottle, 1 qt., rye, #107 stopper	300.00
Bottle, 4 oz., bitters, w/short tube	175.00
Bottle, 4 oz., cologne, w/#108 stopper	75.00
w/drip stop	150.00
Bottle, syrup, w/drip & cut top	135.00
Bowl, 7½ quart, punch	120.00
Bowl, 2", indiv. swan nut (or ash tray)	20.00
Bowl, 3", indiv. nut, hdld.	20.00
Bowl, 4½", dessert (or nappy)	20.00
Bowl, 5", preserve	20.00
Bowl, 5", 1000 island dressing, ruffled top	30.00
Bowl, 5½", dessert	14.00
Bowl, 6", oval jelly, 4 ft.	22.00
Bowl, 6", preserve, 2 hdld.	20.00
Bowl, 7", shell praline	35.00
Bowl, 8", dessert (sauce)	30.00
Bowl, 8", 2 pt. conserve, hdld.	55.00
Bowl, 9", leaf pickle	30.00
Bowl, 10", salad, rnd.	50.00
Bowl, 11", w/attached mayonnaise (chip 'n dip)	225.00
Bowl, 12", gardenia, shallow	65.00
Bowl, 13", oval floral, deep	60.00
Candle block, 1-lite, sq.	20.00
Candle block, 1-lite, swirl	20.00
Candlestick, 1-lite, ftd.	25.00
Candlestick, 1-lite, w/#4233, 5", vase	35.00
Candlestick, 2-lite	35.00
Candlestick, 2-lite, bobeche & 10 "D" prisms	65.00
Candlestick sans vase, 3-lite	45.00
Candlestick, w/#4233, 5", vase, 3-lite	55.00
Candy, 5½", shell and cover	55.00
Candy box, w/cover, 7", 3 part	70.00
Candy box, w/cover, 7"	60.00
Cheese, 5½", ftd.	27.00
Cigarette box, w/cover, 4"	35.00
Cigarette box, w/cover, 4½"	40.00
Cigarette holder, ftd.	35.00
Cigarette holder, oval	25.00
Cigarette holder, rnd.	25.00
Cigarette lighter	30.00
Coaster, 4"	12.00
Cocktail shaker, 1 qt. w/#1 strainer; #86 stopper	325.00
Comport, 5", ftd., deep, #5003, blown rare	300.00
Creamer, indiv.	20.00
Creamer, reg.	30.00
Creamer, round	40.00
Cup	22.00
Cup, punch or custard	9.00
Hurricane block, 1-lite, sq.	40.00
Hurricane block, w/#4061, 10" plain globe, 1-lite, sq.	100.00
Ice tub, w/silver plate handle	120.00

	Crystal
Jar, covered cherry	110.00
Jam jar, w/cover	70.00
Ladle, glass, punch	35.00
Ladle, plastic	10.00
Mayonnaise, 5½", shell, 3 ft.	35.00
Mayonnaise, 6", oval, hdld.	40.00
Mayonnaise ladle	12.00
Mustard & cover	55.00
Oil bottle, 3 oz.	45.00
Oil bottle, w/stopper, 2 oz.	35.00
Oval creamer, sugar, w/tray, set	70.00
Pitcher, ½ gallon, ice, blown	140.00
Pitcher, 2 quart swan, ice lip	700.00
Plate, 7", salad	15.00
Plate, 7", shell	32.00
Plate, 7", underliner for 1000 island dressing bowl	20.00
Plate, 7½", coupe	40.00
Plate, 8", oval, mayonnaise liner	20.00
Plate, 8½", salad	20.00
Plate, 10½", dinner	100.00
Plate, 11", ftd., cake salver	350.00
Plate, 11", torte	40.00
Plate, 12", sand.	45.00
Plate, 13", shell torte	100.00
Plate, 14", sand.	55.00
Plate, 14", torte	50.00
Plate, 20", buffet or punch liner	125.00
Puff box, w/cover, 4¾"	75.00
Salad dressing set, 3 pc.	38.00
Salt & pepper, pr.	45.00
Saucer	6.00
Stem, 1 oz., cordial, wide optic, blown, #5003	130.00
Stem, 3½ oz., cocktail, w.o., blown, #5003	28.00
Stem, 3½ oz., claret, w.o., blown, #5003	38.00
Stem, 3½ oz., oyster cocktail, w.o. blown, #5003	28.00
Stem, 6 oz., sherbet/saucer champagne, #5003	18.00
Stem, 10 oz., water, #1503, pressed	500.00
Stem, 10 oz., w.o., blown, #5003	35.00
Sugar, indiv.	20.00
Sugar, reg.	30.00
Sugar, round	40.00
Syrup pitcher, drip cut	135.00
Tray, 5½", oval, liner indiv. creamer/sugar set	40.00
Tray, 9", 4 pt., leaf relish	40.00
Tray, 10", 5 pt., rnd. relish	45.00
Tray, 12", 3 pt., relish, oval	35.00
Tray, 12", rect., celery	38.00
Tray, 12", rect., celery/olive	35.00
Tumbler, 5 oz., ftd., juice, w.o., blown, #5003	38.00
Tumbler, 8 oz., pressed, #5003	60.00
Tumbler, 10 oz., pressed	70.00
Tumbler, 10 oz., iced tea, w.o., blown, #5003	40.00
Tumbler, 12 oz., ftd., iced tea, w.o., blown, #5003	38.00
Urn, 7", flower	75.00
Vase, 3", short stem	45.00
Vase, 6", ftd.	35.00
Vase, 12"	225.00

and Glass Co., 1926 – 1940s

Colors: crystal, French crystal, frosted crystal, green and frosted green, pink and frosted pink, Ruby flashed, white and assorted ceramic colors

"Dance of the Nudes" is the only name I had ever heard this pattern called; I've found out that the original name was Dancing Nymph. It's hard to buck traditional names, but at least you now know the proper one. When the pricey Ruba Rombic was introduced six years ago, bargains in that pattern disappeared overnight. Will this nymph dance to that tune? These prices are presently more reasonable when compared to many of Consolidated's patterns.

This will serve only as an introduction to Dancing Nymph; we will try to delve deeper next time. Let's cover colors to start. First, that green has a blue cast to it as illustrated in the photograph. French Crystal is clear nudes with etched background like the plate in row 3. The other colors are self-explanatory except for the unusual ceramic colors. Ceramic colors were obtained by covering the bottom of a crystal plate with color, wiping the nude designs clear, and firing the plate. The Honey (yellow) plate in row 3 is an example. These ceramic colors are highly desirable and expensive! Other colors with this process are Sepia (brown), white, dark blue, light blue, pinkish lavender, and light green. You may also find an ice blue colored plate with frosted background; it is rarely seen.

The first production of this pattern lasted from its introduction in 1926 until Consolidated closed in 1932. Upon reopening in 1936, the cupped up saucer and sherbet plates were added to the line. You can see the cupped saucer in row two and the cupped sherbet plates in row 3. These sherbet plates are like a shallow bowl. The flatter version is shown in row 1 with sherbets atop them. Sherbet plates are rarer than 8" plates and should actually sell for more due to scarcity. Interestingly enough, even Fire-King collectors pay three to four times the price of salad plates for 6" plates in some patterns. Collectors of Elegant glass have been slow to accept that.

Candlesticks in Dancing Nymph are very rare; I paid a fortune for a pair to photograph. Not two months later, I found a group of 23 pieces including a pair of candles for half of what I had paid for the candlesticks alone. That sometimes happens; but that way you have pieces to sell! Additionally, the 16" palace bowl and the 18" palace plate are rarely found. Be on the lookout for them; so will I, for the next book!

	Crystal	Frosted Crystal French Crystal	*Frosted Pink or Green	Ceramic Colors
Bowl, 4½"	35.00	65.00	85.00	110.00
Bowl, 8"	75.00	125.00	200.00	275.00
Bowl, 16", palace.........................	600.00	1200.00		1500.00
Candle, pr.	325.00	500.00		700.00
Cup...	35.00	55.00	85.00	110.00
Plate, 6", cupped			75.00	
Plate, 6", sherbet..........................	25.00	45.00	75.00	100.00
Plate, 8", salad	35.00	65.00		125.00
Plate, 10"....................................	60.00	95.00	140.00	195.00
Platter, 18", palace.......................	600.00	1000.00		1250.00
Saucer, coupe			35.00	
Saucer, flat..................................	12.50	20.00	35.00	40.00
Sherbet...	35.00	65.00	85.00	
Tumbler, 3½", cocktail	35.00	65.00		
Tumbler, 5½", goblet	45.00	75.00	125.00	175.00
Vase, 5½", crimped......................	75.00	125.00		150.00
Vase, 5½", fan	75.00	125.00		150.00

*Subtract 10% to 15% for unfrosted.

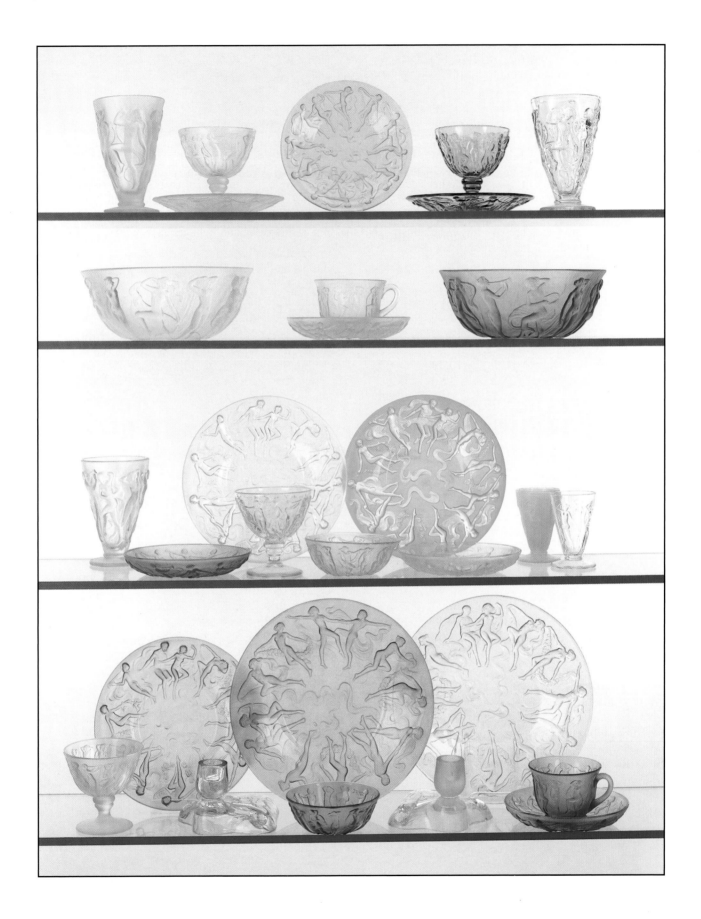

Colors: Emerald green, Peach-Blo, Carmen, Royal blue, Amber, Moonlight blue, Ebony

Decagon is the name of the blank on which many of Cambridge's etchings are found. This ten-sided blank is noticed whenever Cleo, Rosalie, and Imperial Hunt Scene patterns are etched on it. However, collectors of those patterns usually see the pattern itself rather than the Decagon blank! Yet, there are some very enthusiastic collectors of this plain, unetched Decagon "pattern."

Royal blue (cobalt) and Moonlight blue (top picture) are the colors most collected. You will find that Peach-Blo (pink), Emerald (green), and amber are more plentiful, but Moonlight blue is the color of choice. Pattern availability is only one important consideration in collecting! Color plays a primary role; and blue usually wins out.

The off-center snack plate and the flat soup are uncommon Decagon pieces and are especially desirable in blue. I still need one blue relish insert to finish that tray pictured. It was broken 14 years ago right before a photography session, and I have never encountered another! Have you?

	Pastel Colors	Red Blue		Pastel Colors	Red Blue
Basket, 7", 2 hdld. (upturned sides)	15.00	25.00	Mayonnaise, w/liner & ladle	18.00	50.00
Bowl, bouillon, w/liner	7.50	25.00	Oil, 6 oz., tall, w/hdld. & stopper	60.00	110.00
Bowl, cream soup, w/liner	20.00	30.00	Plate, 6¼", bread/butter	3.00	5.00
Bowl, 2½", indiv., almond	22.00	40.00	Plate, 7", 2 hdld.	9.00	15.00
Bowl, 3¾", flat rim, cranberry	17.00	27.50	Plate, 7½"	4.00	10.00
Bowl, 3½" belled, cranberry	17.00	27.50	Plate, 8½", salad	10.00	18.00
Bowl, 5½", 2 hdld., bonbon	10.00	20.00	Plate, 9½", dinner	45.00	65.00
Bowl, 5½", belled, fruit	5.50	15.00	Plate, 10", grill	25.00	40.00
Bowl, 5¾", flat rim, fruit	8.00	15.00	Plate, 10", service	25.00	35.00
Bowl, 6", belled, cereal	15.00	25.00	Plate, 12½", service	25.00	50.00
Bowl, 6", flat rim, cereal	15.00	25.00	Relish, 6 inserts	85.00	150.00
Bowl, 6", ftd., almond	25.00	45.00	Salt dip, 1½", ftd.	17.00	28.00
Bowl, 6¼", 2 hdld., bonbon	12.00	20.00	Sauce boat & plate	55.00	90.00
Bowl, 8½", flat rim, soup "plate"	22.00	40.00	Saucer	1.50	3.00
Bowl, 9", rnd., veg.	28.00	45.00	Server, center hdld.	20.00	30.00
Bowl, 9", 2 pt., relish	25.00	37.50	Stem, 1 oz., cordial	40.00	65.00
Bowl, 9½", oval, veg.	30.00	40.00	Stem, 3½ oz., cocktail	14.00	22.00
Bowl, 10", berry	30.00	40.00	Stem, 6 oz., low sherbet	10.00	16.00
Bowl, 10½", oval, veg.	30.00	40.00	Stem, 6 oz., high sherbet	12.00	22.00
Bowl, 11", rnd. veg.	30.00	42.00	Stem, 9 oz., water	17.00	30.00
Bowl, 11", 2 pt., relish	35.00	32.00	Sugar, lightning bolt handles	7.00	12.00
Comport, 5¾"	20.00	27.50	Sugar, ftd.	9.00	20.00
Comport, 6½", low ft.	20.00	30.00	Sugar, scalloped edge	9.00	20.00
Comport, 7", tall	25.00	42.50	Sugar, tall, lg. ft.	20.00	35.00
Creamer, ftd.	10.00	20.00	Tray, 8", 2 hdld., flat pickle	20.00	35.00
Creamer, scalloped edge	9.00	18.00	Tray, 9", pickle	20.00	35.00
Creamer, lightning bolt handles	7.00	12.00	Tray, 11", oval, service	20.00	40.00
Creamer, tall, lg. ft.	10.00	22.00	Tray, 11", celery	20.00	40.00
Cup	6.00	10.00	Tray, 12", center handled	20.00	35.00
French dressing bottle, "Oil/Vinegar"	70.00	125.00	Tray, 12", oval, service	22.00	40.00
Gravy boat, w/2 hdld. liner (like spouted cream soup)	70.00	110.00	Tray, 13", 2 hdld., service	25.00	40.00
Ice bucket	35.00	65.00	Tray, 15", oval, service	35.00	65.00
Ice tub	35.00	55.00	Tumbler, 2½ oz., ftd.	18.00	28.00
Mayonnaise, 2 hdld., w/2 hdld. liner and ladle	27.00	45.00	Tumbler, 5 oz., ftd.	10.00	18.00
			Tumbler, 8 oz., ftd.	12.00	22.00
			Tumbler, 10 oz., ftd.	15.00	25.00
			Tumbler, 12 oz., ftd.	20.00	35.00

Colors: light amber, green, pink, black, crystal

Examine the Black Forest pattern shot if you confuse these two patterns. Deer and trees are the prevalent theme of "Deerwood," whereas Black Forest depicts moose and trees.

There is no mayonnaise listed although I have had several reports of one. It was actually listed in old company catalogs as a whipped cream pail instead of a mayonnaise. Terminology of the old glass companies often differs. I don't believe either mayonnaise or whipped cream would have kept very well in those days of ice boxes!

Gold decorated, black "Deerwood" is quickly being bought by people who are not necessarily collectors, but just like its looks. This has caused some upward price adjustments! Not much of this is being found, but gold decorated pieces really make the pattern stand out. See the sugar pattern shot. Green and pink make up the large settings this time!

That flat, three-part, pink candy in the bottom photo is a Paden City blank and not U.S. Glass. This makes a researcher's job more "fun" than needed! A U.S. Glass etching on a Paden City candy! There is catalog documentation for "Deerwood." It makes you wonder if some other company did some etchings of "Deerwood." It definitely was produced at Tiffin, but maybe some of the contracts were sublet. The reason I say this is because a collector friend met a man who told her his job used to be running moulds back and forth between different glass factories. He said he moved them as many as three days a week and because of the cost of the moulds, he had to be bonded to get the job. He also said that, "Sometimes the other companies changed the mould a bit; but, often as not, they just ran it as it was." It probably will not make purists very happy, but that would explain a lot of "mysteries" of glass production!

	*Black	Amber	Green	Pink
Bowl, 10", straight edge				45.00
Bowl, 12", console			55.00	60.00
Bowl, 10", footed	125.00			
Cake plate, low pedestal			60.00	60.00
Candlestick, 2½"	55.00		35.00	
Candlestick, 4"				50.00
Candy dish, w/cover, 3 part, flat				100.00
Candy jar, w/cover, ftd. cone			110.00	110.00
Celery, 12"			60.00	
Cheese and cracker			95.00	95.00
Comport, 10", low, ftd., flared	110.00			55.00
Creamer, 2 styles	60.00		40.00	40.00
Cup				70.00
Plate, 5½"			12.00	12.00
Plate, 7½", salad				22.00
Plate, 9½", dinner				70.00
Plate, 10¼", 2 hdld.	125.00			
Saucer				20.00
Server, center hdld.			40.00	40.00
Stem, 2 oz., wine, 4½"				40.00
Stem, 6 oz., sherbet, 4¾"			27.50	
Stem, 6 oz., cocktail, 5"			32.50	
Stem, 9 oz., water, 7"	110.00		45.00	45.00
Sugar, 2 styles	60.00		40.00	40.00
Tumbler, 9 oz.			37.50	37.50
Tumbler, 12 oz., tea, 5½"		45.00		
Vase, 7", sweet pea, rolled edge			95.00	95.00
Vase, 10", ruffled top			110.00	100.00
Vase, 12", 2 handles	135.00			
Whipped cream pail, w/ladle			45.00	45.00

*Add 20% for gold decorated.

Colors: crystal; some pink, yellow, blue, Heatherbloom, Emerald green, amber, Crown Tuscan

Diane is a Cambridge pattern that appears in an abundance of colors; but it is not feasible to acquire a set except in crystal. With good fortune, you might discover a luncheon set in yellow, green, or amber; but colored Diane appears only occasionally.

This time I have chosen to show a wide range of crystal. There are several rarely seen items pictured on the next page. The dinner bell, bitters bottle, and round ball shaker are difficult to find. The ball shaker has a square, screwed-on glass base that is often damaged. It must be difficult to fill these as they have to be turned upside down to put salt or pepper in them — and unless your fingers cover the holes, it flows out while you are trying to pour into it!

Note the two styles of shot or whiskey glasses. The "barrel" shot style is usually found with round decanters and the sham bottom with footed decanters. The item between the ball shaker and the small sugar left of center is a cigarette holder.

You have several choices for stemware collecting in Diane; pick whichever you like. I tend to prefer the Regency style pictured next to the bitters bottle in the back. Cambridge has only a few etched lines that use this ornate stem line, but Diane is one of them!

	Crystal		Crystal
Basket, 6", 2 hdld., ftd.	20.00	Comport, 5½"	27.50
Bottle, bitters	145.00	Comport, 5⅜", blown	37.50
Bowl, #3106, finger, w/liner	37.50	Creamer	14.00
Bowl, #3122	25.00	Creamer, indiv., #3500 (pie crust edge)	15.00
Bowl, #3400, cream soup, w/liner	35.00	Creamer, indiv., #3900, scalloped edge	15.00
Bowl, 3", indiv. nut, 4 ftd.	50.00	Creamer, scroll handle, #3400	15.00
Bowl, 5", berry	20.00	Cup	20.00
Bowl, 5¼", 2 hdld., bonbon	20.00	Decanter, ball	210.00
Bowl, 6", 2 hdld., ftd., bonbon	20.00	Decanter, lg. ftd.	185.00
Bowl, 6", 2 pt., relish	20.00	Decanter, short ft., cordial	215.00
Bowl, 6", cereal	30.00	Hurricane lamp, candlestick base	135.00
Bowl, 6½", 3 pt. relish	25.00	Hurricane lamp, keyhole base w/prisms	225.00
Bowl, 7", 2 hdld., ftd., bonbon	25.00	Ice bucket, w/chrome hand.	65.00
Bowl, 7", 2 pt., relish	22.00	Mayonnaise, div., w/liner & ladles	45.00
Bowl, 7", relish or pickle	25.00	Mayonnaise (sherbet type w/ladle)	35.00
Bowl, 9", 3 pt., celery or relish	35.00	Mayonnaise, w/liner, ladle	40.00
Bowl, 9½", pickle (like corn)	30.00	Oil, 6 oz., w/stopper	125.00
Bowl, 10", 4 ft., flared	45.00	Pitcher, ball	155.00
Bowl, 10", baker	45.00	Pitcher, Doulton	300.00
Bowl, 11", 2 hdld.	40.00	Pitcher, martini	650.00
Bowl, 11", 4 ftd.	45.00	Pitcher, upright	185.00
Bowl, 11½", tab hdld., ftd.	45.00	Plate, 6", 2 hdld., plate.	7.00
Bowl, 12", 3 pt., celery & relish	35.00	Plate, 6", sq., bread/butter	5.00
Bowl, 12", 4 ft.	45.00	Plate, 6½", bread/butter	5.00
Bowl, 12", 4 ft., flared	45.00	Plate, 8", 2 hdld., ftd., bonbon	11.00
Bowl, 12", 4 ft., oval	55.00	Plate, 8", salad	10.00
Bowl, 12", 4 ft., oval, w/"ears" hdld.	55.00	Plate, 8½"	11.00
Bowl, 12", 5 pt., celery & relish	37.50	Plate, 10½", dinner	65.00
Butter, rnd.	145.00	Plate, 12", 4 ft., service	40.00
Cabinet flask	265.00	Plate, 13", 4 ft., torte	40.00
Candelabrum, 2-lite, keyhole	27.50	Plate, 13½", 2 hdld.	35.00
Candelabrum, 3-lite, keyhole	35.00	Plate, 14", torte	45.00
Candlestick, 1-lite, keyhole	20.00	Platter, 13½"	70.00
Candlestick, 5"	20.00	Salt & pepper, ftd., w/glass tops, pr.	35.00
Candlestick, 6", 2-lite, "fleur-de-lis"	32.50	Salt & pepper, pr., flat	35.00
Candlestick, 6", 3-lite	40.00	Saucer	5.00
Candy box, w/cover, rnd.	85.00	Stem, #1066, 1 oz., cordial	55.00
Cigarette urn	45.00	Stem, #1066, 3 oz., cocktail	16.00
Cocktail shaker, glass top	150.00	Stem, #1066, 3 oz., wine	30.00
Cocktail shaker, metal top	95.00	Stem, #1066, 3½ oz., tall cocktail	17.50
Cocktail icer, 2 pc.	65.00	Stem, #1066, 4½ oz., claret	45.00

	Crystal
Stem, #1066, 5 oz., oyster/cocktail	15.00
Stem, #1066, 7 oz., low sherbet	14.00
Stem, #1066, 7 oz., tall sherbet	15.00
Stem, #1066, 11 oz., water	25.00
Stem, #3122, 1 oz., cordial	55.00
Stem, #3122, 2½ oz., wine	30.00
Stem, #3122, 3 oz., cocktail	14.00
Stem, #3122, 4½ oz., claret	45.00
Stem, #3122, 4½ oz., oyster/cocktail	16.00
Stem, #3122, 7 oz., low sherbet	14.00
Stem, #3122, 7 oz., tall sherbet	18.00
Stem, #3122, 9 oz., water goblet	25.00
Sugar, indiv., #3500 (pie crust edge)	13.00
Sugar, indiv., #3900, scalloped edge	13.00
Sugar, scroll handle, #3400	14.00
Tumbler, 2½ oz., sham bottom	45.00
Tumbler, 5 oz., ft., juice	30.00
Tumbler, 5 oz., sham bottom	32.50
Tumbler, 7 oz., old-fashioned, w/sham bottom	45.00
Tumbler, 8 oz., ft.	25.00
Tumbler, 10 oz., sham bottom	32.00
Tumbler, 12 oz., sham bottom	35.00
Tumbler, 13 oz.	32.00
Tumbler, 14 oz., sham bottom	40.00

	Crystal
Tumbler, #1066, 3 oz.	22.00
Tumbler, #1066, 5 oz., juice	14.00
Tumbler, #1066, 9 oz., water	15.00
Tumbler, #1066, 12 oz., tea	22.00
Tumbler, #3106, 3 oz., ftd.	22.00
Tumbler, #3106, 5 oz., ftd., juice	20.00
Tumbler, #3106, 9 oz., ftd., water	14.00
Tumbler, #3106, 12 oz., ftd., tea	22.00
Tumbler, #3122, 2½ oz.	30.00
Tumbler, #3122, 5 oz., juice	15.00
Tumbler, #3122, 9 oz., water	17.00
Tumbler, #3122, 12 oz., tea	20.00
Tumbler, #3135, 2½ oz., ftd., bar	35.00
Tumbler, #3135, 10 oz., ftd., tumbler	16.00
Tumbler, #3135, 12 oz., ftd., tea	28.00
Vase, 5", globe	35.00
Vase, 6", high ft., flower	45.00
Vase, 8", high ft., flower	60.00
Vase, 9", keyhole base	65.00
Vase, 10", bud	50.00
Vase, 11", flower	70.00
Vase, 11", ped. ft., flower	80.00
Vase, 12", keyhole base	85.00
Vase, 13", flower	110.00

Note: See pages 228 – 229 for stem identification.

Colors: crystal

Elaine is often confused with Chantilly. You need to know the difference if for no other reason than Elaine sells much faster because there are more collectors searching for it! The design of Elaine has a thin and angled scroll... like the capital letter "E" (for Elaine) as you write it in script. You will find additional pieces not listed here. I have used as much listing space as I have. Many pieces listed under Rose Point are found etched Elaine. Remember the prices for Elaine will be 30% to 50% lower than those for Rose Point due to collector demand.

	Crystal		Crystal
Basket, 6", 2 hdld. (upturned sides)	22.00	Salt & pepper, ftd., pr	35.00
Bowl, #3104, finger, w/liner	35.00	Salt & pepper, hdld., pr	40.00
Bowl, 3", indiv. nut, 4 ftd.	55.00	Saucer	3.00
Bowl, 5¼", 2 hdld., bonbon	15.00	Stem, #1402, 1 oz., cordial	60.00
Bowl, 6", 2 hdld., ftd., bonbon	20.00	Stem, #1402, 3 oz., wine	25.00
Bowl, 6", 2 pt., relish	20.00	Stem, #1402, 3½ oz., cocktail	20.00
Bowl, 6½", 3 pt., relish	20.00	Stem, #1402, 5 oz., claret	32.50
Bowl, 7", 2 pt., pickle or relish	20.00	Stem, #1402, low sherbet	14.00
Bowl, 7", ftd., tab hdld., bonbon	30.00	Stem, #1402, tall sherbet	15.00
Bowl, 7", pickle or relish	25.00	Stem, #1402, goblet	20.00
Bowl, 9", 3 pt., celery & relish	35.00	Stem, #3104 (very tall stems), ¾ oz., brandy	150.00
Bowl, 9½", pickle (like corn dish)	25.00	Stem, #3104, 1 oz., cordial	150.00
Bowl, 10", 4 ftd., flared	30.00	Stem, #3104, 1 oz., pousse-cafe	150.00
Bowl, 11", tab hdld.	40.00	Stem, #3104, 2 oz., sherry	125.00
Bowl, 11½", ftd., tab hdld.	40.00	Stem, #3104, 2½ oz., creme de menthe	125.00
Bowl, 12", 3 pt., celery & relish	35.00	Stem, #3104, 3 oz., wine	100.00
Bowl, 12", 4 ftd., flared	40.00	Stem, #3104, 3½ oz., cocktail	65.00
Bowl, 12", 4 ftd., oval, "ear" hdld.	47.50	Stem, #3104, 4½ oz., claret	85.00
Bowl, 12", 5 pt. celery & relish	45.00	Stem, #3104, 5 oz., roemer	85.00
Candlestick, 5"	20.00	Stem, #3104, 5 oz., tall hock	80.00
Candlestick, 6", 2-lite	35.00	Stem, #3104, 7 oz., tall sherbet	70.00
Candlestick, 6", 3-lite	42.50	Stem, #3104, 9 oz., goblet	125.00
Candy box, w/cover, rnd.	90.00	Stem, #3121, 1 oz., cordial	60.00
Cocktail icer, 2 pc.	60.00	Stem, #3121, 3 oz., cocktail	24.00
Comport, 5½"	30.00	Stem, #3121, 3½ oz., wine	35.00
Comport, 5⅜", #3500 stem	40.00	Stem, #3121, 4½ oz., claret	45.00
Comport, 5⅜", blown	42.00	Stem, #3121, 4½ oz., oyster cocktail	18.00
Creamer (several styles)	12.00	Stem, #3121, 5 oz., parfait, low stem	30.00
Creamer, indiv.	15.00	Stem, #3121, 6 oz., low sherbet	16.00
Cup	20.00	Stem, #3121, 6 oz., tall sherbet	18.00
Decanter, lg., ftd.	195.00	Stem, #3121, 10 oz., water	25.00
Hat, 9"	325.00	Stem, #3500, 1 oz., cordial	60.00
Hurricane lamp, candlestick base	125.00	Stem, #3500, 2½ oz., wine	35.00
Hurricane lamp, keyhole ft., w/prisms	210.00	Stem, #3500, 3 oz., cocktail	24.00
Ice bucket, w/chrome handle	65.00	Stem, #3500, 4½ oz., claret	45.00
Mayonnaise (cupped sherbet w/ladle)	35.00	Stem, #3500, 4½ oz., oyster cocktail	18.00
Mayonnaise (div. bowl, liner, 2 ladles)	45.00	Stem, #3500, 5 oz., parfait, low stem	30.00
Mayonnaise, w/liner & ladle	40.00	Stem, #3500, 7 oz., low sherbet	16.00
Oil, 6 oz., hdld., w/stopper	95.00	Stem, #3500, 7 oz., tall sherbet	18.00
Pitcher, ball	160.00	Stem, #3500, 10 oz., water	25.00
Pitcher, Doulton	300.00	Sugar (several styles)	10.00
Pitcher, upright	185.00	Sugar, indiv.	12.00
Plate, 6", 2 hdld.	10.00	Tumbler, #1402, 9 oz., ftd., water	18.00
Plate, 6½", bread/butter	7.00	Tumbler, #1402, 12 oz., tea	30.00
Plate, 8", 2 hdld., ftd.	18.00	Tumbler, #1402, 12 oz., tall ftd., tea	30.00
Plate, 8", salad	15.00	Tumbler, #3121, 5 oz., ftd., juice	22.00
Plate, 8", tab hdld., bonbon	18.00	Tumbler, #3121, 10 oz., ftd., water	25.00
Plate, 10½", dinner	65.00	Tumbler, #3121, 12 oz., ftd., tea	30.00
Plate, 11½" 2 hdld., ringed "Tally Ho" sand.	30.00	Tumbler, #3500, 5 oz., ftd., juice	20.00
Plate, 12", 4 ftd., service	30.00	Tumbler, #3500, 10 oz., ftd., water	22.00
Plate, 13", 4 ftd., torte	35.00	Tumbler, #3500, 12 oz., ftd., tea	30.00
Plate, 13½", tab hdld., cake	35.00	Vase, 6", ftd.	40.00
Plate, 14", torte	35.00	Vase, 8", ftd.	60.00
Salt & pepper, flat, pr.	35.00	Vase, 9", keyhole, ftd.	75.00

Note: see pages 228 – 229 for stem identification.

Colors: Flamingo pink, Sahara yellow, Moongleam green, cobalt, and Alexandrite; some Tangerine

Shown is a shelf shot of Alexandrite Empress. Observe that crystal is no longer exhibited here. You will find crystal listings under the name Queen Ann. When the colors were made, this pattern was called Empress; but later on, when crystal was produced, the pattern name was changed to Queen Ann. Prices for the Alexandrite have been flourishing in all pieces except the ever present plates.

Row 1: 7", 3-part relish, shaker, cup and saucer, shaker, 7" round plate
Row 2: 6" mint, nut dish, 6" square plate, sugar, creamer
Row 3: Mayonnaise w/ladle, 10" celery tray, 11" floral bowl
Row 4: 8" square plate, ash tray, 7" candlestick (#135), 9" vase

	Flam.	Sahara	Moon.	Cobalt	Alexan.
Ash tray.	175.00	185.00	375.00	300.00	225.00
Bonbon, 6"	20.00	25.00	30.00		
Bowl, cream soup	30.00	30.00	50.00		110.00
Bowl, cream soup, w/sq. liner	40.00	40.00	55.00		175.00
Bowl, frappe, w/center	45.00	60.00	75.00		
Bowl, nut, dolphin ftd., indiv.	30.00	32.00	45.00		170.00
Bowl, 4½", nappy	25.00	30.00	35.00		
Bowl, 5", preserve, 2 hdld.	20.00	25.00	30.00		
Bowl, 6", ftd., jelly, 2 hdld.	20.00	25.00	30.00		
Bowl, 6", dolphin ftd., mint	35.00	40.00	45.00		230.00
Bowl, 6", grapefruit, sq. top, grnd. bottom	12.50	20.00	25.00		
Bowl, 6½", oval, lemon, w/cover	65.00	80.00	90.00		
Bowl, 7", 3 pt., relish, triplex	40.00	45.00	50.00		300.00
Bowl, 7", 3 pt., relish, ctr. hand.	45.00	50.00	75.00		
Bowl, 7½", dolp. ftd., nappy	65.00	65.00	80.00	300.00	350.00
Bowl, 7½", dolp. ftd., nasturtium	130.00	130.00	150.00	350.00	425.00
Bowl, 8", nappy	35.00	37.00	45.00		
Bowl, 8½", ftd., floral, 2 hdld	45.00	50.00	70.00		
Bowl, 9", floral, rolled edge	40.00	42.00	50.00		
Bowl, 9", floral, flared	70.00	75.00	90.00		
Bowl, 10", 2 hdld., oval dessert	50.00	60.00	70.00		
Bowl, 10", lion head, floral	550.00	550.00	700.00		
Bowl, 10", oval, veg.	50.00	55.00	75.00		
Bowl, 10", square, salad, 2 hdld.	55.00	60.00	80.00		
Bowl, 10", triplex, relish	50.00	55.00	65.00		
Bowl, 11", dolphin ftd., floral	65.00	75.00	100.00	375.00	500.00
Bowl, 13", pickle/olive, 2 pt.	35.00	45.00	50.00		
Bowl, 15", dolp. ftd., punch	900.00	900.00	1,100.00		
Candlestick, low, 4 ftd., w/2 hdld.	100.00	100.00	170.00		
Candlestick, 6", dolphin ftd.	150.00	100.00	155.00	260.00	265.00
Candy, w/cover, 6", dolphin ftd.	150.00	150.00	200.00	450.00	
Comport, 6", ftd.	110.00	70.00	100.00		
Comport, 6", square	70.00	75.00	85.00		
Comport, 7", oval	70.00	75.00	80.00		
Compotier, 6", dolphin ftd.	260.00	225.00	275.00		
Creamer, dolphin ftd.	50.00	40.00	45.00		250.00
Creamer, indiv.	45.00	45.00	50.00		210.00
Cup	30.00	30.00	35.00		115.00
Cup, after dinner	60.00	60.00	70.00		
Cup, bouillon, 2 hdld.	35.00	35.00	45.00		
Cup, 4 oz., custard or punch	30.00	35.00	45.00		
Cup, #1401½, has rim as demi-cup	28.00	32.00	40.00		
Grapefruit, w/square liner	30.00	30.00	35.00		
Ice tub, w/metal handles	100.00	150.00	165.00		
Jug, 3 pint, ftd.	200.00	210.00	250.00		

	Flam.	Sahara	Moon.	Cobalt	Alexan.
Jug, flat			175.00		
Marmalade, w/cover, dolphin ftd.	200.00	90.00	225.00		
Mayonnaise, 5½", ftd. with ladle	85.00	90.00	100.00		400.00
Mustard, w/cover	85.00	80.00	95.00		
Oil bottle, 4 oz.	125.00	125.00	135.00		
Plate, bouillon liner	12.00	15.00	17.50		25.00
Plate, 4½"	10.00	15.00	20.00		
Plate, 6"	11.00	14.00	16.00		40.00
Plate, 6", square	10.00	13.00	15.00		40.00
Plate, 7"	12.00	15.00	17.00		50.00
Plate, 7", square	12.00	15.00	17.00	60.00	65.00
Plate, 8", square	18.00	22.00	35.00	70.00	75.00
Plate, 8"	16.00	20.00	24.00	70.00	75.00
Plate, 9"	25.00	35.00	40.00		
Plate, 10½"	100.00	100.00	140.00		335.00
Plate, 10½", square	100.00	100.00	140.00		335.00
Plate, 12"	45.00	55.00	65.00		
Plate, 12", muffin, sides upturned	55.00	80.00	90.00		
Plate, 12", sandwich, 2 hdld.	35.00	45.00	60.00		180.00
Plate, 13", hors d'oeuvre, 2 hdld.	50.00	60.00	70.00		
Plate, 13", square, 2 hdld.	40.00	45.00	55.00		
Platter, 14"	40.00	45.00	80.00		
Salt & pepper, pr.	100.00	110.00	135.00		450.00
Saucer, square	10.00	10.00	15.00		25.00
Saucer, after dinner	10.00	10.00	15.00		
Saucer, rnd.	10.00	10.00	15.00		25.00
Stem, 2½ oz., oyster cocktail	20.00	25.00	30.00		
Stem, 4 oz., saucer champagne	35.00	40.00	60.00		
Stem, 4 oz., sherbet	22.00	28.00	35.00		
Stem, 9 oz., Empress stemware, unusual	55.00	65.00	75.00		
Sugar, indiv.	45.00	45.00	50.00		210.00
Sugar, dolphin ftd., 3 hdld.	50.00	40.00	45.00		250.00
Tray, condiment & liner for indiv. sugar/creamer	40.00	35.00	50.00		
Tray, 10", 3 pt., relish	50.00	55.00	65.00		
Tray, 10", 7 pt., hors d'oeuvre	160.00	150.00	200.00		
Tray, 10", celery	25.00	35.00	40.00		150.00
Tray, 12", ctr. hdld., sand.	48.00	57.00	65.00		
Tray, 12", sq. ctr. hdld., sand.	52.00	60.00	67.50		
Tray, 13", celery	30.00	40.00	45.00		
Tray, 16", 4 pt., buffet relish	75.00	75.00	86.00		160.00
Tumbler, 8 oz., dolphin ftd., unusual	150.00	170.00	160.00		
Tumbler, 8 oz., grnd. bottom	60.00	50.00	70.00		
Tumbler, 12 oz., tea, grnd. bottom	70.00	65.00	75.00		
Vase, 8", flared	120.00	130.00	190.00		
Vase, 9", dolphin ftd.	150.00	165.00	200.00		850.00

FOSTORIA STEMS AND SHAPES

Top Row: Left to Right
1. Water, 10 oz., 8¼"
2. Claret, 4 oz., 6"
3. Wine, 3 oz., 5½"
4. Cordial, C\v oz., 4"
5. Sherbet, low, 6 oz., 4¼"
6. Cocktail, 3 oz., 5¼"
7. Sherbet, high, 6 oz., 6"

Bottom Row: Left to Right
1. Grapefruit and liner
2. Ice tea tumbler, 12 oz., 6"
3. Water tumbler, 9 oz., 5¼"
4. Parfait, 6 oz., 5¼"
5. Juice tumbler, 5 oz., 4½"
6. Oyster cocktail, 5½ oz.
7. Bar tumbler, 2½ oz.

Color: crystal

First Love is Duncan & Miller's best known etching! Different mould lines were incorporated into this extensive pattern. These include #30 (Pall Mall), #111 (Terrace), #115 (Canterbury), #117 (Three Feathers), #126 (Venetian), and #5111½ (Terrace blown stemware). Terrace can be see on pages 202 and 203. I have included three catalog pages (93 – 95) that show you examples of these mould lines.

Let me know what you think of the colored background on page 91. We keep experimenting to try to show the patterns to the fullest advantage, and this is the latest attempt. If the pattern can be seen better than it was in previous editions, then we have accomplished what we intended. If not, then it's back to the drawing board on photography backdrops!

	Crystal
Ash tray, 3½" sq., #111	17.50
Ash tray, 3½" x 2½", #30	16.50
Ash tray, 5" x 3", #12, club	37.50
Ash tray, 5" x 3¼", #30	24.00
Ash tray, 6½" x 4¼", #30	35.00
Basket, 9¼" x 10" x 7¼", #115	150.00
Basket, 10" x 4¼" x 7", oval hdld., #115	175.00
Bottle, oil w/stopper, 8", #5200	60.00
Bowl, 3" x 5", rose, #115	40.00
Bowl, 4" x 1½", finger, #30	32.00
Bowl, 4¼", finger, #5111½	35.00
Bowl, 6" x 2½", oval, olive, #115	25.00
Bowl, 6¾" x 4¼", ftd., flared rim, #111	30.00
Bowl, 7½" x 3", 3 pt., ftd., #117	35.00
Bowl, 8" sq. x 2½", hdld., #111	55.00
Bowl, 8½" x 4", #115	37.50
Bowl, 9" x 4½", ftd., #111	42.00
Bowl, 9½" x 2½", hdld., #111	45.00
Bowl, 10" x 3¾", ftd., flared rim, #111	55.00
Bowl, 10" x 4½", #115	45.00
Bowl, 10½" x 5", crimped, #115	44.00
Bowl, 10½" x 7" x 7", #126	60.00
Bowl, 10¾" x 4¾", #115	42.50
Bowl, 11" x 1¾", #30	55.00
Bowl, 11" x 3¼", flared rim, #111	62.50
Bowl, 11" x 5¼", flared rim, #6	67.50
Bowl, 11½" x 8¼", oval, #115	45.00
Bowl, 12" x 3½", #6	65.00
Bowl, 12" x 3¼", flared, #115	60.00
Bowl, 12" x 4" x 7½", oval, #117	65.00
Bowl, 12½", flat, ftd., #126	75.00
Bowl, 13" x 3¼" x 8¾", oval, flared, #115	55.00
Bowl, 13" x 7" x 9¼", #126	67.50
Bowl, 13" x 7", #117	62.50
Bowl, 14" x 7½" x 6", oval, #126	65.00
Box, candy w/lid, 4¾" x 6¼"	60.00
Butter or cheese, 7" sq. x 1¼", #111	115.00
Candelabra, 2-lite, #41	35.00
Candelabrum, 6", 2-lite w/prisms, #30	60.00
Candle, 3", 1-lite, #111	25.00
Candle, 3", low, #115	25.00
Candle, 3½", #115	25.00
Candle, 4", cornucopia, #117	25.00
Candle, 4", low, #111	25.00
Candle, 5¼", 2-lite, globe, #30	35.00
Candle, 6", 2-lite, #30	35.00
Candy box, 6" x 3½", 3 hdld., 3 pt., w/lid, #115	75.00
Candy box, 6" x 3½", 3 pt., w/lid, crown finial, #106	80.00

	Crystal
Candy jar, 5" x 7¼", w/lid, ftd., #25	80.00
Candy, 6½", w/5" lid, #115	65.00
Carafe, w/stopper, water, #5200	145.00
Cheese stand, 3" x 5¼", #111	25.00
Cheese stand, 5¾" x 3½", #115	25.00
Cigarette box w/lid, 4" x 4¼"	32.00
Cigarette box w/lid, 4½" x 3½", #30	35.00
Cigarette box w/lid, 4¾" x 3¾"	35.00
Cocktail shaker, 14 oz., #5200	125.00
Cocktail shaker, 16 oz., #5200	125.00
Cocktail shaker, 32 oz., #5200	165.00
Comport w/lid, 8¾" x 5½", #111	125.00
Comport, 3½"x 4¾"W, #111	30.00
Comport, 5" x 5½", flared rim, #115	32.00
Comport, 5¼" x 6¾", flat top, #115	32.00
Comport, 6" x 4¾", low #115	37.50
Creamer, 2½", individual, #115	18.00
Creamer, 3", 10 oz., #111	18.00
Creamer, 3¾", 7 oz., #115	15.00
Creamer, sugar w/butter pat lid, breakfast set, #28	65.00
Cruet, #25	90.00
Cruet, #30	90.00
Cup, #115	18.00
Decanter w/stopper, 16 oz., #5200	135.00
Decanter w/stopper, 32 oz., #30	165.00
Decanter w/stopper, 32 oz., #5200	165.00
Hat, 4½", #30	360.00
Hat, 5½" x 8½" x 6¼", #30	335.00
Honey dish, 5" x 3", #91	30.00
Ice bucket, 6", #30	100.00
Lamp, hurricane, w/prisms, 15", #115	155.00
Lamp shade only, #115	110.00
Lid for candy urn, #111	35.00
Mayonnaise, 4¾" x 4½", div. w/7½" underplate	35.00
Mayonnaise, 5¼" x 3", div. w/6½" plate, #115	35.00
Mayonnaise, 5½" x 2½", ftd., hdld., #111	35.00
Mayonnaise, 5½" x 2¾", #115	35.00
Mayonnaise, 5½" x 3½", crimped, #11	32.00
Mayonnaise, 5¾" x 3", w/dish hdld. tray, #111	35.00
Mayonnaise, w/7" tray hdld., #111	35.00
Mustard w/lid & underplate	57.50
Nappy, 5" x 1", w/bottom star, #25	20.00
Nappy, 5" x 1¾", one hdld., #115	18.00
Nappy, 5½" x 2", div., hdld., #111	18.00
Nappy, 5½" x 2", one hdld., heart, #115	28.00
Nappy, 6" x 1¾", hdld., #111	22.00

	Crystal
Perfume tray, 8" x 5", #5200	25.00
Perfume, 5", #5200	75.00
Pitcher, #5200	155.00
Pitcher, 9", 80 oz., ice lip, #5202	165.00
Plate, 6", #111	12.00
Plate, 6", #115	12.00
Plate, 6", hdld., lemon, #111	14.00
Plate, 6", sq., #111	14.00
Plate, 7", #111	17.50
Plate, 7½", #111	18.00
Plate, 7½", #115	18.00
Plate, 7½", mayonnaise liner, hdld. #115	15.00
Plate, 7½", sq., #111	19.00
Plate, 7½", 2 hdld., #115	19.00
Plate, 8½", #30	20.00
Plate, 8½", #111	20.00
Plate, 8½", #115	20.00
Plate, 11", #111	47.50
Plate, 11", 2 hdld., sandwich, #115	30.00
Plate, 11", hdld., #111	40.00
Plate, 11", hdld., cracker w/ring, #115	40.00
Plate, 11", hdld., cracker w/ring, #111	40.00
Plate, 11", hdld., sandwich, #111	40.00
Plate, 11¼", dinner, #115	55.00
Plate, 12", egg, #30	125.00
Plate, 12", torte, rolled edge, #111	40.00
Plate, 13", torte, flat edge, #111	50.00
Plate, 13", torte, rolled edge, #111	57.50
Plate, 13¼", torte, #111	57.50
Plate, 13½", cake, hdld., #115	50.00
Plate, 14", #115	50.00
Plate, 14", cake, #115	50.00
Plate, 14½", cake, lg. base, #30	55.00
Plate, 14½", cake, sm. base, #30	55.00
Relish, 6" x 1¾", hdld., 2 pt., #111	20.00
Relish, 6" x 1¾", hdld., 2 pt., #115	20.00
Relish, 8" x 4½", pickle, 2 pt., #115	25.00
Relish, 8", 3 pt., hdld., #115	25.00
Relish, 9" x 1½", 2 pt. pickle, #115	25.00
Relish, 9" x 1½", 3 hdld, 3 pt., #115	32.50
Relish, 9" x 1½", 3 hdld., flared, #115	32.50
Relish, 10", 5 pt. tray, #30	65.00
Relish, 10½" x 1½", hdld., 5 pt., #111	80.00
Relish, 10½" x 1¼", 2 hdld, 3 pt., #115	57.50
Relish, 10½" x 7", #115	37.50
Relish, 11¾", tray, #115	45.00
Relish, 12", 4 pt., hdld., #111	40.00
Relish, 12", 5 pt., hdld., #111	50.00
Salt and pepper pr., #30	30.00
Salt and pepper pr., #115	40.00
Sandwich tray, 12" x 5¼", ctr. handle, #115	80.00
Saucer, #115	8.50
Stem, 3¾", 1 oz., cordial, #5111½	60.00
Stem, 3¾", 4½ oz., oyster cocktail, #5111½	22.50
Stem, 4", 5 oz., ice cream, #5111½	14.00
Stem, 4¼", 3 oz., cocktail, #115	22.50

	Crystal
Stem, 4½", 3½ oz., cocktail, #5111½	22.50
Stem, 5", 5 oz., saucer champagne, #5111½	18.00
Stem, 5¼", 3 oz., wine, #5111½	32.50
Stem, 5¼", 5 oz., ftd. juice, #5111½	24.00
Stem, 5¾", 10 oz., low luncheon goblet, #5111½	17.50
Stem, 6", 4½ oz., claret, #5111½	45.00
Stem, 6½", 12 oz., ftd. ice tea, #5111½	35.00
Stem, 6¾", 14 oz., ftd. ice tea, #5111½	35.00
Stem, cordial, #111	20.00
Sugar, 2½", individual, #115	14.00
Sugar, 3", 7 oz., #115	14.00
Sugar, 3", 10 oz., #111	15.00
Tray, 8" x 2", hdld. celery, #111	17.50
Tray, 8" x 4¾", individual sug/cr., #115	17.50
Tray, 8¾", celery, #91	30.00
Tray, 11", celery, #91	40.00
Tumbler, 2", 1½ oz., whiskey, #5200	60.00
Tumbler, 2½" x 3⅜", sham, Teardrop, ftd.	60.00
Tumbler, 3", sham, #5200	32.50
Tumbler, 4¾", 10 oz., sham, #5200	37.50
Tumbler, 5½", 12 oz., sham, #5200	37.50
Tumbler, 6", 14 oz., sham, #5200	37.50
Tumbler, 8 oz., flat, #115	30.00
Urn, 4½" x 4½", #111	27.50
Urn, 4½" x 4½", #115	27.50
Urn, 4¾", rnd ft.	27.50
Urn, 5", #525	37.50
Urn, 5½", ring hdld, sq. ft.	60.00
Urn, 5½", sq. ft.	37.50
Urn, 6½", sq. hdld.	70.00
Urn, 7", #529	37.50
Vase, 4", flared rim, #115	25.00
Vase, 4½" x 4¾", #115	30.00
Vase, 5" x 5", crimped, #115	35.00
Vase, 6", #507	55.00
Vase, 8" x 4¾", cornucopia, #117	65.00
Vase, 8", ftd., #506	90.00
Vase, 8", ftd., #507	90.00
Vase, 8½" x 2¾", #505	100.00
Vase, 8½" x 6", #115	90.00
Vase, 9" x 4½", #505	95.00
Vase, 9", #509	90.00
Vase, 9", bud, #506	80.00
Vase, 9½" x 3½", #506	110.00
Vase, 10" x 4¾", #5200	90.00
Vase, 10", #507	95.00
Vase, 10", ftd., #111	115.00
Vase, 10", ftd., #505	115.00
Vase, 10", ftd., #506	115.00
Vase, 10½" x 12 x 9½", #126	145.00
Vase, 10½", #126	135.00
Vase, 11" x 5¼", #505	145.00
Vase, 11½ x 4½", #506	140.00
Vase, 12", flared #115	145.00
Vase, 12", ftd., #506	145.00
Vase, 12", ftd., #507	145.00

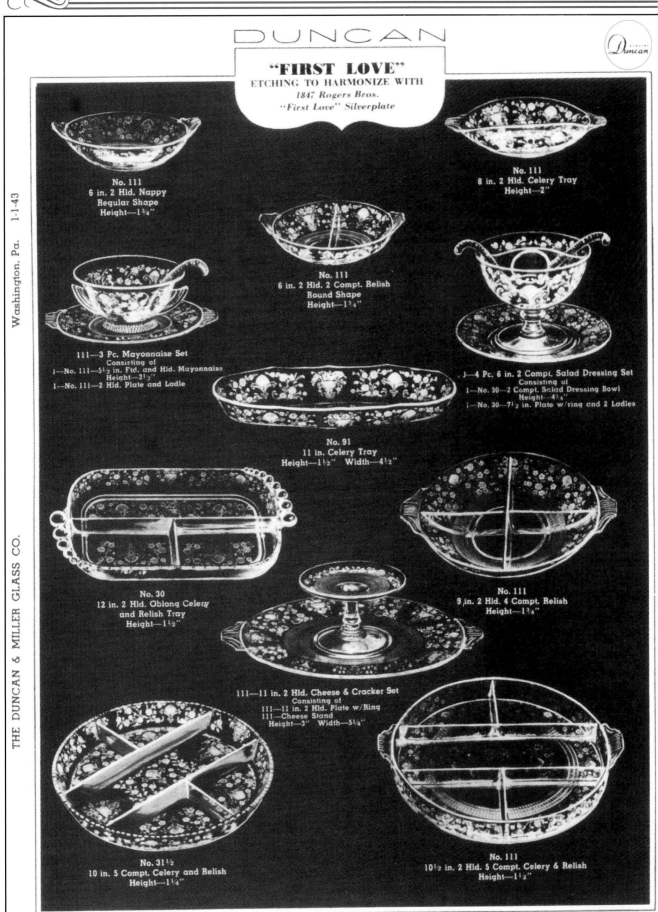

DUNCAN

"FIRST LOVE"
ETCHING TO HARMONIZE WITH
1847 Rogers Bros.
"First Love" Silverplate

No. 111
6 in. 2 Hld. Nappy
Regular Shape
Height—1¾"

No. 111
8 in. 2 Hld. Celery Tray
Height—2"

No. 111
6 in. 2 Hld. 2 Compt. Relish
Round Shape
Height—1¾"

111—3 Pc. Mayonnaise Set
Consisting of
1—No. 111—5½ in. Ftd. and Hld. Mayonnaise
Height—2½"
1—No. 111—2 Hld. Plate and Ladle

J—4 Pc. 6 in. 2 Compt. Salad Dressing Set
Consisting of
1—No. 30—2 Compt. Salad Dressing Bowl
Height—4½"
1—No. 30—7½ in. Plate w/ring and 2 Ladles

No. 91
11 in. Celery Tray
Height—1½" Width—4½"

No. 30
12 in. 2 Hld. Oblong Celery
and Relish Tray
Height—1½"

No. 111
9 in. 2 Hld. 4 Compt. Relish
Height—1¾"

111—11 in. 2 Hld. Cheese & Cracker Set
Consisting of
111—11 in. 2 Hld. Plate w/Ring
111—Cheese Stand
Height—3" Width—5¼"

No. 31½
10 in. 5 Compt. Celery and Relish
Height—1¼"

No. 111
10½ in. 2 Hld. 5 Compt. Celery & Relish
Height—1½"

Washington, Pa. 1-1-43

THE DUNCAN & MILLER GLASS CO.

DUNCAN

"FIRST LOVE"
ETCHING TO HARMONIZE WITH
1847 Rogers Bros.
"First Love" Silverplate

No. 5111½
10 oz. Tall Goblet
Height—6¾"

No. 5111½
5 oz. Saucer Champagne
Height—5"

No. 5111½
3½ oz. Liquor Cocktail
Height—4½"

No. 5111½
3 oz. Wine
Height—5¼"

No. 5111½
4½ oz. Claret
Height—6"

No. 5111½
1 oz. Cordial
Height—3¾"

No. 5111½
12 oz. Ftd. Ice Tea
Height—6½"

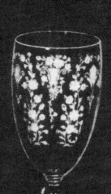

No. 5111½
14 oz. Ftd. Ice Tea
Height—6¾"

No. 5111½
10 oz. Low Luncheon Goblet
Height—5¾"

No. 5111½
4½ oz. Oyster Cocktail
Height—3¾"

No. 5111½
5 oz. Ftd. Orange Juice
Height—5¼"

No. 5111½
5 oz. Ice Cream
Height—4"

No. 5200
1½ oz. Whiskey or Cordial
Tumbler, Sham
Height—2"

No. 5200
3½ oz. Cocktail Tumbler,
Sham
Height—3"

No. 5200
14 oz. Tumbler, Sham
Height—4¾"
Also made 12 oz. and 10 oz.

No. 5111½
Fingerbowl
Diameter—4¼"

DUNCAN

"FIRST LOVE"
ETCHING TO HARMONIZE WITH
1847 Rogers Bros.
"First Love" Silverplate

No. 111
4 in. Low Candlestick

No. 111
4 in. Low Candlestick

No. 111
11 in. Flared Bowl
Height—3¼" Width—11"

No. 30
2 Light Candlestick
Height—6" Width—7"

No. 41
5 in. 2 Light Candlestick
Width—8½"

No. 6
12 in. Flower Bowl, Flared
Height—3½"

No. 126
14 in. Oval Bowl
Height—7½" Width—6"

No. 30
2 Light Candelabrum
w prisms
Height—6" Width—8"

No. 30
2 Light Candelabrum
w prisms
Height—6" Width—8"

Colors: crystal, pink, yellow

Tiffin's Flanders is consistently confused with Cambridge's Gloria by collectors, particularly in yellow and crystal. Refer to Gloria to view the differences in the floral designs.

Flanders stemware is generally found on Tiffin's #17024 blank. Usually these have a crystal foot and stem with tops of crystal, pink, or yellow. Color combinations seen infrequently include green foot with pink stems, and pink tumblers as well as pitchers with crystal handle and foot. A green Flanders vase did surface a couple of years ago and can be seen in *Very Rare Glassware of the Depression Years, Fifth Series.*

Shakers continue to be the most evasive item in Flanders. I have only seen six pink, three crystal, and none in yellow. I have had a few reports of yellow, but I have never seen them. New pieces are being found all the time and the listings are continuing to grow! Thanks are due readers and dealers for postcards sent with this information!

Round plates are Tiffin's line #8800 and each size plate has a different number. Scalloped plates are line #5831. Pitchers were sold both with and without a cover. Remember that the pitcher top is plain with no pattern etched on it.

Note the lamp. So far, these have been found only in crystal. This cylindrical shade is sometimes found on a candlestick and referred to as a Chinese hurricane lamp.

The bouillon cup was placed next to the sugar for comparison. Those handled parfaits are my favorite piece! The footed almond and whiskey are sought by collectors of those items.

	Crystal	Pink	Yellow
Ash tray, 2¼x3¾" w/cigarette rest	45.00		
Bowl, 2 hdld., bouillon	40.00	125.00	75.00
Bowl, finger, w/liner	25.00	75.00	45.00
Bowl, 2 hdld., bonbon	20.00	60.00	35.00
Bowl, 11", ftd., console	35.00	95.00	60.00
Bowl, 12", flanged rim, console	35.00	95.00	60.00
Candlestick, 2 styles	30.00	65.00	40.00
Candy jar, w/cover, flat	125.00	325.00	225.00
Candy jar, w/cover, ftd.	90.00	225.00	165.00
Celery, 11"	25.00	70.00	45.00
Cheese & cracker	40.00	125.00	85.00
Comport, 3½"	25.00	65.00	35.00
Comport, 6"	50.00	145.00	85.00
Creamer, flat	40.00	125.00	80.00
Creamer, ftd.	35.00	115.00	65.00
Cup, 2 styles	48.00	85.00	55.00
Decanter	150.00	325.00	225.00
Electric lamp	300.00		
Grapefruit, w/liner	50.00	125.00	75.00

	Crystal	Pink	Yellow
Hurricane lamp, Chinese style	225.00		
Mayonnaise, w/liner	30.00	85.00	60.00
Nut cup, ftd., blown	30.00	70.00	55.00
Oil bottle & stopper	135.00	325.00	235.00
Parfait, 5⅝", hdld.	60.00	165.00	95.00
Pitcher & cover	200.00	350.00	275.00
Plate, 6"	4.00	12.00	9.00
Plate, 8"	9.00	15.00	12.50
Plate, 10¼", dinner	35.00	80.00	55.00
Relish, 3 pt.	25.00	75.00	50.00
Salt & pepper, pr.	150.00	300.00	250.00
Sandwich server, center hdld.		150.00	
Saucer	8.00	15.00	10.00
Stem, 4½", oyster cocktail	15.00	40.00	25.00
Stem, 4½", sherbet	10.00	28.00	17.50
Stem, 4¾", cocktail	15.00	40.00	30.00
Stem, 5", cordial	55.00	95.00	75.00
Stem, 5⅝", parfait	30.00	95.00	60.00
Stem, 6⅛", wine	28.00	70.00	40.00
Stem, 6¼", saucer champagne	15.00	35.00	20.00
Stem, claret	40.00	135.00	75.00
Stem, 8¼", water	15.00	45.00	27.50
Sugar, flat	40.00	125.00	75.00
Sugar, ftd.	35.00	115.00	60.00
Tumbler, 2¾", 2½ oz., ftd.	40.00	80.00	50.00
Tumbler, 4¾", 9 oz., ftd., water	14.00	40.00	22.00
Tumbler, 4¾", 10 oz., ftd.	17.00	45.00	28.00
Tumbler, 5⅞", 12 oz., ftd., tea	22.00	55.00	32.00
Vase, bud	30.00	80.00	45.00
Vase, ftd.	85.00	225.00	145.00
Vase, Dahlia style	125.00	250.00	185.00
Vase, fan	85.00	225.00	135.00

Colors: crystal

Tiffin's Fuchsia continues to amaze collectors by the new pieces being discovered! Believe me, there are some enthusiastic collectors trying to buy all items available! Because of this, dealers are searching every shop niche and flea market which may explain why so many new pieces are being found!

Most of the items in the top picture are readily found except for the bell and the plate behind the creamer and sugar. The bowl on the plate in the middle is one style of mayonnaise. It is rather small, more like a berry bowl.

In the bottom photo are the rarely seen bitters bottle and the icer and liner on the left. The Chinese hurricane shade can be seen here. That cylinder cover can also be used on the lamp pictured in Flanders. The oval tray in the foreground was found with a sugar and creamer. On the right are the rarely seen cup and saucer and two styles of finger bowls, footed and flat. In between the finger bowls is a footed mayonnaise. There are three styles of double candlesticks shown — the pointed knob being the most difficult on to find!

Of the three known stemware lines for Fuchsia, #15083 is the most often found though you cannot prove it by my photos which omitted all but one, a #17457.

	Crystal		Crystal
Ash tray, 2¼" x 3¾" w/cigarette rest	32.00	Plate, 9½", dinner, #5902	60.00
Bell, 5", #15083	75.00	Plate, 10½", 2 hdld., cake, #5831	55.00
Bitters bottle	325.00	Plate, 10½", muffin tray, pearl edge	55.00
Bowl, 4", finger, ftd., #041	50.00	Plate, 13", lily rolled and crimped edge	65.00
Bowl, 4½" finger, w/#8814 liner	65.00	Plate, 14¼", sandwich, #8833	50.00
Bowl, 5³⁄₁₆", 2 hdld., #5831	27.50	Relish, 6⅜", 3 pt., #5902	25.00
Bowl, 6¼", cream soup, ftd., #5831	50.00	Relish, 9¼", square, 3 pt.	40.00
Bowl, 7¼", salad, #5902	40.00	Relish, 10½" x 12½", hdld., 3 pt., #5902	60.00
Bowl, 8⅜", 2 hdld., #5831	55.00	Relish, 10½" x 12½", hdld., 5 pt.	70.00
Bowl, 9¾", deep salad	75.00	Salt and pepper, pr., #2	100.00
Bowl, 10", salad	65.00	Saucer, #5831	15.00
Bowl, 10½", console, fan shaped sides, #319	65.00	Stem, 4¹⁄₁₆", cordial, #15083	32.50
Bowl, 11⅞", console, flared, #5902	80.00	Stem, 4⅛", sherbet, #15083	12.00
Bowl, 12", flanged rim, console, #5831	60.00	Stem, 4¼", cocktail, #15083	18.00
Bowl, 12⅝", console, flared, #5902	90.00	Stem, 4⅝", 3½ oz., cocktail, #17453	37.50
Bowl, 13", crimped, #5902	75.00	Stem, 4⅞", saucer champagne, hollow stem	75.00
Candlestick, 2-lite, w/pointed center, #5831	75.00	Stem, 5¹⁄₁₆", wine, #15083	30.00
Candlestick, 2-lite, tapered center, #15306	75.00	Stem, 5¼", claret, #15083	37.50
Candlestick, 5", 2-lite, ball center	75.00	Stem, 5⅜", cocktail, "S" stem, #17457	45.00
Candlestick, 5⅝", 2-lite, w/fan center, #5902	75.00	Stem, 5⅜", cordial, "S" stem, #17457	110.00
Candlestick, single, #348	40.00	Stem, 5⅜", 7 oz., saucer champagne, #17453	30.00
Celery, 10", oval, #5831	35.00	Stem, 5⅜", saucer champagne, #15083	15.00
Celery, 10½", rectangular, #5902	37.50	Stem, 5⅜", saucer champagne, "S" stem, #17457	37.50
Cigarette box, w/lid, 4" x 2¾", #9305	110.00	Stem, 5¹⁵⁄₁₆", parfait, #15083	35.00
Cocktail shaker, 8", w/metal top	235.00	Stem, 6¼", low water, #15083	25.00
Comport, 6¼", #5831	30.00	Stem, 7⅜", 9 oz., water, #17453	40.00
Comport, 6½", w/beaded stem, #15082	35.00	Stem, 7½", water, high, #15083	25.00
Creamer, 2⅞", individual, #5831	40.00	Stem, 7⅝", water, "S" stem, #17457	60.00
Creamer, 3⅜", flat w/beaded handle, #5902	27.50	Sugar, 2⅞", individual, #5831	40.00
Creamer, 4½", ftd., #5831	22.50	Sugar, 3⅜", flat, w/beaded handle, #5902	27.50
Cup, #5831	75.00	Sugar, 4½", ftd., #5831	22.50
Electric lamp	300.00	Tray, sugar/creamer	50.00
Hurricane, 12", Chinese style	225.00	Tray, 9½", 2 hdld. for cream/sugar	45.00
Icer, with insert	145.00	Tumbler, 2⁷⁄₁₆", 2 oz., bar, flat, #506	60.00
Mayonnaise, flat, w/6¼" liner, #5902 w/ladle	45.00	Tumbler, 3⁵⁄₁₆", oyster cocktail, #14196	14.00
Mayonnaise, ftd., w/ladle, #5831	45.00	Tumbler, 3⅜", old-fashioned, flat, #580	45.00
Nut dish, 6¼"	35.00	Tumbler, 4¹³⁄₁₆" flat, juice	27.50
Pickle, 7⅜", #5831	40.00	Tumbler, 4⁵⁄₁₆", 5 oz., ftd., juice, #15083	18.00
Pitcher & cover, #194	350.00	Tumbler, 5⅛", water, flat, #517	27.50
Pitcher, flat	350.00	Tumbler, 5⁵⁄₁₆", 9 oz., ftd., water, #15083	15.00
Plate, 6¼", bread and butter, #5902	8.00	Tumbler, 6⁵⁄₁₆", 12 oz., ftd., tea, #15083	30.00
Plate, 6¼", sherbet, #8814	10.00	Vase, 6½", bud, #14185	30.00
Plate, 6⅜", 2 hdld., #5831	12.50	Vase, 8¹³⁄₁₆", flared, crimped	85.00
Plate, 7", marmalade, 3-ftd., #310½	27.50	Vase, 8¼", bud, #14185	35.00
Plate, 7⅞", clam soup or mayo liner, #5831	12.50	Vase, 10½", bud, #14185	45.00
Plate, 7⅞", salad, #8814	15.00	Vase, 10¾", bulbous bottom, #5872	175.00
Plate, 7½", salad, #5831	15.00	Vase, 10⅞", beaded stem, #15082	75.00
Plate, 8¼", luncheon, #5902	17.50	Vase, 11¾", urn, 2 hdld., trophy.	105.00
Plate, 8⅛", luncheon, #8833	22.50	Whipped cream, 3-ftd., #310	40.00
Plate, 8⅜", bonbon, pearl edge	27.50		

GAZEBO, Paden City Glass Company, 1930s

Colors: black, blue, crystal, yellow

Gazebo and another pattern, Utopia, are two very similar Paden City designs. The designs on Utopia are larger and fuller than Gazebo. This may have been a dry run (to use a Kentucky moonshine term) to see if the public would "take" to the design. You probably will not find many pieces of this.

Paden City patterns all have the same misfortune, there is limited availability; but there is enough to titillate your desire for it. As we shopped, we have found few dealers who knew what the pattern was; but all pieces were priced a minimum of $45.00! I guess it looks old and elegant and thus is never priced inexpensively.

Several different mould lines were used for this etching. All measurements are taken from actual pieces. Recently, we acquired some punch cups and we have seen a punch bowl with a floral cutting (not Gazebo). There are several new listings including two styles of double candles, another style of center handle server, footed juice or cocktail, cake stand, and a divided bowl.

I found another blue cheese dish, but I have not spotted one in crystal yet. I have seen that cheese in Ruby, but without an etching! All pieces may not be found in color! Blue seems only to be found on the beaded edge pieces. Please keep me informed of any unlisted items you find!

	Crystal	Blue		Crystal	Blue
Bowl, 9", fan handles	45.00		Mayonnaise, bead handles	25.00	
Bowl, 9", bead handles	45.00	65.00	Plate, 10¾"	45.00	
Bowl, 13", flat edge	55.00		Plate, 12½", bead handles	55.00	75.00
Bowl, 14", low flat	55.00		Plate, 13", fan handles	50.00	
Candlestick, 5¼"	45.00		Plate, 16", beaded edge		85.00
Candlestick, double	55.00		Relish, 9¾", three part	35.00	55.00
Candy w/lid, 10¼", small	75.00	100.00	Server, 10", swan handle	50.00	
Candy w/lid, 11", large	90.00		Server, 11", center handle	40.00	65.00
Cheese dish and cover	85.00	175.00	Sugar	22.50	
Cocktail shaker, w/glass stopper	90.00		Tumbler, ftd. juice	20.00	
Creamer	22.50		Vase, 10¼"	75.00	150.00*
Mayonnaise liner	15.00				

*Black or yellow

Colors: crystal, yellow, Peach-Blo, green, Emerald green, amber, blue, Heatherbloom

Cambridge's Gloria is often confused with Tiffin's Flanders. Look closely at these two similar patterns and notice that the flower on Gloria bends the stem. They are easily identified once you place them side by side.

Yellow and crystal Gloria sets can be built with work and perseverance, but any other color will take more than patience. Yellow Gloria is more available than crystal; so if you like that color, this would be a pattern to consider. I have seen luncheon sets in blue and Peach-Blo (pink), but larger sets may not be possible to assemble. I prefer the dark Emerald green, but not much of that color was made! Gold decorated items fetch about 20% to 25% more than those without gold. However, pieces with worn gold are difficult to sell at that premium price.

Note the amber footed, yellow stem. There is a diminutive amount of this color combination available. I have only found that one piece, but a collector told me he had other stems. Gloria is an ideal pattern in which to mix colors, since so many are rarely seen in quantity. The Peach-Blo basket on the bottom of 105 was found in Oregon. I am amazed at the Elegant glass that is being found in the West! Every year when I travel out there, I seem to see some glassware that I never see in the East. Distribution of patterns was definitely geographical, and there is no better way to find this out than to visit different areas!

The pitchers shown atop page 105 are all rarely seen. The amber one is a Doulton style and is usually found in color without an etching! That ball jug in (dark) Emerald green is one of the few pieces of glass I have ever regretted selling.

	Crystal	Green, Pink/ Yellow		Crystal	Green, Pink/ Yellow
Basket, 6", 2 hdld. (sides up)	20.00	35.00	Comport, 5", 4 ftd.	17.00	37.50
Bowl, 3", indiv. nut, 4 ftd.	55.00	75.00	Comport, 6", 4 ftd.	20.00	40.00
Bowl, 3½", cranberry	25.00	55.00	Comport, 7", low	30.00	65.00
Bowl, 5", ftd., crimped edge, bonbon	20.00	34.00	Comport, 7", tall	35.00	80.00
Bowl, 5", sq., fruit, "saucer"	15.00	25.00	Comport, 9½", tall, 2 hdld., ftd. bowl	65.00	140.00
Bowl, 5½", bonbon, 2 hdld.	20.00	32.00	Creamer, ftd.	12.00	20.00
Bowl, 5½", bonbon, ftd.	15.00	28.00	Creamer, tall, ftd.	13.00	25.00
Bowl, 5½", flattened, ftd., bonbon	15.00	28.00	Cup, rnd. or sq.	15.00	27.00
Bowl, 5½", fruit, "saucer"	15.00	25.00	Cup, 4 ftd., sq.	25.00	65.00
Bowl, 6", rnd., cereal	20.00	35.00	Cup, after dinner (demitasse), rnd.		
Bowl, 6", sq., cereal	16.00	32.00	or sq.	65.00	110.00
Bowl, 8", 2 pt., 2 hdld., relish	20.00	32.00	Fruit cocktail, 6 oz., ftd. (3 styles)	9.00	17.50
Bowl, 8", 3 pt., 3 hdld., relish	22.50	38.00	Ice pail, metal handle w/tongs	45.00	90.00
Bowl, 8¾", 2 hdld., figure, "8" pickle	17.50	37.50	Icer, w/insert	60.00	90.00
Bowl, 8¾", 2 pt., 2 hdld., figure "8"			Mayonnaise, w/liner & ladle		
relish	20.00	40.00	(4 ftd. bowl)	35.00	65.00
Bowl, 9", salad, tab hdld.	35.00	75.00	Oil, w/stopper, tall, ftd., hdld.	90.00	195.00
Bowl, 9½", 2 hdld., veg.	55.00	90.00	Oyster cocktail, #3035, 4½ oz.	12.00	20.00
Bowl, 10", oblong, tab hdld., "baker"	37.50	70.00	Oyster cocktail, 4½ oz., low stem	12.00	20.00
Bowl, 10", 2 hdld.	35.00	75.00	Pitcher, 67 oz., middle indent	150.00	275.00
Bowl, 11", 2 hdld., fruit	35.00	75.00	Pitcher, 80 oz., ball	160.00	260.00
Bowl, 12", 4 ftd., console	35.00	65.00	Pitcher, w/cover, 64 oz.	175.00	335.00
Bowl, 12", 4 ftd., flared rim	35.00	65.00	Plate, 6", 2 hdld.	9.00	15.00
Bowl, 12", 4 ftd., oval	35.00	75.00	Plate, 6", bread/butter	6.00	9.00
Bowl, 12", 5 pt., celery & relish	35.00	60.00	Plate, 7½", tea	8.00	12.00
Bowl, 13", flared rim	35.00	65.00	Plate, 8½"	9.00	15.00
Bowl, cream soup, w/rnd. liner	22.00	40.00	Plate, 9½", dinner	55.00	80.00
Bowl, cream soup, w/sq. saucer	22.00	40.00	Plate, 10", tab hdld., salad	18.00	37.50
Bowl, finger, flared edge, w/rnd. plate	27.00	38.00	Plate, 11", 2 hdld.	20.00	45.00
Bowl, finger, ftd.	20.00	30.00	Plate, 11", sq., ftd. cake	85.00	235.00
Bowl, finger, w/rnd. plate	27.00	40.00	Plate, 11½", tab hdld., sandwich	17.50	40.00
Butter, w/cover, 2 hdld.	125.00	295.00	Plate, 14", chop or salad	40.00	75.00
Candlestick, 6", ea.	20.00	37.50	Plate, sq., bread/butter	6.00	9.00
Candy box, w/cover, 4 ftd., w/tab hdld.	70.00	120.00	Plate, sq., dinner	60.00	85.00
Cheese compote w/11½" cracker plate,			Plate, sq., salad	7.00	12.00
tab hdld.	35.00	65.00	Plate, sq., service	22.00	45.00
Cocktail shaker, grnd. stopper, spout			Platter, 11½"	55.00	115.00
(like pitcher)	110.00	210.00	Salt & pepper, pr., short	40.00	75.00
Comport, 4", fruit cocktail	13.00	26.00	Salt & pepper, pr., w/glass top, tall	42.00	125.00

GLORIA

	Crystal	Green Pink/ Yellow		Crystal	Green Pink/ Yellow
Salt & pepper, ftd., metal tops..............	50.00	125.00	Tray, 4 pt., ctr. hdld., relish.................	30.00	45.00
Saucer, rnd...	2.00	4.00	Tray, 9", pickle, tab hdld.	16.00	45.00
Saucer, rnd. after dinner	8.00	15.00	Tumbler, #3035, 5 oz., high ftd.	11.00	20.00
Saucer, sq., after dinner (demitasse)....	10.00	17.00	Tumbler, #3035, 10 oz., high ftd.	12.00	22.00
Saucer, sq.	2.00	3.00	Tumbler, #3035, 12 oz., high ftd.	17.00	30.00
Stem, #3035, 2½ oz., wine	20.00	40.00	Tumbler, #3115, 5 oz., ftd., juice	12.00	20.00
Stem, #3035, 3 oz., cocktail	17.50	28.00	Tumbler, #3115, 8 oz., ftd.	12.00	20.00
Stem, #3035, 3½ oz., cocktail	17.00	27.00	Tumbler, #3115, 10 oz., ftd.	13.00	21.00
Stem, #3035, 4½ oz., claret	30.00	55.00	Tumbler, #3115, 12 oz., ftd.	17.00	30.00
Stem, #3035, 6 oz., low sherbet	11.00	16.00	Tumbler, #3120, 2½ oz., ftd. (used		
Stem, #3035, 6 oz., tall sherbet	12.50	18.00	w/cocktail shaker)	25.00	45.00
Stem, #3035, 9 oz., water	15.00	30.00	Tumbler, #3120, 5 oz., ftd.	12.00	20.00
Stem, #3035, 3½ oz., cocktail	17.00	30.00	Tumbler, #3120, 10 oz., ftd.	12.00	20.00
Stem, #3115, 9 oz., goblet	15.00	30.00	Tumbler, #3120, 12 oz., ftd.	17.00	30.00
Stem, #3120, 1 oz., cordial...................	60.00	135.00	Tumbler, #3120, 2½ oz., ftd. (used		
Stem, #3120, 4½ oz., claret	30.00	55.00	w/shaker)	25.00	45.00
Stem, #3120, 6 oz., low sherbet	10.00	15.00	Tumbler, #3130, 5 oz., ftd.	12.00	20.00
Stem, #3120, 6 oz., tall sherbet.............	11.00	16.00	Tumbler, #3130, 10 oz., ftd.	13.00	20.00
Stem, #3120, 9 oz., water	15.00	25.00	Tumbler, #3130, 12 oz., ftd.	15.00	25.00
Stem, #3130, 2½ oz., wine	20.00	42.50	Tumbler, #3135, 5 oz., juice	12.00	20.00
Stem, #3130, 6 oz., low sherbet	10.00	15.00	Tumbler, #3135, 10 oz., water..............	12.00	20.00
Stem, #3130, 6 oz., tall sherbet.............	11.00	16.00	Tumbler, #3135, 12 oz., tea	17.00	30.00
Stem, #3130, 8 oz., water	18.00	30.00	Tumbler, 12 oz., flat (2 styles), one		
Stem, #3135, 1 oz., cordial...................	65.00	145.00	indent side to match 67 oz. pitcher.	18.00	35.00
Stem, #3135, 6 oz., low sherbet	11.00	15.00	Vase, 9", oval, 4 indent........................	85.00	165.00
Stem, #3135, 6 oz., tall sherbet.............	12.00	16.00	Vase, 10", keyhole base	60.00	120.00
Stem, #3135, 8 oz., water	18.00	30.00	Vase, 10", squarish top	75.00	165.00
Sugar, ftd...	11.00	18.00	Vase, 11"..	55.00	110.00
Sugar, tall, ftd.	11.00	20.00	Vase, 11", neck indent	75.00	135.00
Sugar shaker, w/glass top.....................	175.00	325.00	Vase, 12", keyhole base, flared rim	60.00	125.00
Syrup, tall, ftd.......................................	65.00	135.00	Vase, 12", squarish top	60.00	130.00
Tray, 11", ctr. hdld., sandwich	20.00	37.50	Vase, 14", keyhole base, flared rim	75.00	165.00
Tray, 2 pt., ctr. hdld., relish.................	25.00	37.50			

Note: See pages 228 – 229 for stem identification.

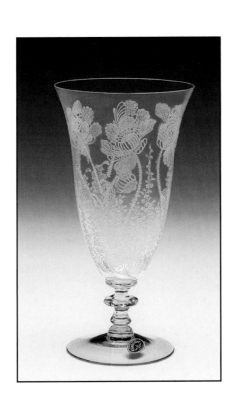

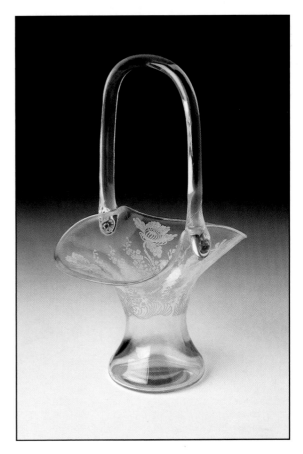

Colors: crystal; Flamingo pink punch bowl and cups only

Greek Key is loved by many collectors, but it is not abundant in today's market. Collections amass slowly.

	Crystal		Crystal
Bowl, finger	40.00	Pitcher, 1 pint (jug)	130.00
Bowl, jelly, w/cover, 2 hdld., ftd	145.00	Pitcher, 1 quart (jug)	210.00
Bowl, indiv., ftd., almond	40.00	Pitcher, 3 pint (jug)	250.00
Bowl, 4", nappy	25.00	Pitcher, ½ gal. (tankard)	240.00
Bowl, 4", shallow, low ft., jelly	40.00	Oil bottle, 2 oz., squat, w/#8 stopper	100.00
Bowl, 4½", nappy	25.00	Oil bottle, 2 oz., w/#6 stopper	110.00
Bowl, 4½", scalloped, nappy	25.00	Oil bottle, 4 oz., squat, w/#8 stopper	100.00
Bowl, 4½", shallow, low ft., jelly	40.00	Oil bottle, 4 oz., w/#6 stopper	100.00
Bowl, 5", ftd., almond	40.00	Oil bottle, 6 oz., w/#6 stopper	100.00
Bowl, 5", ftd., almond, w/cover	110.00	Oil bottle, 6 oz., squat, w/#8 stopper	100.00
Bowl, 5", hdld., jelly	95.00	Plate, 4½"	20.00
Bowl, 5", low ft., jelly, w/cover	110.00	Plate, 5"	25.00
Bowl, 5", nappy	30.00	Plate, 5½"	25.00
Bowl, 5½", nappy	40.00	Plate, 6"	35.00
Bowl, 5½", shallow nappy, ftd.	65.00	Plate, 6½"	35.00
Bowl, 6", nappy	30.00	Plate, 7"	50.00
Bowl, 6", shallow nappy	30.00	Plate, 8"	70.00
Bowl, 6½", nappy	35.00	Plate, 9"	90.00
Bowl, 7", low ft., straight side	90.00	Plate, 10"	110.00
Bowl, 7", nappy	80.00	Plate, 16", orange bowl liner	180.00
Bowl, 8", low ft., straight side	70.00	Puff box, #1, w/cover	175.00
Bowl, 8", nappy	70.00	Puff box, #3, w/cover	175.00
Bowl, 8", scalloped nappy	65.00	Salt & pepper, pr.	125.00
Bowl, 8", shallow, low ft.	75.00	Sherbet, 4½ oz., ftd., straight rim	30.00
Bowl, 8½", shallow nappy	75.00	Sherbet, 4½ oz., ftd., flared rim	30.00
Bowl, 9", flat, banana split	45.00	Sherbet, 4½ oz., high ft., shallow	30.00
Bowl, 9", ftd., banana split	55.00	Sherbet, 4½ oz., ftd., shallow	30.00
Bowl, 9", low ft., straight side	65.00	Sherbet, 4½ oz., ftd., cupped rim	30.00
Bowl, 9", nappy	70.00	Sherbet, 6 oz., low ft.	35.00
Bowl, 9", shallow, low ft.	70.00	Spooner, lg.	100.00
Bowl, 9½", shallow nappy	70.00	Spooner, 4½" (or straw jar)	90.00
Bowl, 10", shallow, low ft.	85.00	Stem, ¾ oz., cordial	250.00
Bowl, 11", shallow nappy	70.00	Stem, 2 oz., wine	110.00
Bowl, 12", orange bowl	500.00	Stem, 2 oz., sherry	200.00
Bowl, 12", punch, ftd.	300.00	Stem, 3 oz., cocktail	50.00
Flamingo	750.00	Stem, 3½ oz., burgundy	125.00
Bowl, 12", orange, flared rim	450.00	Stem, 4½ oz., saucer champagne	60.00
Bowl, 14½", orange, flared rim	500.00	Stem, 4½ oz., claret	170.00
Bowl, 15", punch, ftd.	400.00	Stem, 7 oz.	95.00
Bowl, 18", punch, shallow	400.00	Stem, 9 oz.	125.00
Butter, indiv. (plate)	35.00	Stem, 9 oz., low ft.	110.00
Butter/jelly, 2 hdld., w/cover	200.00	Straw jar, w/cover	350.00
Candy, w/cover, ½ lb.	140.00	Sugar	50.00
Candy, w/cover, 1 lb.	170.00	Sugar, oval, hotel	55.00
Candy, w/cover, 2 lb.	210.00	Sugar, rnd., hotel	50.00
Cheese & cracker set, 10"	150.00	Sugar & creamer, oval, individual	140.00
Compote, 5"	90.00	Tray, 9", oval celery	50.00
Compote, 5", w/cover	130.00	Tray, 12", oval celery	60.00
Creamer	50.00	Tray, 12½", French roll	140.00
Creamer, oval, hotel	55.00	Tray, 13", oblong	260.00
Creamer, rnd., hotel	50.00	Tray, 15", oblong	300.00
Cup, 4½ oz., punch	20.00	Tumbler, 2½ oz. (or toothpick)	450.00
Cup, punch, Flamingo	45.00	Tumbler, 5 oz., flared rim	50.00
Coaster	20.00	Tumbler, 5 oz., straight side	50.00
Egg cup, 5 oz.	80.00	Tumbler, 5½ oz., water	50.00
Hair receiver	170.00	Tumbler, 7 oz., flared rim	60.00
Ice tub, lg., tab hdld.	150.00	Tumbler, 7 oz., straight side	60.00
Ice tub, sm., tab hdld.	130.00	Tumbler, 8 oz., w/straight, flared, cupped, shallow	60.00
Ice tub, w/cover, hotel	220.00	Tumbler, 10 oz., flared rim	90.00
Ice tub, w/cover, 5", individual, w/5" plate	200.00	Tumbler, 10 oz., straight wide	90.00
Jar, 1 qt., crushed fruit, w/cover	400.00	Tumbler, 12 oz., flared rim	100.00
Jar, 2 qt., crushed fruit, w/cover	400.00	Tumbler, 12 oz., straight side	100.00
Jar, lg. cover, horseradish	140.00	Tumbler, 13 oz., straight side	100.00
Jar, sm. cover, horseradish	130.00	Tumbler, 13 oz., flared rim	100.00
Jar, tall celery	140.00	Water bottle	210.00
Jar, w/knob cover, pickle	160.00		

Colors: Amber, Azure (blue), crystal, Ebony, green, Topaz, Wisteria

My listings are from a Fostoria catalog that had January 1, 1933, entered on the front page in pencil. Not all pieces were made in all colors according to this catalog. If there is no price listed, it means that no piece is supposed to have been made. If you have such an item, please let me know!

I was told that a set of Wisteria Hermitage was impossible to attain; so I set out to see if I could find enough for a picture in that color. Enjoy!

	Crystal	Amber/Green/Topaz	Azure	Wisteria
Ash tray holder, #2449	5.00	8.00	12.00	
*Ash tray, #2449	3.00	5.00	8.00	
Bottle, 3 oz., oil, #2449	17.50	35.00		
Bottle, 27 oz., bar w/stopper, #2449	45.00			
Bowl, 4½", finger, #2449½	4.00	6.00	10.00	20.00
Bowl, 5", fruit, #2449½	5.00	8.00	12.00	
Bowl, 6", cereal, #2449½	6.00	10.00	20.00	
Bowl, 6½", salad, #2449½	6.00	9.00	14.00	
Bowl, 7", soup, #2449½	8.00	12.00	22.00	35.00
Bowl, 7½", salad, #2449½	8.00	12.00	22.00	
Bowl, 8", deep, ped., ft., #2449	17.50	32.00	60.00	
Bowl, 10", ftd., #2449	20.00	35.00		95.00
Bowl, grapefruit, w/crystal liner, #2449	20.00	35.00		
Candle, 6", #2449	12.50	22.00	35.00	
Coaster, 5⅝", #2449	5.00	7.50	11.00	
Comport, 6", #2449	12.00	17.50	27.50	40.00
Creamer, ftd., #2449	4.00	6.00	10.00	30.00
Cup, ftd., #2449	6.00	10.00	15.00	22.00
Decanter, 28 oz., w/stopper, #2449	35.00	50.00	95.00	
Fruit cocktail, 2⅜", 5 oz., ftd., #2449	5.00	7.50	12.00	
Ice tub, 6", #2449	17.50	35.00	50.00	150.00
Icer, #2449	10.00	18.00	30.00	50.00
Mayonnaise, 5⅝" w/7" plate, #2449	20.00	35.00		
Mug, 9 oz., ftd., #2449	12.50			
Mug, 12 oz., ftd., #2449	15.00			
Mustard w/cover & spoon, #2449	17.50	35.00		
Pitcher, pint, #2449	22.50	40.00	60.00	600.00
Pitcher, 3 pint, #2449	30.00	60.00	150.00	
Plate, 6", #2449½	3.00	5.00	8.00	
Plate, 7", ice dish liner	4.00	6.00	10.00	
Plate, 7", #2449½	4.00	6.00	10.00	
Plate, 7⅜", crescent salad, #2449	10.00	17.50	30.00	
Plate, 8", #2449½	6.00	10.00	15.00	22.00
Plate, 9", #2449½	12.50	20.00	30.00	
Plate, 12", sandwich, #2449		12.50	20.00	
Relish, 6", 2 pt., #2449	6.00	10.00	15.00	25.00
Relish, 7¼", 3 pt., #2449	8.00	11.00	17.50	50.00
Relish, 8", pickle, #2449	8.00	11.00	17.50	
Relish, 11", celery, #2449	10.00	15.00	25.00	50.00
Salt & pepper, 3⅜", #2449	20.00	40.00	65.00	
Salt, indiv., #2449	4.00	6.00	10.00	
Saucer, #2449	2.00	3.50	5.00	8.00
Sherbet, 3", 7 oz., low, ftd., #2449	6.00	8.00	12.50	20.00
Stem, 3¼", 5½ oz., high sherbet, #2449	8.00	11.00	17.50	25.00
Stem, 4⅝", 4 oz., claret, #2449	10.00	15.00		
Stem, 5¼", 9 oz., water goblet, #2449	10.00	15.00	25.00	40.00
Sugar, ftd., #2449	4.00	6.00	10.00	30.00
Tray, 6½", condiment, #2449	6.00	12.00	20.00	30.00
Tumbler, 2½", 2 oz., #2449½	4.00	6.00	14.00	20.00
Tumbler, 2½", 2 oz., ftd., #2449	5.00	8.00		
Tumbler, 3", 4 oz., cocktail, ftd., #2449	5.00	7.50	12.00	18.00
Tumbler, 3¼", 6 oz. old-fashioned, #2449½	6.00	10.00	18.00	25.00
Tumbler, 3⅞", 5 oz., #2449½	5.00	8.00	12.00	20.00
Tumbler, 4", 5 oz., ftd., #2449	5.00	8.00	12.00	20.00
Tumbler, 4⅛", 9 oz., ftd., #2449	6.00	10.00	15.00	25.00
Tumbler, 4¾", 9 oz., #2449½	6.00	10.00	15.00	30.00
Tumbler, 5¼", 12 oz., ftd., iced tea, #2449	10.00	16.00	28.00	
Tumbler, 5⅞", 13 oz., #2449½	10.00	16.00	28.00	
Vase, 6", ftd.	22.00	32.50		

* Ebony – $12.00

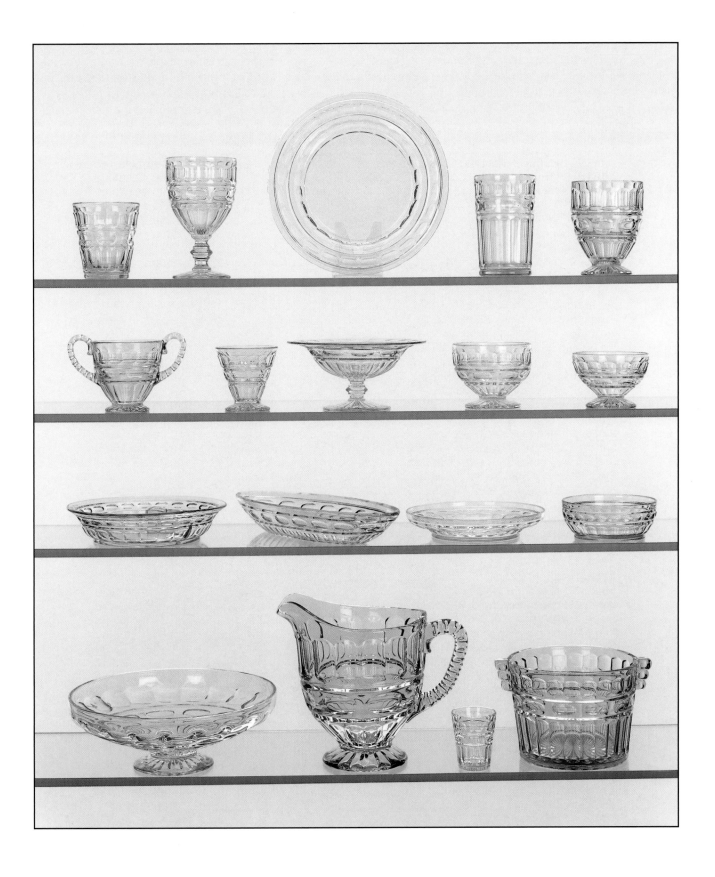

Colors: amber, black, crystal, Emerald green, green, pink, Willow blue

Imperial Hunt Scene cups, saucers, creamers, sugars, and shakers are not easily found, You can see all but the creamer on the next page, thanks to a collector from Ohio who bought a luncheon set in an antique mall a few years ago! There is quite an assortment of Peach-Blo (pink) on the next page. It has been a while since I had enough pink to have a photo of that color. Stems are abundant in most sizes except for cordials and clarets. You will find bi-colored Hunt Scene stemware. Pink bowl with a green stem is the typical form. Serving pieces are infrequently seen. This is another Cambridge pattern that is found with gold decorated ware. Gold decoration adds 10% to the price listed. Be wary of worn gold; it is not very desirable!

A crystal #1402 Tally-Ho cup is pictured; now, I need a crystal Tally-Ho saucer with Imperial Hunt Scene etching!

Black and Emerald green (dark) with gold decorations sell 25% to 50% higher than prices listed.

	Crystal	Colors
Bowl, 6", cereal	15.00	28.00
Bowl, 8"	35.00	70.00
Bowl, 8½", 3 pt.	25.00	65.00
Candlestick, 2-lite, keyhole	17.50	37.50
Candlestick, 3-lite, keyhole	27.50	65.00
Comport, 5½", #3085		40.00
Creamer, flat	12.00	35.00
Creamer, ftd.	15.00	35.00
Cup	45.00	55.00
Decanter		235.00
Finger bowl, w/plate, #3085		45.00
Humidor, tobacco		375.00
Ice bucket	50.00	95.00
Ice tub	40.00	85.00
Mayonnaise, w/liner	30.00	65.00
Pitcher, w/cover, 63 oz., #3085		295.00
Pitcher, w/cover, 76 oz., #711	150.00	275.00
Plate, 8"	12.00	22.00
Salt & pepper, pr.	50.00	150.00
Saucer	10.00	15.00
Stem, 1 oz., cordial, #1402	60.00	
Stem, 2½ oz., wine, #1402	45.00	
Stem, 3 oz., cocktail, #1402	40.00	
Stem, 6 oz., tomato, #1402	40.00	
Stem, 6½ oz., sherbet, #1402	35.00	
Stem, 7½ oz., sherbet, #1402	40.00	
Stem, 10 oz., water, #1402	40.00	
Stem, 14 oz., #1402	50.00	
Stem, 18 oz., #1402	60.00	
Stem, 1 oz., cordial, #3085		185.00
Stem, 2½ oz., cocktail, #3085		40.00
Stem, 2½ oz., wine, #3085		55.00
Stem, 4½ oz., claret, #3085		67.50
Stem, 5½ oz., parfait, #3085		65.00
Stem, 6 oz., low sherbet, #3085		22.50
Stem, 6 oz., high sherbet, #3085		27.50
Stem, 9 oz., water, #3085		45.00
Sugar, flat w/ lid	40.00	95.00
Sugar, ftd.	15.00	35.00
Tumbler, 2½ oz., 2⅞", flat, #1402	25.00	
Tumbler, 5 oz., flat, #1402	20.00	
Tumbler, 7 oz., flat, #1402	20.00	
Tumbler, 10 oz., flat, #1402	23.00	
Tumbler, 10 oz., flat, tall, #1402	25.00	
Tumbler, 15 oz., flat, #1402	35.00	
Tumbler, 2½ oz., ftd., #3085		45.00
Tumbler, 5 oz., 3⅞", ftd., #3085		30.00
Tumbler, 8 oz., ftd., #3085		30.00
Tumbler, 10 oz., ftd., #3085		35.00
Tumbler, 12 oz., 5⅜", ftd., #3085		40.00

Colors: crystal, Flamingo pink, Sahara yellow, Moongleam green, cobalt, and Alexandrite

To save answering several dozen letters, I will repeat that if you find any colored piece of Ipswich, other than those listed above, it was made at Imperial and not Heisey. Even if it is marked Heisey, it was still manufactured at Imperial. Mostly, I get letters on (Alexandrite) candy jars that are actually Imperial's Heather (purple) color.

Moongleam has been the color of choice with collectors of Ipswich for some time now. There is a scarcity of tumblers in all sizes; therefore, you will have to pay more when, and if, you see them. The pitcher is the most difficult Moongleam piece to find, followed closely by the candlestick with center piece vase. This candlestick is shown complete as a pattern shot on the bottom of page 113. You can also find this candlestick in cobalt blue. Remember, the little footed vase is the difficult piece to find. Don't let someone talk you into buying these candles without that vase unless the price is very inexpensive. The prices listed include that vase; keep that in mind when out shopping!

The Ipswich goblet was the only piece made in Alexandrite. If you have any problem determining whether a piece you have is Alexandrite or not, look in the back of this book on page 230. We have been able to show this color more consistently than any other book ever has. You can also take an Alexandrite piece outside in natural light where it will look pink, and then near a fluorescent bulb where it will change to a blue hue. Fostoria's Wisteria, Tiffin's Twilight, and Cambridge's Heatherbloom all have similar color characteristics; do not confuse them with Heisey's Alexandrite.

	Crystal	Pink	Sahara	Green	Cobalt	Alexandrite
Bowl, finger, w/underplate	40.00	90.00	80.00	120.00		
Bowl, 11", ftd., floral	70.00		300.00		400.00	
Candlestick, 6", 1-lite	150.00	275.00	200.00	300.00	400.00	
Candlestick centerpiece, ftd., vase, "A" prisms, complete	160.00	300.00	350.00	450.00	500.00	
Candy jar, ¼ lb., w/cover	175.00					
Candy jar, ½ lb., w/cover	175.00	325.00	300.00	400.00		
Cocktail shaker, 1 quart, strainer, #86 stopper	225.00	600.00	700.00	800.00		
Creamer	35.00	70.00	60.00	125.00		
Stem, 4 oz., oyster cocktail, ftd	25.00	60.00	50.00	70.00		
Stem, 5 oz., saucer champagne (knob in stem)	25.00	60.00	50.00	70.00		
Stem, 10 oz., goblet (knob in stem)	30.00	85.00	70.00	90.00		750.00
Stem, 12 oz., schoppen, flat bottom	100.00					
Pitcher, ½ gal.	150.00	250.00	350.00	750.00		
Oil bottle, 2 oz., ftd., #86 stopper	125.00	285.00	275.00	300.00		
Plate, 7", square	30.00	60.00	50.00	70.00		
Plate, 8", square	35.00	65.00	55.00	75.00		
Sherbet, 4 oz., ftd. (knob in stem)	15.00	35.00	30.00	45.00		
Sugar	35.00	70.00	60.00	125.00		
Tumbler, 5 oz., ftd. (soda)	30.00	45.00	40.00	75.00		
Tumbler, 8 oz., ftd. (soda)	30.00	45.00	40.00	85.00		
Tumbler, 10 oz., cupped rim, flat bottom	70.00	110.00	100.00	140.00		
Tumbler, 10 oz., straight rim, flat bottom	70.00	110.00	100.00	140.00		
Tumbler, 12 oz., ftd. (soda)	40.00	80.00	70.00	95.00		

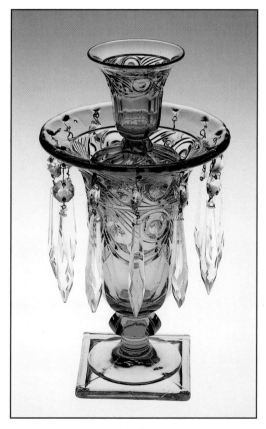

Dalzell Viking Glass Company 1996...

Colors: crystal, Cobalt, Ruby, Light Blue, Emerald, Amethyst

Janice was a newly listed pattern in the last book; now I have some unfortunate news to report. Dalzell Viking is making or recently made the candlestick pictured on the end of Row 2. These were made in cobalt blue and red that I can confirm. The light blue shown here was not made and I do not know about crystal, but it is highly likely that crystal was made also. I will study the old and new to let you know how to tell them apart for the next book; for now, just be wary!

There is a separate line of swan handled items in the Janice pattern that I have not included here. I have not had any volunteers who are willing or knowledgeable enough to help in pricing swan handled items! I hope to address that in the future. If you are an advanced collector of Janice, let me know what additional pieces you have found and be sure to suggest any pricing ideas you may have when you write!

One of the blue candy jars in the bottom row has an etched pattern. I have only seen this etching on blue and crystal. Be on the lookout for baskets, pitchers and footed ice buckets. They seem to be the creme de la creme of this pattern.

I have found that red items are found less often than blue, but there seem to be more collectors seeking blue at the present time. That tends to balance the pricing for those colors. Demand will make up for scarcity in **every** instance!

	Crystal	Blue/ Red		Crystal	Blue/ Red
Basket, 6½", 9" high	65.00	125.00	Ice tub, 6", ftd.	85.00	235.00
Basket, 11"	75.00	160.00	Jam jar w/cover, 6"	20.00	45.00
Basket, 12", oval, 10" high	85.00	185.00	Mayonnaise liner, 7", 2 hdl.	9.00	14.00
Bonbon, 5½", 2 hdl., 4½" high	18.00	30.00	Mayonnaise plate, 6"	7.50	12.50
Bonbon, 6", 2 hdl., 4" high	20.00	33.00	Mayonnaise, 6", 2 hdl.	18.00	30.00
Bonbon, 7", 2 hdl., 4¾" high	25.00	40.00	Mayonnaise, round	15.00	27.50
Bowl, 5½", flower, w/eight crimps	22.00	35.00	Oil, 5 oz., w/stopper	35.00	95.00
Bowl, 6", 2 hdl., crimped	20.00	33.00	Pitcher, 15 oz., berry cream	37.50	110.00
Bowl, 9½", cupped	35.00	55.00	Plate, 7", 2 hdl.	9.00	14.00
Bowl, 9½", flared	35.00	55.00	Plate, 8½", salad	10.00	17.50
Bowl, 9", 2 hdl.	37.50	65.00	Plate, 11", cheese	22.50	40.00
Bowl, 10"	37.50	65.00	Plate, 11", ftd., rolled edge	27.50	50.00
Bowl, 10½", cupped, 3 toed	45.00	75.00	Plate, 12", 2 hdl.	25.00	45.00
Bowl, 10½", flared, 3 toed	45.00	75.00	Plate, 13"	30.00	60.00
Bowl, 11", oval	40.00	75.00	Plate, 13", 2 hdl.	32.50	65.00
Bowl, 11", cupped, ftd.	45.00	75.00	Plate, 14", ftd., rolled edge	37.50	75.00
Bowl, 11", flared	40.00	65.00	Plate, 15"	40.00	
Bowl, 12", flared	42.50	70.00	Plate, 15", rolled edge torte	45.00	
Bowl, 12", fruit, ruffled top	50.00	85.00	Platter, 13", oval	32.50	70.00
Bowl, 12", oval	42.50	70.00	Relish, 6", 2 part, 2 -hdl.	15.00	37.50
Bowl, 12", salad, scalloped top	50.00	85.00	Salt and pepper, pr.	35.00	75.00
Bowl, 12", six crimps	52.50	95.00	Saucer	2.00	4.50
Bowl, 13", flared	50.00	80.00	Sherbet	12.00	26.00
Canape set: tray w/ftd. juice	30.00		Sugar, 6 oz.	12.00	20.00
Candelbra, 5", 2-lt., 5" wide	40.00		Sugar, individual, flat	10.00	20.00
Candlestick, 5½", 1-lt., 5" wide	35.00		Sugar, individual, ftd.	12.50	22.50
Candlestick, 6", 1-lt., 4½" wide	37.50		Sugar, tall	15.00	35.00
Candy box w/cover, 5½"	55.00	150.00	Syrup, w/dripcut top	55.00	
Celery, 11"	20.00	45.00	Tray, oval, 2 hdl., ind. sug/cr	12.00	20.00
Comport, cracker for cheese plate	14.00	25.00	Tray, oval, 2 hdl., cr/sug	15.00	25.00
Condiment set: tray and 2 cov. jars	55.00	125.00	Tumbler	12.00	27.50
Creamer, 6 oz.	12.00	20.00	Vase, 4", ivy, 3½" high	22.00	40.00
Creamer, individual, flat	12.00	20.00	Vase, 4", ivy, 4½" high, w/base peg	25.00	50.00
Creamer, individual, ftd.	12.50	22.50	Vase, 7", ftd.	35.00	65.00
Creamer, tall	15.00	35.00	Vase, 8", ball, 7½" high	45.00	95.00
Cup	8.00	23.00	Vase, 8", cupped, 3 toed	50.00	100.00
Guest set: bottle w/tumbler	75.00		Vase, 8", flared, 3 toed	50.00	100.00
Ice pail, 10", hld.	65.00	165.00	Vase, 9", ball	55.00	110.00

Colors: crystal, Azure blue, Topaz yellow, Rose pink

June is the most collected etched Fostoria pattern. Blue June has been the star, but pink is rapidly gaining momentum. Both colors have seen major price increases while crystal and yellow have remained steady.

Shakers came with both glass and metal tops. Collectors prefer the glass ones first used by the company.

If you will refer to Versailles (page 212), I have listed all the Fostoria line numbers for each piece. Since these are essentially the same listings as June, you can use the item number listings from Versailles. Be sure to see the stemware illustrations on page 89. You would not want to pay for a claret and receive a high sherbet!

	Crystal	Rose, Blue	Topaz
Ash tray	25.00	50.00	35.00
Bottle, salad dressing, #2083 or #2375	195.00	850.00	375.00
Bowl, baker, 9", oval	35.00	125.00	65.00
Bowl, baker, 10", oval	40.00	135.00	75.00
Bowl, bonbon	12.50	30.00	23.00
Bowl, bouillon, ftd.	12.00	38.00	23.00
Bowl, finger, w/liner	32.50	60.00	30.00
Bowl, mint, 3 ftd., 4½"	10.00	42.00	28.00
Bowl, 6", nappy, 3 ftd., jelly	12.00	40.00	23.00
Bowl, 6½", cereal	20.00	65.00	35.00
Bowl, 7", soup	50.00	175.00	150.00
Bowl, lg., dessert, hdld.	30.00	135.00	75.00
Bowl, 10"	30.00	115.00	65.00
Bowl, 10", Grecian	40.00	115.00	60.00
Bowl, 11", centerpiece	30.00	80.00	50.00
Bowl, 12", centerpiece, three types	35.00	100.00	55.00
Bowl, 13", oval centerpiece, w/flower frog	65.00	225.00	110.00
Candlestick, 2"	14.00	30.00	22.00
Candlestick, 3"	12.00	35.00	22.00
Candlestick, 3", Grecian	20.00	50.00	30.00
Candlestick, 5", Grecian	25.00	65.00	35.00
Candy, w/cover, 3 pt.		295.00	
Candy, w/cover, ½ lb., ¼ lb.			185.00
Celery, 11½"	25.00	95.00	45.00
Cheese & cracker set, #2368 or #2375	40.00	120.00	65.00
Comport, 5", #2400	20.00	60.00	35.00
Comport, 6", #5298 or #5299	22.00	85.00	45.00
Comport, 7", #2375	25.00	110.00	50.00
Comport, 8", #2400	40.00	140.00	60.00
Cream soup, ftd.	18.00	45.00	32.50
Creamer, ftd.	12.00	25.00	17.50
Creamer, tea	25.00	60.00	45.00
Cup, after dinner	25.00	80.00	45.00
Cup, ftd.	15.00	30.00	22.00
Decanter	400.00	2,000.00	575.00
Goblet, claret, 6", 4 oz.	40.00	150.00	75.00
Goblet, cocktail, 5¼", 3 oz.	20.00	45.00	32.50
Goblet, cordial, 4", ¾ oz.	50.00	135.00	70.00
Goblet, water, 8¼", 10 oz.	30.00	60.00	40.00
Goblet, wine, 5½", 3 oz.	25.00	95.00	50.00
Grapefruit	30.00	100.00	65.00
Grapefruit liner	25.00	80.00	40.00
Ice bucket	50.00	150.00	80.00
Ice dish	25.00	65.00	42.00
Ice dish liner (tomato, crab, fruit)	5.00	20.00	10.00
Mayonnaise, w/liner	25.00	65.00	40.00
Oil, ftd.	200.00	650.00	335.00
Oyster cocktail, 5½ oz.	16.00	35.00	25.00
Parfait, 5¼"	35.00	125.00	65.00
Pitcher	225.00	575.00	325.00
Plate, canape	15.00	45.00	25.00
Plate, lemon	14.00	25.00	20.00
Plate, 6", bread/butter	4.50	12.00	6.00
Plate, 6", finger bowl liner	4.50	12.00	8.00
Plate, 7½", salad	5.00	9.00	8.00
Plate, 7½, cream soup	4.00	12.00	7.50
Plate, 8¾", luncheon	6.00	18.00	12.00
Plate, 9½", sm. dinner	10.00	38.00	24.00
Plate, 10", grill	35.00	110.00	70.00
Plate, 10", cake, hdld (no indent)	20.00	60.00	40.00
Plate, 10", cheese with indent, hdld.	20.00	60.00	40.00
Plate, 10¼", dinner	35.00	110.00	70.00
Plate, 13", chop	22.00	80.00	55.00
Plate, 14", torte		100.00	70.00
Platter, 12"	30.00	120.00	70.00
Platter, 15"	65.00	225.00	125.00
Relish, 8½", 3 part	20.00		35.00
Sauce boat	40.00	275.00	100.00
Sauce boat liner	15.00	75.00	35.00
Saucer, after dinner	6.00	20.00	10.00
Saucer	4.00	7.50	5.00
Shaker, ftd., pr	60.00	195.00	120.00
Sherbet, high, 6", 6 oz.	17.50	35.00	25.00
Sherbet, low, 4¼", 6 oz.	15.00	30.00	20.00
Sugar, ftd., straight or scalloped top	12.00	25.00	20.00
Sugar cover	50.00	225.00	130.00
Sugar pail	65.00	225.00	135.00
Sugar, tea	25.00	60.00	45.00
Sweetmeat	15.00	35.00	20.00
Tray, service and lemon		325.00	275.00
Tray, 11", ctr. hdld.	20.00	45.00	35.00
Tumbler, 2½ oz., ftd.	20.00	75.00	45.00
Tumbler, 5 oz., 4½", ftd.	15.00	45.00	28.00
Tumbler, 9 oz., 5¼", ftd.	15.00	45.00	25.00
Tumbler, 12 oz., 6", ftd.	20.00	68.00	35.00
Vase, 8", 2 styles	75.00	295.00	195.00
Vase, 8½", fan, ftd.	75.00	250.00	150.00
Whipped cream bowl	10.00	20.00	14.00
Whipped cream pail	75.00	210.00	135.00

Note: See stemware identification on page 89.

Colors: Topaz yellow, green; some blue

Kashmir has few collectors when compared to the numbers that seek other Fostoria etched patterns. Availability is a major consideration for collectors and Kashmir would rate only a 1 or 2 on a scale of 10 when it comes to that. More Kashmir is found in the Midwest, but you can see from my pictures how well green Kashmir has avoided me; and I have been looking for it! Still, what is found does not instantaneously vanish as do some of the other Fostoria patterns. The right collector has to come along; and since there are so few Kashmir admirers, it often takes awhile to sell!

If you want to buy a Fostoria set, this may be it. While everyone else is running up the price on June and Versailles, you could sneak up on a beautiful set without much rivalry. I see settings of yellow for sale; yet, there are few buyers! You could complete a set of yellow Kashmir cheaper than any other etched, yellow Fostoria pattern.

The stemware and tumbler line is #5099 which is the same line on which Trojan is found. This is the cascading waterfall stem.

Both styles of after dinner cups are shown in the picture of blue. The square saucer set is more difficult to find than the round. Those two green cup and saucer sets are all I have ever been able to find!

	Yellow, Green	Blue
Ash tray	25.00	30.00
Bowl, cream soup	22.00	25.00
Bowl, finger	15.00	20.00
Bowl, 5", fruit	13.00	15.00
Bowl, 6", cereal	30.00	35.00
Bowl, 7", soup	35.00	65.00
Bowl, 8½", pickle	20.00	30.00
Bowl, 9", baker	37.50	45.00
Bowl, 10"	40.00	45.00
Bowl, 12", centerpiece	40.00	50.00
Candlestick, 2"	15.00	17.50
Candlestick, 3"	20.00	25.00
Candlestick, 5"	22.50	27.50
Candlestick, 9½"	40.00	60.00
Candy, w/cover	85.00	125.00
Cheese and cracker set	65.00	85.00
Comport, 6"	35.00	45.00
Creamer, ftd.	17.50	20.00

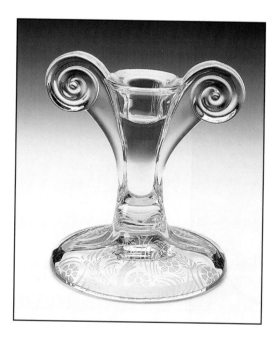

	Yellow, Green	Blue
Cup	15.00	20.00
Cup, after dinner, flat	38.00	
Cup, after dinner, ftd.	38.00	55.00
Grapefruit	50.00	
Grapefruit liner	40.00	
Ice bucket	65.00	90.00
Oil, ftd.	275.00	450.00
Pitcher, ftd.	275.00	395.00
Plate, 6", bread & butter	5.00	6.00
Plate, 7", salad, rnd.	6.00	7.00
Plate, 7", salad, sq.	6.00	7.00
Plate, 8", salad	8.00	10.00
Plate, 9" luncheon	9.00	12.00
Plate, 10", dinner	45.00	65.00
Plate, 10", grill	35.00	50.00
Plate, cake, 10"	35.00	
Salt & pepper, pr.	110.00	165.00
Sandwich, center hdld.	35.00	40.00
Sauce boat, w/liner	75.00	125.00
Saucer, rnd.	5.00	10.00
Saucer, after dinner, sq.	8.00	
Saucer, after dinner, rnd.	8.00	15.00
Stem, ¾ oz., cordial	85.00	115.00
Stem, 2½ oz., ftd.	30.00	45.00
Stem, 2 oz., ftd., whiskey	30.00	50.00
Stem, 2½ oz., wine	32.00	40.00
Stem, 3 oz., cocktail	22.00	25.00
Stem, 3½ oz., ftd., cocktail	22.00	25.00
Stem, 4 oz., claret	35.00	55.00
Stem, 4½ oz., oyster cocktail	16.00	18.00
Stem, 5½ oz., parfait	30.00	40.00
Stem, 5 oz., ftd., juice	15.00	25.00
Stem, 5 oz., low sherbet	13.00	20.00
Stem, 6 oz., high sherbet	17.50	22.50
Stem, 9 oz., water	20.00	35.00
Stem, 10 oz., ftd., water	22.00	30.00
Stem, 11 oz.	22.50	
Stem, 12 oz., ftd.	25.00	35.00
Stem, 13 oz., ftd., tea	25.00	
Stem, 16 oz., ftd., tea	35.00	
Sugar, ftd.	15.00	20.00
Sugar lid	50.00	85.00
Vase, 8"	90.00	145.00

Note: See stemware identification on page 89.

Colors: crystal; rare in black and amber

Lariat prices have slowed from the dramatic jumps of two years ago; but the rarer pieces are still going up because when one appears in the market place, it is rapidly snapped up by a collector who has been waiting. The cutting most often seen on Lariat is Moonglo. Many non-Lariat collectors adore this cut, but few Lariat collectors corral it! We have tried to stimulate your interest with the number of pieces shown. Enjoy! The ads that I have previously shown are becoming collectible themselves. Watch for them in women's magazines of the 1940s and 1950s.

	Crystal
Ash tray, 4"	15.00
Basket, 7½", bonbon	100.00
Basket, 8½", ftd.	165.00
Basket, 10", ftd.	195.00
Bowl, 2 hdld., cream soup	50.00
Bowl, 7 quart, punch	130.00
Bowl, 4", nut, individual	32.00
Bowl, 7", 2 pt., mayo	24.00
Bowl, 7", nappy	20.00
Bowl, 8", flat, nougat	24.00
Bowl, 9½", camellia	28.00
Bowl, 10", hdld., celery	35.00
Bowl, 10½", 2 hdld., salad	38.00
Bowl, 10½", salad	40.00
Bowl, 11", 2 hdld., oblong, relish	30.00
Bowl, 12", floral or fruit	40.00
Bowl, 13", celery	50.00
Bowl, 13", gardenia	35.00
Bowl, 13", oval, floral	35.00
Candlestick, 1-lite, individual	30.00
Candlestick, 2-lite	40.00
Candlestick, 3-lite	45.00
Candy box, w/cover, caramel	75.00
Candy, w/cover, 7"	90.00
Candy, w/cover, 8", w/horsehead finial (rare)	1,500.00
Cheese, 5", ftd., w/cover	50.00
Cheese dish, w/cover, 8"	60.00
Cigarette box	55.00
Coaster, 4"	12.00
Cologne	95.00

	Crystal
Compote, 10", w/cover	100.00
Creamer	20.00
Creamer & sugar, w/tray, indiv.	45.00
Cup	20.00
Cup, punch	8.00
Ice tub	75.00
Jar, w/cover, 12", urn	175.00
Lamp & globe, 7", black-out	120.00
Lamp & globe, 8", candle, handled	95.00
Mayonnaise, 5" bowl, 7" plate w/ladle set	60.00
Oil bottle, 4 oz., hdld., w/#133 stopper	180.00
Oil bottle, 6 oz., oval	75.00
Plate, 6", finger bowl liner	8.00
Plate, 7", salad	14.00
Plate, 8", salad	22.00
Plate, 10½", dinner	125.00
Plate, 11", cookie	35.00
Plate, 12", demi-torte, rolled edge	40.00
Plate, 13", deviled egg, round	220.00
Plate, 14", 2 hdld., sandwich	50.00
Plate, 15", deviled egg, oval	220.00
Plate, 21", buffet	70.00
Platter, 15", oval	60.00
Salt & pepper, pr.	200.00
Saucer	5.00
Stem, 1 oz., cordial, double loop	250.00
Stem, 1 oz., cordial blown, single loop	150.00
Stem, 2½ oz., wine, blown	25.00
Stem, 3½ oz., cocktail, pressed	20.00
Stem, 3½ oz., cocktail, blown	20.00
Stem, 3½ oz., wine, pressed	24.00
Stem, 4 oz., claret, blown	28.00
Stem, 4¼ oz., oyster cocktail or fruit	18.00
Stem, 4½ oz., oyster cocktail, blown	18.00
Stem, 5½ oz., sherbet/saucer champagne, blown	17.00
Stem, 6 oz., low sherbet	10.00
Stem, 6 oz., sherbet/saucer champagne, pressed	17.00
Stem, 9 oz., pressed	22.00
Stem, 10 oz., blown	22.00
Sugar	20.00
Tray, rnd., center hdld., w/ball finial	165.00
Tray for sugar & creamer, 8", 2 handled	24.00
Tumbler, 5 oz., ftd., juice	22.00
Tumbler, 5 oz., ftd., juice, blown	22.00
Tumbler, 12 oz., ftd., ice tea	28.00
Tumbler, 12 oz., ftd., ice tea, blown	28.00
Vase, 7", ftd., fan	30.00
Vase, swung	135.00

Color: crystal

Duncan's Lily of the Valley is one pattern that garners compliments from non-collectors. I admired a cordial when I first started collecting stems about 20 years ago. I had to be told it was Lily of the Valley, but bought it for my cordial collection without hesitation because of its beauty! Stemware has the Lily of the Valley cut into the stem itself, but the bowls atop the stem are found with or without the cutting. Duncan's designation for this stem was D-4 and the cut variety was DC-4. Prices below are for cut (DC-4) bowl items; deduct about a third (or more) for plain bowl stems. Once you see this pattern, you will understand why collectors want the cut version!

As with First Love, Canterbury #115 and Pall Mall #30 blanks were used for this cutting. The mayonnaise pictured is #30 and the bowl and plate are #115. I have not found anyone who has seen a cup or saucer in this cut. Those would be a find!

The box pictured below contained an original cut set. It was found in the St. Louis area last year. Although not a fancy box, it does chronicle a set for the collector. There may be additional pieces than those listed. Help me document them! I suspect there are candlesticks to go with the bowl.

	Crystal		Crystal
Ash tray, 3"	18.00	Plate, 8"	20.00
Ash tray, 6"	25.00	Plate, 9"	40.00
Bowl, 12"	55.00	Stem, cocktail	22.00
Candy, w/lid	75.00	Stem, cordial	75.00
Cheese and cracker	55.00	Stem, high sherbet	20.00
Creamer	25.00	Stem, water goblet	35.00
Mayonnaise	30.00	Stem, wine	40.00
Mayonnaise ladle	8.00	Sugar	25.00
Mayonnaise liner	15.00		

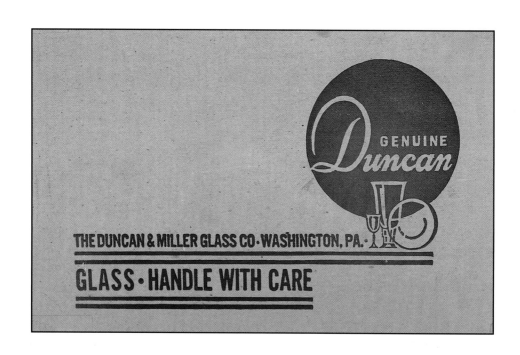

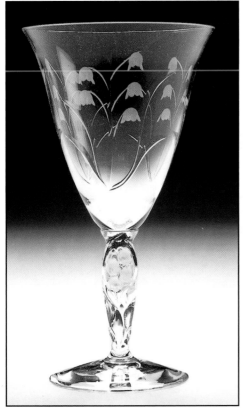

Color: Dawn

This Heisey pattern in the Dawn color only is named Lodestar. Crystal pieces in the same design are called Satellite and the prices decline sensationally! Each piece has the star-like shape for its base. Dawn is not inexpensive as you can see by the prices listed below. These are realistic selling prices, not hoped for or asking prices!

	Dawn
Ash tray	95.00
Bowl, 4½", sauce dish, #1626	40.00
Bowl, 5", mayonnaise	85.00
Bowl, 6¾", #1565	60.00
Bowl, 8"	65.00
Bowl, 11", crimped	100.00
Bowl, 12", deep floral	90.00
Bowl, 14", shallow	130.00
Candleblock, 2¾" tall, 1-lite star, #1543, pr. (Satellite)	275.00
Candlestick, 2" tall, 1-lite centerpiece, pr.	130.00
Candlestick, 5¾" tall, 2-lite, pr.	600.00
Candy jar, w/cover, 5"	135.00
Celery, 10"	60.00
Creamer	50.00
Creamer, w/handle	90.00
Jar, w/cover, 8", #1626	160.00
Pitcher, 1 qt., #1626	170.00
Plate, 8½"	65.00
Plate, 14"	90.00
Relish, 7½", 3 pt.	60.00
Sugar	50.00
Sugar, w/handles	90.00
Tumbler, 6 oz., juice	50.00
Vase, 8", #1626	160.00
Vase, 8", crimped, #1626	180.00

SYMPHONE Blank, #5010, et. al.; A.H. Heisey & Co., 1939 – 1950s

Colors: crystal

Minuet is one Heisey pattern where prices have remained somewhat stable. There have been a few price hikes, namely for dinner plates. By the way, they are listed as service plates in the catalogs. I have always been fond of the apple marmalade pictured in row 2. These are difficult to sell without the ladle. Actually, Heisey ladles and spoons have become a collectible themselves. Do not hesitate to buy one! Of course, colored ones are preferred, but marked crystal sell well also.

Minuet stemware is copious, but tumblers are elusive. Also, serving pieces are troublesome to acquire except for the three-part relish and the three-footed bowl, pictured in the bottom row. You will have enthusiastic competition searching for this pattern.

	Crystal
Bell, dinner, #3408	75.00
Bowl, finger, #3309	50.00
Bowl, 6", ftd., mint	25.00
Bowl, 6", ftd., 2 hdld., jelly	30.00
Bowl, 6½", salad dressings	35.00
Bowl, 7", salad dressings	40.00
Bowl, 7", triplex, relish	60.00
Bowl, 7½", sauce, ftd.	70.00
Bowl, 9½", 3 pt., "5 o'clock," relish	70.00
Bowl, 10", salad, #1511 TOUJOURS	65.00
Bowl, 11", 3 pt., "5 o'clock," relish	80.00
Bowl, 11", ftd., floral	110.00
Bowl, 12", oval, floral, #1511 TOUJOURS	65.00
Bowl, 12", oval, #1514	65.00
Bowl, 13", floral, #1511 TOUJOURS	60.00
Bowl, 13", pickle & olive	45.00
Bowl, 13½", shallow salad	75.00
Candelabrum, 1-lite, w/prisms	110.00
Candelabrum, 2-lite, bobeche & prisms	175.00
Candlestick, 1-lite, #112	35.00
Candlestick, 2-lite, #1511 TOUJOURS	150.00
Candlestick, 3-lite, #142 CASCADE	75.00
Candlestick, 5", 2-lite, #134 TRIDENT	60.00
Centerpiece vase & prisms, #1511 TOUJOURS	200.00
Cocktail icer, w/liner, #3304 UNIVERSAL	225.00
Comport, 5½", #5010	40.00
Comport, 7½", #1511 TOUJOURS	60.00
Creamer, #1511 TOUJOURS	50.00
Creamer, dolphin ft.	42.50
Creamer, indiv., #1509 QUEEN ANN	37.50
Creamer, indiv., #1511 TOUJOURS	70.00
Cup	30.00
Ice bucket, dolphin ft.	160.00
Marmalade, w/cover, #1511 TOUJOURS (apple shape)	160.00
Mayonnaise, 5½", dolphin ft.	50.00
Mayonnaise, ftd., #1511 TOUJOURS	75.00
Pitcher, 73 oz., #4164	300.00
Plate, 7", mayonnaise liner	10.00

	Crystal
Plate, 7", salad	18.00
Plate, 7", salad, #1511 TOUJOURS	15.00
Plate, 8", luncheon	30.00
Plate, 8", luncheon, #1511 TOUJOURS	25.00
Plate, 10½", service	190.00
Plate, 12", rnd., 2 hdld., sandwich	150.00
Plate, 13", floral, salver, #1511 TOUJOURS	60.00
Plate, 14", torte, #1511 TOUJOURS	60.00
Plate, 15", sand., #1511 TOUJOURS	65.00
Plate, 16", snack rack, w/#1477 center	80.00
Salt & pepper, pr. (#10)	75.00
Saucer	10.00
Stem, #5010, SYMPHONE, 1 oz., cordial	135.00
Stem, #5010, 2½ oz., wine	50.00
Stem, #5010, 3½ oz., cocktail	35.00
Stem, #5010, 4 oz., claret	40.00
Stem, #5010, 4½ oz., oyster cocktail	25.00
Stem, #5010, 6 oz., saucer champagne	25.00
Stem, #5010, 6 oz., sherbet	25.00
Stem, #5010, 9 oz., water	35.00
Sugar, indiv., #1511 TOUJOURS	70.00
Sugar, indiv., #1509 QUEEN ANN	37.50
Sugar dolphin ft., #1509 QUEEN ANN	40.00
Sugar, #1511 TOUJOURS	50.00
Tray, 12", celery, #1511 TOUJOURS	50.00
Tray, 15", social hour	90.00
Tray for indiv. sugar & creamer	30.00
Tumbler, #5010, 5 oz., fruit juice	34.00
Tumbler, #5010, 9 oz., low ftd., water	35.00
Tumbler, #5010, 12 oz., tea	60.00
Tumbler, #2351, 12 oz., tea	60.00
Vase, 5", #5013	50.00
Vase, 5½", ftd., #1511 TOUJOURS	60.00
Vase, 6", urn, #5012	70.00
Vase, 7½", urn, #5012	85.00
Vase, 8", #4196	85.00
Vase, 9", urn, #5012	95.00
Vase, 10", #4192	100.00
Vase, 10", #4192, SATURN optic	110.00

Colors: amethyst, black, blue, crystal, green, pink, lilac, crystal stems w/color bowls

Morgan has attracted many new collectors since its inclusion in the last book. With everyone searching for this sparsely distributed pattern, it has been even more difficult to find additional pieces to include in this book. Cups and saucers are the nemesis of this Central Glass Works pattern. Only crystal and pink are being found with crystal leading the way.

Morgan was designed in 1920 by Joseph O. Balda, who was better known for his Heisey designs. The pattern allegedly was adopted for use in the governor's mansion by a West Virginia governing family named Morgan. Thus, the very masculine pattern name attached to a swinging, angelic design.

The gold decorated bud vase shown as a pattern shot below is applied against an amethyst background. We have now found this gold design on a black bud vase. Does anyone have a gold decorated piece other than a bud vase? I've still only seen two whiskey sets; one is pictured on the ribbed, square tray in the bottom photo. Both sets were on the identical unetched tray; apparently that is the appropriate one.

Even stemware has become more difficult to find, with the blue stems I have seen exhibiting some royal prices. No one seems to be buying at those enormous prices; and, if anything, they may be self-defeating by stifling would be collectors. It's called sticker shock! Prices can skyrocket so fast that new collectors search for other patterns. It has happened before, an example being Lancaster's Jubilee.

Blue and lilac are the rarer colors, but I doubt you can find enough of either color buying a piece at a time. You might get lucky though and find a set. If you have knowledge of additional pieces, please share the knowledge!

	*All Colors
Bonbon, 6", two handled	35.00
Bowl, 4¼", ftd., fruit	30.00
Bowl, 10", console	50.00
Bowl, 13", console	65.00
Candlestick, pr.	75.00
Candy w/lid, diamond shaped, 4 ftd.	200.00
Comport, 6½" tall, 5" wide	40.00
Comport, 6½" tall, 6" wide	45.00
Creamer, ftd.	40.00
Cup	85.00
Decanter, w/stopper	195.00
Ice bucket, 4¾" x7½", 2 hdld.	110.00
Mayonnaise	45.00

	*All Colors
Mayonnaise liner	12.50
Oil bottle	95.00
Pitcher	195.00
Plate, 6½", fruit bowl liner	8.00
Plate, 7¼", salad	12.00
Plate, 8½", luncheon	20.00
Plate, 9¼", dinner	30.00
Saucer	15.00
Server, 9½", octagonal, center handle	65.00
Server, 10⅜", round, center handle	65.00
Server, 11", octagonal, flat, center handle	65.00
Stem, 3¼", sherbet	15.00
Stem, 4⅜", sherbet, beaded stem	25.00
Stem, 5⅛", cocktail, beaded stem	30.00
Stem, 5⅜", high, sherbet, beaded stem	35.00
Stem, 5⅞", high sherbet, straight stem	35.00
Stem, 5⅞", wine	40.00
Stem, 7¼", 10 oz., water	45.00
Stem, 8¼", water	45.00
Sugar, ftd.	40.00
Tumbler, oyster cocktail	15.00
Tumbler, 2⅛", whiskey	50.00
Tumbler, 10 oz., flat water	25.00
Tumbler, 4⅜", ftd. juice	25.00
Tumbler, 5⅜", ftd., 10 oz., water	25.00
Tumbler, 5¾", ftd., water	25.00
Tumbler, 5⅞", ftd., 12 oz., tea	30.00
Vase, 8", drape optic	85.00
Vase, 9⅞", straight w/flared top	135.00
** Vase, 10", bud	150.00

* Crystal 10% to 20% lower.
　Blue, lilac 10% to 20% higher.
** Gold decorated $250.00

Colors: amber, crystal, Carmen, Royal Blue, Heatherbloom, Emerald green (light and dark); rare in Violet

True, the diverse colors in Mt. Vernon give collectors a selection, but you can only finish a large setting in amber or crystal. You could acquire luncheon sets in red, cobalt blue, and Heatherbloom; only a few accessory pieces are obtainable in those colors. However, prices for those three colors will fetch up to double the prices listed for amber and crystal. Many collectors are mixing their crystal Mt. Vernon with a spattering of colored wares. Give it a try!

	Amber/Crystal
Ash tray, 3½", #63	8.00
Ash tray, 4", #68	12.00
Ash tray, 6" x 4½", oval, #71	12.00
Bonbon, 7", ftd., #10	12.50
Bottle, bitters, 2½ oz., #62	55.00
Bottle, 7 oz., sq., toilet, #18	65.00
Bowl, finger, #23	10.00
Bowl, 4½", ivy ball or rose, ftd., #12	27.50
Bowl, 5¼", fruit, #6	10.00
Bowl, 6", cereal, #32	12.50
Bowl, 6", preserve, #76	12.00
Bowl, 6½", rose, #106	18.00
Bowl, 8", pickle, #65	17.50
Bowl, 8½", 4 pt., 2 hdld., sweetmeat, #105	32.00
Bowl, 10", 2 hdld., #39	20.00
Bowl, 10½", deep, #43	30.00
Bowl, 10½", salad, #120	25.00
Bowl, 11", oval, 4 ftd., #136	27.50
Bowl, 11", oval, #135	25.00
Bowl, 11½", belled, #128	30.00
Bowl, 11½", shallow, #126	30.00
Bowl, 11½", shallow cupped, #61	30.00
Bowl, 12", flanged, rolled edge, #129	32.50
Bowl, 12", oblong, crimped, #118	32.50
Bowl, 12", rolled edge, crimped, #117	32.50
Bowl, 12½", flanged, rolled edge, #45	35.00
Bowl, 12½", flared, #121	35.00
Bowl, 12½", flared, #44	35.00
Bowl, 13", shallow, crimped, #116	35.00
Box, 3", w/cover, round, #16	30.00
Box, 4", w/cover, sq., #17	32.50
Box, 4½", w/cover, ftd., round, #15	37.50
Butter tub, w/cover, #73	65.00
Cake stand, 10½" ftd., #150	35.00
Candelabrum, 13½", #38	125.00
Candlestick, 4", #130	10.00
Candlestick, 5", 2-lite, #110	25.00
Candlestick, 8", #35	27.50
Candy, w/cover, 1 lb., ftd., #9	65.00
Celery, 10½", #79	15.00
Celery, 11", #98	17.50
Celery, 12", #79	20.00
Cigarette box, 6", w/cover, oval, #69	32.00
Cigarette holder, #66	15.00
Coaster, 3", plain, #60	5.00
Coaster, 3", ribbed, #70	5.00
Cocktail icer, 2 pc., #85	27.50
Cologne, 2½ oz., w/stopper, #1340	37.50
Comport, 4½", #33	12.00
Comport, 5½", 2 hdld., #77	15.00
Comport, 6", #34	15.00
Comport, 6½", #97	17.50
Comport, 6½", belled, #96	22.50
Comport, 7½" #11	25.00
Comport, 8", #81	25.00
Comport, 9", oval, 2 hdld., #100	35.00

	Amber/Crystal
Comport, 9½", #99	30.00
Creamer, ftd., #8	10.00
Creamer, indiv., #4	10.00
Creamer, #86	10.00
Cup, #7	6.50
Decanter, 11 oz., #47	50.00
Decanter, 40 oz., w/stopper, #52	70.00
Honey jar, w/cover (marmalade), #74	35.00
Ice bucket, w/tongs, #92	35.00
Lamp, 9" hurricane, #1607	70.00
Mayonnaise, divided, 2 spoons, #107	25.00
Mug, 14 oz., stein, #84	30.00
Mustard, w/cover, 2½ oz., #28	25.00
Pickle, 6", 1 hdld., #78	12.00
Pitcher, 50 oz., #90	80.00
Pitcher, 66 oz., #13	85.00
Pitcher, 80 oz., ball, #95	95.00
Pitcher, 86 oz., #91	115.00
Plate, finger bowl liner, #23	4.00
Plate, 6", bread & butter, #4	3.00
Plate, 6⅜", bread & butter, #19	4.00
Plate, 8½", salad, #5	7.00
Plate, 10½", dinner, #40	35.00
Plate, 11½", hdld., #37	20.00
Relish, 6", 2 pt., 2 hdld., #106	12.00
Relish, 8", 2 pt., hdld., #101	17.50
Relish, 8", 3 pt., 3 hdld., #103	20.00
Relish, 11", 3 part, #200	25.00
Relish, 12", 2 part, #80	30.00
Relish, 12", 5 part, #104	30.00
Salt, indiv., #24	7.00
Salt, oval, 2 hdld., #102	12.00
Salt & pepper, pr., #28	22.50
Salt & pepper, pr., short, #88	20.00
Salt & pepper, tall, #89	25.00
Salt dip, #24	9.00
Sauce boat & ladle, tab hdld., #30-445	60.00
Saucer, #7	7.50
Stem, 3 oz., wine, #27	15.00
Stem, 3½ oz., cocktail, #26	9.00
Stem, 4 oz., oyster cocktail, #41	9.00
Stem, 4½ oz., claret, #25	13.50
Stem, 4½ oz., low sherbet, #42	7.50
Stem, 6½ oz., tall sherbet, #2	10.00
Stem, 10 oz., water, #1	15.00
Sugar, ftd., #8	10.00
Sugar, indiv., #4	12.00
Sugar, #86	10.00
Tray, for indiv., sugar & creamer, #4	10.00
Tumbler, 1 oz., ftd., cordial, #87	22.00
Tumbler, 2 oz., whiskey, #55	10.00
Tumbler, 3 oz., ftd., juice, #22	9.00
Tumbler, 5 oz., #56	12.00
Tumbler, 5 oz., ftd., #21	12.00
Tumbler, 7 oz., old-fashioned, #57	15.00
Tumbler, 10 oz., ftd., water, #3	15.00

	Amber/Crystal			Amber/Crystal
Tumbler, 10 oz., table, #51	12.00		Vase, 5", #42	15.00
Tumbler, 10 oz., tall, #58	12.00		Vase, 6", crimped, #119	20.00
Tumbler, 12 oz., barrel shape, #13	15.00		Vase, 6", ftd., #50	25.00
Tumbler, 12 oz., ftd., tea, #20	17.00		Vase, 6½", squat, #107	27.50
Tumbler, 14 oz., barrel shape, #14	20.00		Vase, 7", #58	30.00
Tumbler, 14 oz., tall, #59	22.00		Vase, 7", ftd., #54	35.00
Urn, w/cover (same as candy), #9	65.00		Vase, 10", ftd., #46	50.00

Color: crystal, blue, blue and pink opalescent

Nautical is a pattern that should be easily recognized, but numerous pieces are not! It is hard to miss those with anchors and rope, but some pieces do not have the anchor which means they can escape all but the watchful eye of knowledgeable seekers. A bar or whiskey glass was bought by a dealer for $2.00 on his way to the 20-30-40 Society's Depression glass show. It had a huge deposit of old glue from the price tag; so, it had been sitting on a shelf for quite a while. Good buys are still around!

Most collectors search for blue, but many of them are inclined to mix the blue with other colors in order to have more choices. I should point out the difference in the decanter and covered jar that are pictured side by side on the next page. The covered jars are shown on each end of row 2 with the decanter pictured next to the one on the right. I confused the decanter with a jar myself when I first saw it. There is a close up view of the decanter at the bottom of the page.

The 7" comport with an anchor for the stem can be found with two different tops. The opalescent one has a pointed edge top while the other style has a plain edge top. I have a blue opalescent one sitting here to show next time. The covered jars, decanter, and comport are the pieces to find as you can see by their prices.

There are some similar pieces to this pattern that are confused with it. You can find a pair of bookends that have a leaning anchor across the base. You will often see this same shaped bookend with a horse head. The anchor bookends can even be found in blue!

	*Blue	Crystal	Opalescent
Ash tray, 3".......................................	15.00	8.00	
Ash tray, 6".......................................	25.00	12.50	
Candy jar, w/lid..............................	500.00	250.00	600.00
Cigarette holder.............................	30.00	15.00	
Cigarette jar....................................	50.00	25.00	
Cocktail shaker (fish design)...........	125.00	60.00	
Comport, 7".....................................	195.00	100.00	495.00
Creamer...	30.00	15.00	
Decanter..	450.00	200.00	550.00
Ice bucket.......................................	95.00	55.00	
Marmalade.......................................	50.00	25.00	
Plate, 6½", 2 hdld., cake.................	25.00	12.00	
Plate, 8"..	20.00	10.00	
Plate, 10"..	50.00	25.00	
Relish, 12", 7 part...........................	65.00	35.00	
Relish, 2-part, 2 hdld.	45.00	22.50	
Shakers, pr.		32.50	
Sugar...	30.00	15.00	
Tumbler, 2 oz., bar..........................	22.50	12.50	
Tumbler, 8 oz., whisky & soda........	20.00	12.00	
Tumbler, 9 oz., water, ftd.	25.00	15.00	
Tumbler, cocktail.............................	20.00	12.00	
Tumbler, ftd., orange juice	25.00	15.00	
Tumbler, high ball	27.50	18.00	

*Add 10% for satinized.

NAVARRE, Plate Etching #327, Fostoria Glass Company, 1937 – 1980

Colors: crystal; all other colors found made very late

Fostoria's Navarre may now be the most collected etched **crystal** pattern made by that company! It has passed Chintz for that honor in the last few years. Of course, American is the most widely collected Fostoria crystal pattern; but it was made for about 70 years and several generations came to know it quite well. Navarre was made for over 40 years; it, too, has lasting recognition. As always, with so many collectors searching for it, prices continue to increase! Harder to find pieces increase in price faster. It is better to buy them when you see them than to take the chance they will cost even more later. Remember, a highly desirable pattern is easier to sell in the event that need arises.

Note the footed shakers in the bottom photo. They came with both glass and metal lids. Metal lids are prevalent. Glass tops were used in the early production years.

Only the older crystal pieces of Navarre are priced in this Elegant book. Colors of pink, blue, and green were all made in the 1970s as were additional crystal pieces not originally made in the late 1930s and 1940s. These later pieces include carafes, roemer wines, continental champagnes, and brandies. You can find these later pieces in my *Collectible Glassware from the 40s, 50s & 60s....* Most of these pieces are signed "Fostoria" although some carried only a sticker. I am telling you this to make you aware of the colors made in Navarre. You will even find a few pieces of Navarre that are signed Lenox. These were made after Fostoria closed. Some collectors shy away from the Lenox pieces; but it does not seem to make much difference to a majority of Navarre devotees. A few Depression era glass shows have not allowed these pieces or colors to be sold since they were of so recent manufacture. However, most shows are changing the rules to allow patterns that began production earlier to be included.

	Crystal		Crystal
Bell, dinner	60.00	Plate, #2440, 7½", salad	15.00
Bowl, #2496, 4", square, hdld.	14.00	Plate, #2440, 8½", luncheon	22.00
Bowl, #2496, 4⅜", hdld.	14.00	Plate, #2440, 9½", dinner	50.00
Bowl, #869, 4½", finger	75.00	Plate, #2496, 10", hdld., cake	55.00
Bowl, #2496, 4⅝", tri-cornered	15.00	Plate, #2440, 10½", oval cake	55.00
Bowl, #2496, 5", hdld., ftd.	18.50	Plate, #2496, 14", torte	75.00
Bowl, #2496, 6", square, sweetmeat	20.00	Plate, #2464, 16", torte	135.00
Bowl, #2496, 6¼", 3 ftd., nut	20.00	Relish, #2496, 6", 2 part, square	32.50
Bowl, #2496, 7⅜", ftd., bonbon	27.50	Relish, #2496, 10" x 7½", 3 part	47.50
Bowl, #2496, 10", oval, floating garden	55.00	Relish, #2496, 10", 4 part	52.50
Bowl, #2496, 10½", hdld., ftd.	75.00	Relish, #2419, 13¼", 5 part	87.50
Bowl, #2470½, 10½", ftd.	60.00	Salt & pepper, #2364, 3¼", flat, pr.	65.00
Bowl, #2496, 12", flared	62.50	Salt & pepper, #2375, 3½", ftd., pr.	110.00
Bowl, #2545, 12½", oval, "Flame"	60.00	Salad dressing bottle, #2083, 6½"	425.00
Candlestick, #2496, 4"	22.00	Sauce dish, #2496, div. mayo., 6½"	40.00
Candlestick, #2496, 4½", double	37.50	Sauce dish, #2496, 6½" x 5¼"	135.00
Candlestick, #2472, 5", double	45.00	Sauce dish liner, #2496, 8", oval	30.00
Candlestick, #2496, 5½"	30.00	Saucer, #2440	5.00
Candlestick, #2496, 6", triple	47.50	Stem, #6106, 1 oz., cordial, 3⅞"	55.00
Candlestick, #2545, 6¾", double, "Flame"	65.00	Stem, #6106, 3¼ oz., wine, 5½"	35.00
Candlestick, #2482, 6¾", triple	60.00	Stem, #6106, 3½ oz., cocktail, 6"	25.00
Candy, w/cover, #2496, 3 part	135.00	Stem, #6106, 4 oz., oyster cocktail, 3⅝"	27.50
Celery, #2440, 9"	35.00	Stem, #6106, 4½ oz., claret, 6½"	42.50
Celery, #2496, 11"	45.00	Stem, #6106, 6 oz., low sherbet, 4⅜"	24.00
Comport, #2496, 3¼", cheese	27.50	Stem, #6106, 6 oz., saucer champagne, 5⅝"	24.00
Comport, #2400, 4½"	30.00		
Comport, #2496, 4¾"	35.00	Stem, #6106, 10 oz., water, 7⅝"	30.00
Cracker, #2496, 11", plate	42.50	Sugar, #2440, 3⅝", ftd.	18.00
Creamer, #2440, 4¼", ftd.	20.00	Sugar, #2496, individual	16.00
Creamer, #2496, individual	17.50	Syrup, #2586, metal cut-off top, 5½"	425.00
Cup, #2440	19.00	Tid bit, #2496, 8¼", 3 ftd., turned up edge	22.00
Ice bucket, #2496, 4⅜" high	130.00	Tray, #2496½", for ind. sugar/creamer	22.00
Ice bucket, #2375, 6" high	150.00	Tumbler, #6106, 5 oz., ftd., juice, 4⅝"	25.00
Mayonnaise, #2375, 3 piece	67.50	Tumbler, #6106, 10 oz., ftd., water, 5⅜"	25.00
Mayonnaise, #2496½, 3 piece	67.50	Tumbler, #6106, 13 oz., ftd., tea, 5⅞"	32.00
Pickle, #2496, 8"	27.50	Vase, #4108, 5"	100.00
Pickle, #2440, 8½"	30.00	Vase, #4121, 5"	100.00
Pitcher, #5000, 48 oz., ftd.	365.00	Vase, #4128, 5"	100.00
Plate, #2440, 6", bread/butter	11.00	Vase, #2470, 10", ftd.	175.00

Colors: crystal, frosted crystal, some cobalt with crystal stem and foot

The double branched candelabrum with bobeches in New Era is probably the most acknowledged Heisey candle. In the market you can find more diverse pricing on these than for any other Heisey item shown in this book. Since almost everyone knows they are Heisey, then, they **think** they have to be extremely valuable! Of course, these were made during both production periods of this pattern; and thus, they are plentiful when compared to other Heisey candles! Since New Era candles are also sought by Art Deco collectors, the price rises even though they are fairly abundant. An ample supply can be made to look scarce when demand is high.

The cobalt stems and tumbler pictured in row 3 are undeniably difficult to find with prices averaging $150.00 to $175.00 each. The after dinner cup and saucer are in short supply. Flawless plates (without scratches in the centers or nicks underneath) are not readily found.

Many pieces in this pattern were monogrammed. Today, these pieces are difficult to sell unless you can find someone with the same three initials! Remember that when you are tempted to buy some at a bargain price. It might not be such a bargain!

	Crystal		Crystal
Ash tray or indiv. nut	50.00	Stem, 1 oz. cordial	45.00
Bottle, rye, w/stopper	150.00	Stem, 3 oz. wine	30.00
Bowl, 11", floral	60.00	Stem, 3½ oz., high, cocktail	15.00
Candelabra, 2-lite, w/2 #4044 bobeche		Stem, 3½ oz., oyster cocktail	15.00
& prisms	140.00	Stem, 4 oz., claret	20.00
Creamer	35.00	Stem, 6 oz., champagne	15.00
Cup	12.00	Stem, 10 oz., goblet	20.00
Cup, after dinner	70.00	Stem, low, 6 oz., sherbet	15.00
Pilsner, 8 oz.	25.00	Sugar	35.00
Pilsner, 12 oz.	30.00	Tray, 13", celery	35.00
Plate, 5½" x 4½", bread & butter	15.00	Tumbler, 5 oz., ftd., soda	15.00
Plate, 9" x 7"	25.00	Tumbler, 8 oz., ftd., soda	15.00
Plate, 10" x 8"	40.00	Tumbler, 12 oz., ftd., soda	15.00
Relish, 13", 3 part	30.00	Tumbler, 14 oz., ftd., soda	18.00
Saucer	5.00	Tumbler, low, footed, 10 oz.	15.00
Saucer, after dinner	10.00		

NEW GARLAND, Plate Etching #284, Fostoria Glass Company, 1930 – 1934

Colors: Amber, Rose, and Topaz

New Garland is one of those Fostoria patterns that dealers are beginning to accumulate in their inventories because customers are asking for it. Pink appears to be the color at the moment, but Topaz has its admirers. I've only found a couple of sets in the last few years, but they sold fast when we displayed them at shows. Basic dinnerware items are available, but serving and accessory pieces seem to be scattered, at best. I have seen few amber pieces which may indicate that color would be difficult to accumulate! A large grouping of New Garland sets a beautiful table. There are few Elegant patterns found on squared shapes.

	Amber/Topaz	Rose
Bonbon, 2 hdld.	15.00	20.00
Bottle, salad dressing	95.00	150.00
Bowl, 5", fruit	10.00	12.50
Bowl, 6", cereal	12.00	18.00
Bowl, 7", soup	22.00	30.00
Bowl, 7½"	25.00	40.00
Bowl, 10", baker	35.00	45.00
Bowl, 11", ftd.	50.00	70.00
Bowl, 12"	50.00	70.00
Candlestick, 2"	15.00	20.00
Candlestick, 3"	17.50	22.50
Candlestick, 9½"	30.00	40.00
Candy jar, cover, ½ lb.	50.00	75.00
Celery, 11"	22.00	30.00
Comport, 6"	20.00	28.00
Comport, tall	30.00	40.00
Cream soup	18.00	22.50
Creamer	12.50	15.00
Creamer, ftd.	15.00	17.50
Creamer, tea	17.50	20.00
Cup, after dinner	20.00	25.00
Cup, ftd.	14.00	17.50
Decanter	125.00	195.00
Finger bowl, #4121	12.00	15.00
Finger bowl, #6002, ftd.	15.00	18.00
Ice bucket	55.00	70.00
Ice dish	20.00	25.00
Jelly, 7"	18.00	22.50
Lemon dish, 2 hdld.	15.00	18.00
Mayonnaise, 2 hdld.	18.00	22.50
Mint, 5½"	12.50	16.00
Nut, individual	10.00	13.00
Oil, ftd.	100.00	150.00
Pickle, 8½"	16.00	20.00
Pitcher, ftd.	195.00	250.00
Plate, 6"	4.00	6.00
Plate, 7"	7.00	10.00
Plate, 8"	12.00	15.00

	Amber/Topaz	Rose
Plate, 9"	25.00	35.00
Plate, 10" cake, 2 hdld.	27.50	35.00
Platter, 12"	35.00	45.00
Platter. 15"	50.00	75.00
Relish, 4 part	20.00	27.50
Relish, 8½"	14.00	18.00
Sauce boat	40.00	55.00
Sauce boat liner	15.00	20.00
Saucer	3.00	4.00
Saucer, after dinner	8.00	10.00
Shaker, pr.	40.00	60.00
Shaker, pr., ftd.	75.00	100.00
Stem, #4120, 2 oz., whiskey	18.00	25.00
Stem, #4120, 3½ oz., cocktail	20.00	24.00
Stem, #4120, 5 oz., low sherbet	14.00	16.00
Stem, #4120, 7 oz., low sherbet	15.00	18.00
Stem, #4120, high sherbet	18.00	20.00
Stem, #4120, water goblet	22.00	25.00
Stem, #6002, claret	25.00	32.50
Stem, #6002, cordial	30.00	37.50
Stem, #6002, goblet	22.00	25.00
Stem, #6002, high sherbet	18.00	20.00
Stem, #6002, low sherbet	14.00	16.00
Stem, #6002, oyster cocktail	16.00	20.00
Stem, #6002, wine	22.00	25.00
Sugar	12.50	15.00
Sugar, ftd.	15.00	17.50
Sugar, tea	17.50	20.00
Tumbler, #4120, 5 oz.	12.00	15.00
Tumbler, #4120, 10 oz.	14.00	17.50
Tumbler, #4120, 13 oz.	15.00	18.00
Tumbler, #4120, 16 oz.	20.00	24.00
Tumbler, #6002, ftd., 2 oz.	18.00	22.00
Tumbler, #6002, ftd., 5 oz.	12.00	15.00
Tumbler, #6002, ftd., 10 oz.	14.00	17.50
Tumbler, #6002, ftd., 13 oz.	15.00	18.00
Vase, 8"	40.00	50.00

Colors: crystal, Flamingo pink, Sahara yellow, Moongleam green, Hawthorne orchid, Marigold deep amber/yellow, and Dawn

Bearing in mind Octagon was regularly marked Heisey, it is one of those patterns that everyone can easily identify, but few collectors buy! It is one of the simpler Heisey patterns, but it does come in an abundance of colors! In the price list below, the only piece that leaps out at you is the 12", four-part tray. Octagon is fairly priced and is generally just waiting for a new home.

Two Marigold Octagon pieces are pictured here. This is the only place that rarely seen Heisey color (Marigold) is portrayed in this book. Be careful when buying Marigold because the color is subject to peeling. At that point, it becomes undesirable to collectors!

	Crystal	Flam.	Sahara	Moon.	Hawth.	Marigold
Basket, 5", #500.	100.00	300.00	300.00	340.00	450.00	
Bonbon, 6", sides up, #1229	10.00	40.00	25.00	25.00	40.00	
Bowl, cream soup, 2 hdld.	10.00	20.00	25.00	30.00	40.00	
Bowl, 2 hdld, ind. nut bowl	10.00	17.50	25.00	20.00	60.00	65.00
Bowl, 5½", jelly, #1229	15.00	25.00	25.00	25.00	50.00	
Bowl, 6", mint, #1229	10.00	20.00	25.00	20.00	45.00	30.00
Bowl, 6", #500	14.00	20.00	22.00	25.00	35.00	
Bowl, 6½", grapefruit	10.00	20.00	22.00	25.00	35.00	
Bowl, 8", ftd., #1229 comport	15.00	25.00	35.00	45.00	55.00	
Bowl, 9", flat soup	10.00	15.00	20.00	27.50	30.00	
Bowl, 9", vegetable	15.00	20.00	25.00	30.00	50.00	
Candlestick, 3", 1-lite	15.00	30.00	30.00	40.00	50.00	
Cheese dish, 6", 2 hdld., #1229	7.00	15.00	10.00	12.00	15.00	
Creamer, #500	10.00	30.00	35.00	35.00	50.00	
Creamer, hotel	10.00	30.00	30.00	35.00	50.00	
Cup, after dinner	10.00	20.00	20.00	25.00	42.00	
Cup, #1231	5.00	15.00	20.00	20.00	35.00	
Dish, frozen dessert, #500	10.00	20.00	20.00	30.00	35.00	50.00
Ice tub, #500	30.00	70.00	75.00	80.00	115.00	150.00
Mayonnaise, 5½", ftd., #1229	10.00	25.00	30.00	35.00	45.00	
Nut, two hdld.	10.00	18.00	18.00	25.00	60.00	70.00
Plate, cream soup liner	3.00	5.00	7.00	9.00	12.00	
Plate, 6"	4.00	8.00	8.00	10.00	15.00	
Plate, 7", bread	5.00	10.00	10.00	15.00	20.00	
Plate, 8", luncheon	7.00	10.00	10.00	15.00	25.00	
Plate, 10", sand., #1229	15.00	20.00	25.00	30.00	80.00	
Plate, 10", muffin, #1229, sides up	15.00	25.00	30.00	35.00	40.00	
Plate, 10½"	17.00	25.00	30.00	35.00	45.00	
Plate, 10½", ctr. hdld., sandwich	25.00	40.00	40.00	45.00	70.00	
Plate, 12", muffin, #1229, sides up	20.00	27.00	30.00	35.00	45.00	
Plate, 13", hors d'oeuvre, #1229	20.00	35.00	35.00	45.00	60.00	
Plate, 14"	22.00	25.00	30.00	35.00	50.00	
Platter, 12¾", oval	20.00	25.00	30.00	40.00	50.00	
Saucer, after dinner	5.00	8.00	10.00	10.00	12.00	
Saucer, #1231	5.00	8.00	10.00	10.00	12.00	
Sugar, #500	10.00	25.00	35.00	35.00	50.00	
Sugar, hotel	10.00	30.00	30.00	35.00	50.00	
Tray, 6", oblong, #500	8.00	15.00	15.00	15.00	30.00	
Tray, 9", celery	10.00	20.00	20.00	25.00	45.00	
Tray, 12", celery	10.00	25.00	25.00	30.00	50.00	
Tray, 12", 4 pt., #500 variety	60.00	120.00	140.00	160.00	250.00	*350.00

*Dawn

A.H. Heisey & Co., 1930 – 1939

Colors: crystal, Flamingo pink, Sahara yellow, Moongleam green, Marigold deep amber/yellow

Due to the abundance of Sahara (yellow), Old Colony pricing will be predicated on Sahara as follows: crystal – Subtract 50%; Flamingo – Subtract 10%; Moongleam – add 10%; Marigold – add 20%.

	Sahara
Bouillon cup, 2 hdld., ftd.	25.00
Bowl, finger, #4075	15.00
Bowl, ftd., finger, #3390	25.00
Bowl, 4½", nappy	14.00
Bowl, 5", ftd., 2 hdld.	24.00
Bowl, 6", ftd., 2 hdld., jelly	30.00
Bowl, 6", dolphin ftd., mint	35.00
Bowl, 7", triplex, dish	35.00
Bowl, 7½", dolphin ftd., nappy	70.00
Bowl, 8", nappy	40.00
Bowl, 8½", ftd., floral, 2 hdld.	60.00
Bowl, 9", 3 hdld.	90.00
Bowl, 10", rnd., 2 hdld., salad	60.00
Bowl, 10", sq., salad, 2 hdld.	55.00
Bowl, 10", oval, dessert, 2 hdld.	50.00
Bowl, 10", oval, veg.	42.00
Bowl, 11", floral, dolphin ft.	80.00
Bowl, 13", ftd., flared	40.00
Bowl, 13", 2 pt., pickle & olive	24.00
Cigarette holder, #3390	44.00
Comport, 7", oval, ftd.	80.00
Comport, 7", ftd., #3368	70.00
Cream soup, 2 hdld.	22.00
Creamer, dolphin ft.	45.00
Creamer, indiv.	40.00
Cup, after dinner	40.00
Cup	32.00
Decanter, 1 pt.	325.00
Flagon, 12 oz., #3390	100.00
Grapefruit, 6"	30.00
Grapefruit, ftd., #3380	20.00
Ice tub, dolphin ft.	115.00
Mayonnaise, 5½", dolphin ft.	70.00
Oil, 4 oz., ftd.	105.00
Pitcher, 3 pt., #3390	230.00

	Sahara
Pitcher, 3 pt., dolphin ft.	240.00
Plate, bouillon	15.00
Plate, cream soup	12.00
Plate, 4½", rnd.	7.00
Plate, 6", rnd.	15.00
Plate, 6", sq.	15.00
Plate, 7", rnd.	20.00
Plate, 7", sq.	20.00
Plate, 8", rnd.	24.00
Plate, 8", sq.	24.00
Plate, 9", rnd.	23.00
Plate, 10½", rnd.	80.00
Plate, 10½", sq.	70.00
Plate, 12", rnd.	75.00
Plate, 12", 2 hdld., rnd., muffin	75.00
Plate, 12", 2 hdld., rnd., sand.	70.00
Plate, 13", 2 hdld., sq., sand.	50.00
Plate, 13", 2 hdld., sq., muffin	50.00
Platter, 14", oval	45.00
Salt & pepper, pr.	125.00
Saucer, sq.	10.00
Saucer, rnd.	10.00
Stem, #3380, 1 oz., cordial	135.00
Stem, #3380, 2½ oz., wine	35.00
Stem, #3380, 3 oz., cocktail	25.00
Stem, #3380, 4 oz., oyster/cocktail	15.00
Stem, #3380, 4 oz., claret	40.00
Stem, #3380, 5 oz., parfait	15.00
Stem, #3380, 6 oz., champagne	15.00
Stem, #3380, 6 oz., sherbet	14.00
Stem, #3380, 10 oz., short soda	18.00
Stem, #3380, 10 oz., tall soda	25.00
Stem, #3390, 1 oz., cordial	125.00
Stem, #3390, 2½ oz., wine	35.00
Stem, #3390, 3 oz., cocktail	20.00

	Sahara
Stem, #3390, 3 oz., oyster/cocktail	20.00
Stem, #3390, 4 oz., claret	30.00
Stem, #3390, 6 oz., champagne	25.00
Stem, #3390, 6 oz., sherbet	25.00
Stem, #3390, 11 oz., low water	25.00
Stem, #3390, 11 oz., tall water	27.00
Sugar, dolphin ft.	45.00
Sugar, indiv.	40.00
Tray, 10", celery	30.00
Tray, 12", ctr. hdld., sand.	75.00
Tray, 12", ctr. hdld., sq.	75.00
Tray, 13", celery	26.00
Tray, 13", 2 hdld., hors d'oeuvre	75.00

	Sahara
Tumbler, dolp. ft.	165.00
Tumbler, #3380, 1 oz., ftd., bar	45.00
Tumbler, #3380, 2 oz., ftd., bar	20.00
Tumbler, #3380, 5 oz., ftd., bar	12.00
Tumbler, #3380, 8 oz., ftd., soda	18.00
Tumbler, #3380, 10 oz., ftd., soda	20.00
Tumbler, #3380, 12 oz., ftd., tea	22.00
Tumbler, #3390, 2 oz., ftd.	24.00
Tumbler, #3390, 5 oz., ftd., juice	20.00
Tumbler, #3390, 8 oz., ftd., soda	25.00
Tumbler, #3390, 12 oz., ftd., tea	27.00
Vase, 9", ftd.	150.00

OLD SANDWICH, Blank #1404, A.H. Heisey & Co.

Colors: crystal, Flamingo pink, Sahara yellow, Moongleam green, cobalt, amber

As with its sister pattern Ipswich, Moongleam is the Old Sandwich color of choice. Sets can be accumulated in crystal, but other colored sets would be nearly impossible. Please notice that Moongleam cup and saucer in the top photo, one of the few ever found in Old Sandwich! That cupped bowl (in the center of the bottom photo) was listed as a popcorn bowl; but at its price, I doubt if anyone still uses it that way!

Cobalt blue pieces of Old Sandwich are rare and **expensive!**

	Crystal	Flam.	Sahara	Moon.	Cobalt
Ash tray, individual...................................	9.00	45.00	35.00	55.00	45.00
Beer mug, 12 oz....................................	35.00	300.00	210.00	400.00	240.00
Beer mug, 14 oz....................................	45.00	325.00	225.00	425.00	250.00
* Beer mug, 18 oz....................................	50.00	400.00	270.00	475.00	300.00
Bottle, catsup, w/#3 stopper (like lg. cruet)......	60.00	200.00	175.00	225.00	
Bowl, finger..	12.00	50.00	60.00	60.00	
Bowl, ftd., popcorn, cupped.......................	45.00	90.00	75.00	125.00	
Bowl, 11", rnd., ftd., floral.......................	50.00	85.00	65.00	100.00	
Bowl, 12", oval, ftd., floral.......................	35.00	80.00	70.00	80.00	
Candlestick, 6"....................................	45.00	100.00	90.00	150.00	235.00
Cigarette holder....................................	50.00	65.00	60.00	65.00	
Comport, 6"..	40.00	95.00	90.00	100.00	
Creamer, oval..	15.00	22.00	25.00	30.00	
Creamer, 12 oz.......................................	32.00	165.00	170.00	175.00	300.00
Creamer, 14 oz.......................................	35.00	175.00	180.00	185.00	
Creamer, 18 oz.......................................	40.00	185.00	190.00	195.00	
Cup..	40.00	65.00	65.00	125.00	
Decanter, 1 pint, w/#98 stopper....................	75.00	185.00	200.00	225.00	425.00
Floral block, #22...................................	15.00	25.00	30.00	35.00	
Oil bottle, 2½ oz., #85 stopper....................	65.00	100.00	95.00	140.00	
Parfait, 4½ oz.......................................	15.00	50.00	50.00	60.00	
Pilsner, 8 oz..	14.00	28.00	32.00	38.00	
Pilsner, 10 oz.......................................	16.00	32.00	37.00	42.00	
Pitcher, ½ gallon, ice lip..........................	85.00	175.00	165.00	185.00	
Pitcher, ½ gallon, reg..............................	85.00	175.00	165.00	185.00	
Plate, 6", sq., ground bottom......................	10.00	20.00	17.00	22.00	
Plate, 7", sq..	10.00	27.00	25.00	30.00	
Plate, 8", sq..	15.00	30.00	27.00	32.00	
Salt & pepper, pr....................................	40.00	65.00	75.00	85.00	
Saucer..	10.00	15.00	15.00	25.00	
Stem, 2½ oz., wine...................................	18.00	45.00	45.00	55.00	
Stem, 3 oz., cocktail...............................	15.00	30.00	32.00	40.00	
Stem, 4 oz., claret.................................	17.00	35.00	35.00	50.00	150.00
Stem, 4 oz., oyster cocktail........................	12.00	27.00	27.00	32.00	
Stem, 4 oz., sherbet.................................	7.00	17.00	17.00	20.00	
Stem, 5 oz., saucer champagne......................	12.00	32.00	32.00	35.00	
Stem, 10 oz., low ft.................................	20.00	30.00	35.00	40.00	
Sugar, oval..	15.00	22.00	25.00	30.00	
Sundae, 6 oz...	18.00	30.00	30.00	35.00	
Tumbler, 1½ oz., bar, ground bottom................	20.00	130.00	120.00	135.00	100.00
Tumbler, 5 oz., juice...............................	7.00	15.00	15.00	25.00	
Tumbler, 6½ oz., toddy..............................	10.00	22.00	22.00	25.00	
Tumbler, 8 oz., ground bottom, cupped & straight rim ..	12.00	35.00	35.00	40.00	
Tumbler, 10 oz.......................................	15.00	40.00	40.00	45.00	
Tumbler, 10 oz., low ft.............................	15.00	40.00	42.00	45.00	
Tumbler, 12 oz., ftd., iced tea.....................	20.00	45.00	45.00	55.00	
Tumbler, 12 oz., iced tea...........................	20.00	45.00	45.00	55.00	

*Amber; 300.00; Round creamer & sugar, $30.00 ea. piece (unusual). Whimsey Basket made from footed soda, $725.00.

A.H. Heisey & Co., 1940 – 1957

Colors: crystal

Orchid is found etched on two Heisey mould blanks. Blank #1519, known as Waverly, is illustrated on page 149 as well as the plate on the left on page 150. Blank #1509, or Queen Ann, is pictured on page 151 along with the plate on the right on page 150. These two patterns have their own listings in this book, but I hope these photos will help alleviate confusion among beginners and novice mall dealers!

Serving pieces and flatware items have risen slowly in price the past two years; but prices on a few pieces of stemware have been slowly dropping! Particularly, water goblets, high sherbets, and iced teas have softened due to an oversupply at present. Remember, I am noting what is going now and not attempting to foretell what will happen if suddenly everyone chooses to collect Orchid. If that happens, then the supply could diminish overnight!

	Crystal		Crystal
Ash tray, 3".	30.00	Bowl, 11", ftd., floral	115.00
Basket, 8½", LARIAT	1,200.00	Bowl, 12", crimped, floral, WAVERLY	85.00
Bell, dinner, #5022 or #5025	135.00	Bowl, 13", floral	115.00
Bottle, 8 oz., French dressings	195.00	Bowl, 13", crimped, floral, WAVERLY	95.00
Bowl, finger, #3309 or #5025	90.00	Bowl, 13", gardenia	70.00
Bowl, 4½", nappy, QUEEN ANN	37.50	Butter, w/cover, ¼ lb., CABOCHON	325.00
Bowl, 5½", ftd., mint, QUEEN ANN	37.50	Butter, w/cover, 6", WAVERLY	175.00
Bowl, 6", jelly, 2 hdld, QUEEN ANN	37.50	Candleholder, 6", deep epernette, WAVERLY	1,000.00
Bowl, 6" oval, lemon, w/cover, QUEEN ANN	295.00	Candlestick, 1-lite, MERCURY	45.00
Bowl, 6", oval, lemon, w/cover, WAVERLY	895.00	Candlestick, 1-lite, QUEEN ANN, w/prisms	135.00
Bowl, 6½", ftd., honey, cheese, QUEEN ANN	42.50	Candlestick, 2-lite, FLAME	160.00
Bowl, 6½", ftd., jelly, WAVERLY	65.00	Candlestick, 5", 2-lite, TRIDENT	55.00
Bowl, 6½", 2 pt., oval, dressings, WAVERLY	50.00	Candlestick, 2-lite, WAVERLY	65.00
Bowl, 7", lily, QUEEN ANN	125.00	Candlestick, 3-lite, CASCADE	85.00
Bowl, 7", salad	60.00	Candlestick, 3-lite, WAVERLY	100.00
Bowl, 7", 3 pt., rnd., relish	55.00	Candy box, w/cover, 6", low ft.	175.00
Bowl, 7", ftd., honey, cheese, WAVERLY	55.00	Candy, w/cover, 5", high ft., WAVERLY	250.00
Bowl, 7", ftd., jelly	45.00	Candy, w/cover, 6", bow knot finial	175.00
Bowl, 7", ftd., oval, nut, WAVERLY	90.00	Cheese (comport) & cracker (11½") plate	135.00
Bowl, 8", mint, ftd., QUEEN ANN	65.00	Cheese & cracker, 14", plate	155.00
Bowl, 8", nappy, QUEEN ANN	70.00	Chocolate, w/cover, 5", WAVERLY	210.00
Bowl, 8", 2 pt., oval, dressings, ladle	55.00	Cigarette box, w/cover, 4", PURITAN	140.00
Bowl, 8", pt., rnd., relish	62.50	Cigarette holder, #4035	85.00
Bowl, 8½", flared, QUEEN ANN	67.50	Cigarette holder, w/cover	165.00
Bowl, 8½", floral, 2 hdld., ftd., QUEEN ANN	65.00	Cocktail icer, w/liner, UNIVERSAL, #3304	250.00
Bowl, 9", 4 pt., rnd., relish	75.00	Cocktail shaker, pt., #4225	275.00
Bowl, 9", ftd., fruit or salad	135.00	Cocktail shaker, qt., #4036 or #4225	225.00
Bowl, 9", gardenia, QUEEN ANN	65.00	Comport, 5½", blown	95.00
Bowl, 9", salad, WAVERLY	175.00	Comport, 6", low ft., WAVERLY	55.00
Bowl, 9½", crimped, floral, QUEEN ANN	75.00	Comport, 6½", low ft., WAVERLY	60.00
Bowl, 9½", epergne	525.00	Comport, 7", ftd., oval	145.00
Bowl, 10", crimped	72.50	Creamer, individual	35.00
Bowl, 10", deep salad	125.00	Creamer, ftd.	35.00
Bowl, 10", gardenia	75.00	Cup, WAVERLY or QUEEN ANN	42.50
Bowl, 10½", ftd., floral	115.00	Decanter, oval, sherry, pt.	250.00
Bowl, 11", shallow, rolled edge	70.00	Decanter, pt., ftd., #4036	325.00
Bowl, 11", 3 ftd., floral, seahorse ft.	150.00	Decanter, pt., #4036½	250.00
Bowl, 11", 3 pt., oblong, relish	70.00	Ice bucket, ftd., QUEEN ANN	250.00
Bowl, 11", 4 ftd., oval	125.00	Ice bucket, 2 hdld., WAVERLY	425.00
Bowl, 11", flared	135.00	Marmalade, w/cover	235.00
Bowl, 11", floral	70.00	Mayonnaise and liner, #1495, FERN	250.00

ORCHID

	Crystal
Mayonnaise, 5½", 1 hdl.	55.00
Mayonnaise, 5½", ftd.	55.00
Mayonnaise, 5½", 1 hdl., div.	50.00
Mayonnaise, 6½", 1 hdl.	65.00
Mayonnaise, 6½", 1 hdl., div.	65.00
Mustard, w/cover, QUEEN ANN	145.00
Oil, 3 oz., ftd.	185.00
Pitcher, 73 oz.	500.00
Pitcher, 64 oz., ice tankard	525.00
Plate, 6"	13.00
Plate, 7", mayonnaise	20.00
Plate, 7", salad	22.00
Plate, 8", salad, WAVERLY	24.00
Plate, 10½", dinner	150.00
Plate, 11", demi-torte	62.50
Plate, 11", sandwich	75.00
Plate, 12", ftd., salver, WAVERLY	250.00
Plate, 12", rnd sandwich, hdld.	70.00
Plate, 14", ftd., cake or salver	300.00
Plate, 14", torte, rolled edge	65.00
Plate, 14", torte, WAVERLY	90.00
Plate, 14", sandwich, WAVERLY	80.00
Plate, 15", sandwich, WAVERLY	75.00
Plate, 15½", QUEEN ANN	110.00
Salt & pepper, pr.	85.00
Salt & pepper, ftd., pr., WAVERLY	80.00
Saucer, WAVERLY or QUEEN ANN	12.50
Stem, #5022 or #5025, 1 oz., cordial	125.00

	Crystal
Stem, #5022 or #5025, 2 oz., sherry	125.00
Stem, #5022 or #5025, 3 oz., wine	80.00
Stem, #5022 or #5025, 4 oz., oyster cocktail	60.00
Stem, #5025, 4 oz., cocktail	40.00
Stem, #5022 or #5025, 4½ oz., claret	145.00
Stem, #5022 or #5025, 6 oz., saucer champagne	30.00
Stem, #5022 or #5025, 6 oz., sherbet	25.00
Stem, #5022 or #5025, 10 oz., low water goblet	37.50
Stem, #5022 or #5025, 10 oz., water goblet	42.50
Sugar, individual	35.00
Sugar, ftd.	35.00
Tray, indiv., creamer/sugar, QUEEN ANN	90.00
Tray, 12", celery	55.00
Tray, 13", celery	60.00
Tumbler, #5022 or #5025, 5 oz., fruit	55.00
Tumbler, #5022 or #5025, 12 oz., iced tea	65.00
Vase, 4", ftd., violet, WAVERLY	120.00
Vase, 6", crimped top	125.00
Vase, 7", ftd., fan	90.00
Vase, 7", ftd.	140.00
Vase, 7", crimped top, LARIAT	120.00
Vase, 8", ftd., bud	215.00
Vase, 8", sq., ftd., bud	225.00
Vase, 10", sq., ftd., bud	295.00
Vase, 12"	375.00
Vase, 14"	695.00

Colors: crystal; rare in amber

I cannot keep Plantation in stock! What few pieces I find, sell at the first show we have them in our booth! This pattern is hot with collectors right now — even pushing the desirable Rose and Orchid patterns aside as Heisey's most avidly sought patterns.

The pressed cordial in the top photo on page 153 is quite rare. I had to buy eight to get one for my collection; but the other seven sold so fast that it made my head spin! The plate in the background picturing a lady with a pineapple on her head, is a coupe plate that sells in the $400.00 range if you should spot one.

You will have a major problem in finding stems and tumblers in Plantation unlike many other Heisey patterns where stemware abounds! All flat tumblers are rare; do not let any escape!

	Crystal
Ash tray, 3½".	45.00
Bowl, 9 qt., Dr. Johnson, punch	600.00
Bowl, 5", nappy	25.00
Bowl, 5½", nappy	35.00
Bowl, 6½", 2 hdld., jelly	45.00
Bowl, 6½", flared, jelly	60.00
Bowl, 6½", ftd., honey, cupped	75.00
Bowl, 8", 4 pt., rnd., relish	70.00
Bowl, 8½", 2 pt., dressing	70.00
Bowl, 9", salad	170.00
Bowl, 9½", crimped, fruit or flower	85.00
Bowl, 9½", gardenia	85.00
Bowl, 11", 3 part, relish	60.00
Bowl, 11½", ftd., gardenia	140.00
Bowl, 12", crimped, fruit or flower	100.00
Bowl, 13", celery	70.00
Bowl, 13", 2 part, celery	60.00
Bowl, 13", 5 part, oval relish	90.00
Bowl, 13", gardenia	90.00
Butter, ¼ lb., oblong, w/cover	110.00
Butter, 5", rnd. (or cov. candy)	150.00
Candelabrum, w/two #1503 bobeche & 10 "A" prisms	180.00
Candle block, hurricane type w/globe	200.00
Candle block, 1-lite	110.00
Candle holder, 5", ftd., epergne	120.00
Candlestick, 1-lite	100.00
Candlestick, 2-lite	80.00
Candlestick, 3-lite	110.00
Candy box, w/cover, 7" length, flat bottom	180.00
Candy, w/cover, 5", tall, ftd.	200.00
Cheese, w/cover, 5", ftd.	90.00
Cigarette box, w/cover	180.00
Coaster, 4"	60.00
Comport, 5"	50.00
Comport, 5", w/cover, deep	100.00
Creamer, ftd.	40.00
Cup	40.00

	Crystal
Cup, punch	35.00
Marmalade, w/cover	190.00
Mayonnaise, 4½", rolled ft.	65.00
Mayonnaise, 5¼", w/liner	55.00
Oil bottle, 3 oz., w/#125 stopper	130.00
Pitcher, ½ gallon, ice lip, blown	400.00
Plate, coupe (rare)	400.00
Plate, 7", salad	25.00
Plate, 8", salad	35.00
Plate, 10½", demi-torte	70.00
Plate, 13", ftd., cake salver	200.00
Plate, 14", sandwich	120.00
Plate, 18", buffet	110.00
Plate, 18", punch bowl liner	120.00
Salt & pepper, pr.	70.00
Saucer	10.00
Stem, 1 oz., cordial	125.00
Stem, 3 oz., wine, blown	75.00
Stem, 3½ oz., cocktail, pressed	35.00
Stem, 4 oz., fruit/oyster cocktail	35.00
Stem, 4½ oz., claret, blown	65.00
Stem, 4½ oz., claret, pressed	65.00
Stem, 4½ oz., oyster cocktail, blown	40.00
Stem, 6½ oz., sherbet/saucer champagne, blown	40.00
Stem, 10 oz., pressed	50.00
Stem, 10 oz., blown	50.00
Sugar, ftd.	40.00
Syrup bottle, w/drip, cut top	140.00
Tray, 8½", condiment/sugar & creamer	90.00
Tumbler, 5 oz., ftd., juice, pressed	60.00
Tumbler, 5 oz., ftd., juice, blown	40.00
Tumbler, 8 oz., water, pressed	125.00
Tumbler, 10 oz., pressed	90.00
Tumbler, 12 oz., ftd., iced tea, pressed	90.00
Tumbler, 12 oz., ftd., iced tea, blown	75.00
Vase, 5", ftd., flared	90.00
Vase, 9", ftd., flared	140.00

Colors: crystal, yellow, Heatherbloom, green, amber, Carmen, and Crown Tuscan w/gold

	Crystal
Basket, 2 hdld. (upturned sides)	20.00
Basket, 7", 1 hdld.	245.00
Bowl, 3", indiv. nut, 4 ftd.	50.00
Bowl, 3½", cranberry	30.00
Bowl, 3½" sq., cranberry	30.00
Bowl, 5¼", 2 hdld., bonbon	20.00
Bowl, 6", 2 pt., relish	18.00
Bowl, 6", ftd., 2 hdld., bonbon	20.00
Bowl, 6", grapefruit or oyster	20.00
Bowl, 6½", 3 pt., relish	20.00
Bowl, 7", 2 pt., relish	22.00
Bowl, 7", ftd., bonbon, tab hdld.	25.00
Bowl, 7", pickle or relish	25.00
Bowl, 9", 3 pt., celery & relish, tab hdld.	35.00
Bowl, 9½", ftd., pickle (like corn bowl)	25.00
Bowl, 10", flared, 4 ftd.	40.00
Bowl, 11", 2 pt., 2 hdld., "figure 8" relish	35.00
Bowl, 11", 2 hdld.	37.50
Bowl, 12", 3 pt., celery & relish, tab hdld.	35.00
Bowl, 12", 5 pt., celery & relish	37.50
Bowl, 12", flared, 4 ftd.	45.00
Bowl, 12", oval, 4 ftd., "ears" handles	45.00
Bowl, finger, w/liner #3124	40.00
Bowl, seafood (fruit cocktail w/liner)	65.00
Candlestick, 5"	22.00
Candlestick, 6", 2-lite, "fleur-de-lis"	37.50
Candlestick, 6", 3-lite	45.00
Candy box, w/cover, rnd.	70.00
Cigarette holder, urn shape	60.00
Cocktail icer, 2 pt.	65.00
Cocktail shaker, w/stopper	95.00
Cocktail shaker, 80 oz., hdld. ball w/chrome top	195.00
Cologne, 2 oz., hdld. ball w/stopper	110.00
Comport, 5½"	27.50
Comport, 5⅜", blown	35.00
Creamer, ftd.	12.00
Creamer, hdld. ball	35.00
Creamer, indiv.	12.50
Cup, ftd. sq.	18.00
Cup, rd.	15.00
Decanter, 29 oz. ftd., sherry, w/stopper	210.00
Hurricane lamp, candlestick base	145.00
Hurricane lamp, keyhole base, w/prisms	195.00
Ice bucket, w/chrome handle	75.00
Ivy ball, 5¼"	65.00
Mayonnaise, div. bowl, w/liner & 2 ladles	45.00
Mayonnaise, w/liner & ladle	40.00
Oil, 6 oz., loop hdld., w/stopper	95.00
Oil, 6 oz., hdld. ball, w/stopper	85.00
Pitcher, ball	155.00
Pitcher, Doulton	325.00
Plate, 6", 2 hdld.	15.00
Plate, 6½", bread/butter	7.50
Plate, 8", salad	12.50
Plate, 8", ftd., 2 hdld.	17.50
Plate, 8", ftd., bonbon, tab hdld.	20.00
Plate, 8½", sq.	15.00
Plate, 10½", dinner	65.00
Plate, 13", 4 ftd., torte	40.00
Plate, 13½", 2 hdld., cake	40.00
Plate, 14", torte	55.00
Puff box, 3½", ball shape, w/lid	175.00
Salt & pepper, pr., flat	25.00

	Crystal
Saucer, sq. or rnd.	3.00
Set: 3 pc. frappe (bowl, 2 plain inserts)	50.00
Stem, #3121, 1 oz., cordial	60.00
Stem, #3121, 1 oz., low ftd., brandy	55.00
Stem, #3121, 2½ oz., wine	35.00
Stem, #3121, 3 oz., cocktail	20.00
Stem, #3121, 4½ oz., claret	40.00
Stem, #3121, 4½ oz., oyster cocktail	15.00
Stem, #3121, 5 oz., parfait	38.00
Stem, #3121, 6 oz., low sherbet	13.50
Stem, #3121, 6 oz., tall sherbet	15.00
Stem, #3121, 10 oz., goblet	22.50
Stem, #3124, 3 oz., cocktail	15.00
Stem, #3124, 3 oz., wine	30.00
Stem, #3124, 4½ oz., claret	40.00
Stem, #3124, 7 oz., low sherbet	14.00
Stem, #3124, 7 oz., tall sherbet	15.00
Stem, #3124, 10 oz., goblet	18.00
Stem, #3126, 1 oz., cordial	60.00
Stem, #3126, 1 oz., low ft., brandy	60.00
Stem, #3126, 2½ oz., wine	35.00
Stem, #3126, 3 oz., cocktail	17.50
Stem, #3126, 4½ oz., claret	40.00
Stem, #3126, 4½ oz., low ft., oyster cocktail	12.50
Stem, #3126, 7 oz., low sherbet	14.00
Stem, #3126, 7 oz., tall sherbet	15.00
Stem, #3126, 9 oz., goblet	20.00
Stem, #3130, 1 oz., cordial	60.00
Stem, #3130, 2½ oz., wine	35.00
Stem, #3130, 3 oz., cocktail	17.50
Stem, #3130, 4½ oz., claret	40.00
Stem, #3130, 4½ oz., fruit/oyster cocktail	15.00
Stem, #3130, 7 oz., low sherbet	14.00
Stem, #3130, 7 oz., tall sherbet	15.00
Stem, #3130, 9 oz., goblet	22.50
Sugar, ftd., hdld. ball	32.50
Sugar, ftd.	12.00
Sugar, indiv.	11.50
Tray, 11", celery	35.00
Tumbler, #3121, 2½ oz., bar	35.00
Tumbler, #3121, 5 oz., ftd., juice	18.00
Tumbler, #3121, 10 oz., ftd., water	16.50
Tumbler, #3121, 12 oz., ftd., tea	25.00
Tumbler, #3124, 3 oz.	15.00
Tumbler, #3124, 5 oz., juice	15.00
Tumbler, #3124, 10 oz., water	15.00
Tumbler, #3124, 12 oz., tea	22.00
Tumbler, #3126, 2½ oz.	35.00
Tumbler, #3126, 5 oz., juice	14.00
Tumbler, #3126, 10 oz., water	15.00
Tumbler, #3126, 12 oz., tea	22.00
Tumbler, #3130, 5 oz., juice	16.00
Tumbler, #3130, 10 oz., water	15.00
Tumbler, #3130, 12 oz., tea	22.00
Tumbler, 12 oz., "roly-poly"	28.00
Vase, 5", globe	45.00
Vase, 6", ftd.	50.00
Vase, 8", ftd.	65.00
Vase, 9", keyhole ft.	75.00
Vase, 10", bud	55.00
Vase, 11", flower	65.00
Vase, 11", pedestal ft.	75.00
Vase, 12", keyhole ft.	95.00
Vase, 13", flower	125.00

Colors: crystal, Limelight green

Limelight colored Provincial was Heisey's attempt at remaking the earlier, popular Zircon color!

	Crystal	Limelight Green
Ash tray, 3" square	12.50	
Bonbon dish, 7", 2 hdld., upturned sides	12.00	45.00
Bowl, 5 quart, punch	120.00	
Bowl, individual, nut/jelly	20.00	40.00
Bowl, 4½", nappy	15.00	70.00
Bowl, 5", 2 hdld., nut/jelly	20.00	
Bowl, 5½", nappy	20.00	40.00
Bowl, 5½", round, hdld., nappy	20.00	
Bowl, 5½", tri-corner, hdld., nappy	20.00	55.00
Bowl, 10", 4 part, relish	40.00	195.00
Bowl, 12", floral	35.00	
Bowl, 13", gardenia	40.00	
Box, 5½", footed, candy, w/cover	85.00	550.00
Butter dish, w/cover	100.00	
Candle, 1-lite, block	35.00	
Candle, 2-lite	80.00	
Candle, 3-lite, #4233, 5", vase	95.00	
Cigarette box w/cover	60.00	
Cigarette lighter	30.00	
Coaster, 4"	15.00	
Creamer, footed	25.00	95.00
Creamer & sugar, w/tray, individual	80.00	
Cup, punch	10.00	
Mayonnaise, 7" (plate, ladle, bowl)	40.00	150.00
Mustard	110.00	
Oil bottle, 4 oz., #1 stopper	45.00	
Oil & vinegar bottle (french dressing)	65.00	
Plate, 5", footed, cheese	20.00	
Plate, 7", 2 hdld., snack	25.00	
Plate, 7", bread	10.00	
Plate, 8", luncheon	15.00	50.00
Plate, 14", torte	45.00	
Plate, 18", buffet	70.00	175.00
Salt & pepper, pr.	40.00	
Stem, 3½ oz., oyster cocktail	15.00	
Stem, 3½ oz., wine	20.00	
Stem, 5 oz., sherbet/champagne	10.00	
Stem, 10 oz.	20.00	
Sugar, footed	25.00	95.00
Tray, 13", oval, celery	22.00	
Tumbler, 5 oz., footed, juice	14.00	60.00
Tumbler, 8 oz.	17.00	
Tumbler, 9 oz., footed	17.00	65.00
Tumbler, 12 oz., footed, iced tea	20.00	80.00
Tumbler, 13", flat, ice tea	20.00	
Vase, 3½", violet	30.00	95.00
Vase, 4", pansy	35.00	
Vase, 6", sweet pea	45.00	

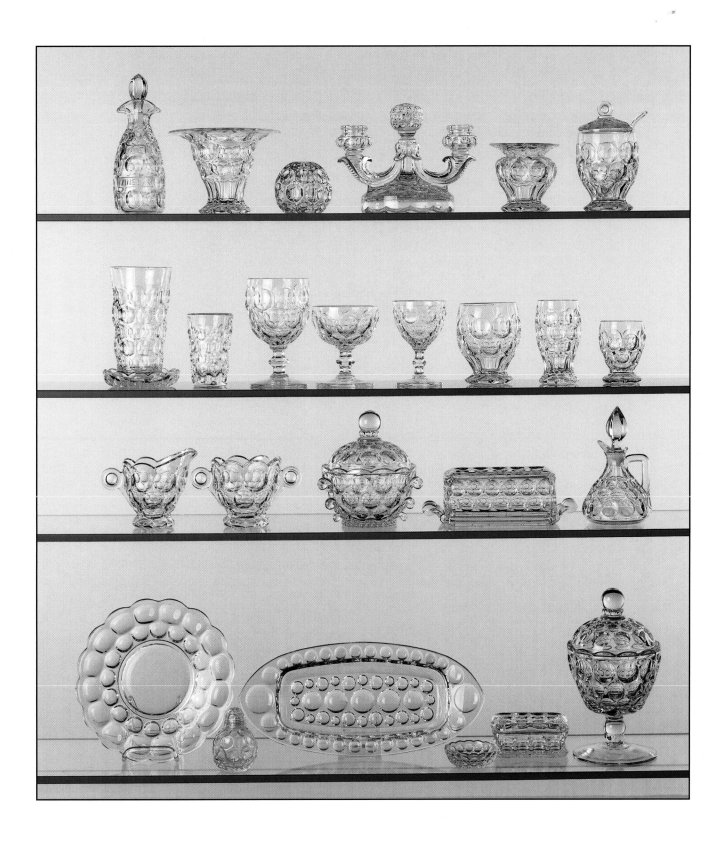

Colors: crystal

When Empress (#1401) is made in crystal it is commonly referred to as Queen Ann (c.1938). Although this has been accepted by most everyone, it is not entirely true. There is a slight difference between the two patterns. This blank was used for several of the etched patterns, i.e., Orchid, Heisey Rose, Minuet, etc. This pattern has been easy to find and inexpensive in the past; however, the prices are now beginning to increase, especially for the unusual pieces.

	Crystal		Crystal
Ash tray.	30.00	Marmalade, w/cover, dolphin ftd.	60.00
Bonbon, 6"	12.00	Mayonnaise, 5½", ftd., w/ladle	30.00
Bowl, cream soup	18.00	Mustard, w/cover	60.00
Bowl, cream soup, w/sq. liner	25.00	Oil bottle, 4 oz.	40.00
Bowl, frappe, w/center	25.00	Plate, bouillon liner	8.00
Bowl, nut, dolphin ftd., indiv.	20.00	Plate, cream soup liner	8.00
Bowl, 4½", nappy	8.00	Plate, 4½"	5.00
Bowl, 5", preserve, 2 hdld.	15.00	Plate, 6"	5.00
Bowl, 6", ftd., jelly, 2 hdld.	15.00	Plate, 6", square	5.00
Bowl, 6", dolp. ftd., mint	18.00	Plate, 7"	8.00
Bowl, 6", grapefruit, sq. top, ground bottom	12.00	Plate, 7", square	7.00
Bowl, 6½", oval, lemon, w/cover	40.00	Plate, 8", square	10.00
Bowl, 7", 3 pt., relish, triplex	18.00	Plate, 8"	9.00
Bowl, 7", 3 pt., relish, ctr. hand.	25.00	Plate, 9"	12.00
Bowl, 7½", dolphin ftd., nappy	28.00	Plate, 10½"	40.00
Bowl, 7½", dolphin ftd., nasturtium	35.00	Plate, 10½", square	40.00
Bowl, 8", nappy	25.00	Plate, 12"	25.00
Bowl, 8½", ftd., floral, 2 hdld.	32.00	Plate, 12", muffin, sides upturned	35.00
Bowl, 9", floral, rolled edge	25.00	Plate, 12", sandwich, 2 hdld.	30.00
Bowl, 9", floral, flared	32.00	Plate, 13", hors d'oeuvre, 2 hdld.	60.00
Bowl, 10", 2 hdld., oval dessert	30.00	Plate, 13", square, 2 hdld.	35.00
Bowl, 10", lion head, floral	250.00	Platter, 14"	30.00
Bowl, 10", oval, veg.	30.00	Salt & pepper, pr.	50.00
Bowl, 10", square, salad, 2 hdld.	35.00	Saucer, square	5.00
Bowl, 10", triplex, relish	25.00	Saucer, after dinner	5.00
Bowl, 11", dolphin ftd., floral	38.00	Saucer	5.00
Bowl, 13", pickle/olive, 2 pt.	20.00	Stem, 2½ oz., oyster cocktail	15.00
Bowl, 15", dolphin ftd., punch	400.00	Stem, 4 oz., saucer champagne	20.00
Candlestick, 3", 3 ftd	50.00	Stem, 4 oz., sherbet	15.00
Candlestick, low, 4 ftd., w/2 hdld.	30.00	Stem, 9 oz., Empress stemware, unusual	40.00
Candlestick, 6", dolphin ftd.	70.00	Sugar, indiv.	20.00
Candy, w/cover, 6", dolphin ftd.	50.00	Sugar, dolphin ftd., 3 hdld.	30.00
Comport, 6", ftd.	25.00	Tray, condiment & liner for indiv. sugar/creamer	20.00
Comport, 6", square	40.00	Tray, 10", 3 pt., relish	20.00
Comport, 7", oval	35.00	Tray, 10", 7 pt., hors d'oeuvre	60.00
Compotier, 6", dolphin ftd.	70.00	Tray, 10", celery	12.00
Creamer, dolphin ftd.	30.00	Tray, 12", ctr. hdld., sand.	30.00
Creamer, indiv.	20.00	Tray, 12", sq. ctr. hdld., sand.	32.50
Cup	15.00	Tray, 13", celery	20.00
Cup, after dinner	20.00	Tray, 16", 4 pt., buffet relish	35.00
Cup, bouillon, 2 hdld.	20.00	Tumbler, 8 oz., dolphin ftd., unusual	75.00
Cup, 4 oz., custard or punch	12.00	Tumbler, 8 oz., ground bottom	20.00
Cup, #1401½, has rim as demi-cup	20.00	Tumbler, 12 oz., tea, ground bottom	20.00
Grapefruit, w/square liner	20.00	Vase, 8", flared	55.00
Ice tub, w/metal handles	60.00		
Jug, 3 pint, ftd.	100.00		

Colors: crystal, Sahara, Zircon, rare

	Crystal
Ash tray, round	14.00
Ash tray, square	10.00
Ash tray, 4", round	22.00
Ash tray, 6", square	35.00
Ash trays, bridge set (heart, diamond, spade, club)	60.00
Basket, bonbon, metal handle	25.00
Bottle, rock & rye, w/#104 stopper	240.00
Bottle, 4 oz., cologne	130.00
Bottle, 5 oz., bitters, w/tube	130.00
Bowl, indiv., nut	15.00
Bowl, oval, indiv., jelly	20.00
Bowl, indiv., nut, 2 part	20.00
Bowl, 4½", nappy, bell or cupped	20.00
Bowl, 4½", nappy, scalloped	20.00
Bowl, 5", lemon, w/cover	65.00
Bowl, 5", nappy, straight	15.00
Bowl, 5", nappy, square	25.00
Bowl, 6", 2 hdld., divided, jelly	20.00
Bowl, 6", 2 hdld., jelly	20.00
Bowl, 7", 2 part, oval, relish	30.00
Bowl, 8", centerpiece	40.00
Bowl, 8", nappy, square	55.00
Bowl, 9", nappy, square	65.00
Bowl, 9", salad	40.00
Bowl, 10", flared, fruit	45.00
Bowl, 10", floral	45.00
Bowl, 11", centerpiece	50.00
Bowl, 11", punch	200.00
Bowl, 11½", floral	50.00
Bowl, 12", oval, floral	55.00
Bowl, 12", flared, fruit	50.00
Bowl, 13", cone, floral	65.00
Bowl, 14", oblong, floral	70.00
Bowl, 14", oblong, swan hdld., floral	280.00
Box, 8", floral	70.00
Candle block, 3", #1469½	30.00
Candle vase, 6"	35.00
Candlestick, 2", 1-lite	35.00
Candlestick, 2-lite, bobeche & "A" prisms	80.00
Candlestick, 7", w/bobeche & "A" prisms	120.00
Cheese, 6", 2 hdld.	20.00
Cigarette box, w/cover, oval	90.00
Cigarette box, w/cover, 6"	35.00
Cigarette holder, oval, w/2 comp. ashtrays	70.00
Cigarette holder, round	14.00
Cigarette holder, square	14.00
Cigarette holder, w/cover	30.00
Coaster or cocktail rest	8.00
Cocktail shaker, 1 qt., w/#1 strainer & #86 stopper	300.00
Comport, 6", low ft., flared	25.00
Comport, 6", low ft., w/cover	40.00
Creamer	30.00
Creamer, indiv.	20.00
Cup	15.00
Cup, beverage	12.00
Cup, punch	10.00
Decanter, 1 pint, w/#95 stopper	210.00
Ice tub, 2 hdld.	85.00
Marmalade, w/cover (scarce)	90.00
Mayonnaise and under plate	55.00

	Crystal
Mustard, w/cover	80.00
Oil bottle, 3 oz., w/#103 stopper	50.00
Pitcher, ½ gallon, ball shape	380.00
Pitcher, ½ gallon, ice lip, ball shape	380.00
Plate, oval, hors d'oeuvres	500.00
Plate, 2 hdld., ice tub liner	50.00
Plate, 6", round	12.00
Plate, 6", square	24.00
Plate, 7", square	24.00
Plate, 8", round	20.00
Plate, 8", square	30.00
Plate, 13½", sandwich	45.00
Plate, 13½", ftd., torte	45.00
Plate, 14", salver	50.00
Plate, 20", punch bowl underplate	140.00
Puff box, 5", and cover	80.00
Salt & pepper, pr.	45.00
Salt dip, indiv.	13.00
Saucer	5.00
Soda, 12 oz., ftd., no knob in stem (rare)	50.00
Stem, cocktail, pressed	25.00
Stem, claret, pressed	50.00
Stem, oyster cocktail, pressed	35.00
Stem, sherbet, pressed	20.00
Stem, saucer champagne, pressed	30.00
Stem, wine, pressed	40.00
Stem, 1 oz., cordial, blown	160.00
Stem, 2 oz., sherry, blown	90.00
Stem, 2½ oz., wine, blown	80.00
Stem, 3½ oz., cocktail, blown	35.00
Stem, 4 oz., claret, blown	55.00
Stem, 4 oz., oyster cocktail, blown	30.00
Stem, 5 oz., saucer champagne, blown	25.00
Stem, 5 oz., sherbet, blown	20.00
Stem, 8 oz., luncheon, low stem	30.00
Stem, 8 oz., tall stem	40.00
Sugar	30.00
Sugar, indiv.	20.00
Tray, for indiv. sugar & creamer	20.00
Tray, 10½", oblong	35.00
Tray, 11", 3 part, relish	45.00
Tray, 12", celery & olive, divided	40.00
Tray, 12", celery	40.00
Tumbler, 2½ oz., bar, pressed	45.00
Tumbler, 5 oz., juice, blown	30.00
Tumbler, 5 oz., soda, ftd., pressed	30.00
Tumbler, 8 oz., #1469¾, pressed	35.00
Tumbler, 8 oz., old-fashioned, pressed	35.00
Tumbler, 8 oz., soda	40.00
Tumbler, 10 oz., #1469½, pressed	45.00
Tumbler, 12 oz., ftd., soda, pressed	50.00
Tumbler, 12 oz., soda, #1469½, pressed	50.00
Tumbler, 13 oz., iced tea, blown	40.00
Vase, #1 indiv., cuspidor shape	40.00
Vase, #2 indiv., cupped top	45.00
Vase, #3 indiv., flared rim	30.00
Vase, #4 indiv., fan out top	55.00
Vase, #5 indiv., scalloped top	55.00
Vase, 3½"	25.00
Vase, 6" (also flared)	35.00
Vase, 8"	75.00
Vase, 8", triangular, #1469¾	110.00

Colors: Amber, Bluebell, Carmen, crystal, Emerald green, Heatherbloom, Peach-Blo, Topaz, Willow blue

Cambridge's #731 line, now known as Rosalie, is a perfect Cambridge introductory pattern for someone to collect without first taking out a loan. Do not let that deceive you into thinking this attractive ware will be effortlessly found. Most Rosalie collectors focus on pink and green, although amber could also be scraped together with work. Conceivably, a small set of Willow Blue is feasible; but Carmen, Bluebell, or Heatherbloom are colors that are too infrequently seen to be gathered into sets. Those colors make great accent pieces with other colored sets, and many collectors are doing that!

Several of the pieces pictured would fetch a fortune in other Cambridge patterns, but Rosalie collectors can gather these difficult pieces for a song — so to speak! The upper photo shows a wafer tray in front. A smaller version of this tray was for sugar cubes. The marmalade jar, salad dressing bottle, and twin spouted gravy boat are highly collectible pieces! These items are gathered by collectors other than Cambridge buffs. They are known as item collectors, those who buy sugar cube trays or salad dressing bottles. I've discovered there are item collectors for almost everything!

	Blue Pink Green	Amber		Blue Pink Green	Amber
Bottle, French dressing	125.00	90.00	Gravy, double, w/platter	150.00	90.00
Bowl, bouillon, 2 hdld.	30.00	15.00	Ice bucket or pail	75.00	50.00
Bowl, cream soup	30.00	20.00	Icer, w/liner	60.00	45.00
Bowl, finger, w/liner	40.00	25.00	Ice tub	75.00	65.00
Bowl, finger, ftd., w/liner	40.00	30.00	Marmalade	125.00	85.00
Bowl, 3½", cranberry	35.00	25.00	Mayonnaise, ftd., w/liner	55.00	25.00
Bowl, 3⅝", w/cover, 3 pt.	55.00	40.00	Nut, 2½", ftd.	60.00	45.00
Bowl, 5½", fruit	18.00	12.00	Pitcher, 62 oz., #955	225.00	175.00
Bowl, 5½", 2 hdld., bonbon	20.00	12.00	Plate, 6¾", bread/butter	7.00	5.00
Bowl, 6¼", 2 hdld., bonbon	22.50	15.00	Plate, 7", 2 hdld.	15.00	7.00
Bowl, 7", basket, 2 hdld.	30.00	20.00	Plate, 7½", salad	10.00	6.00
Bowl, 8½", soup	45.00	30.00	Plate, 8⅜"	15.00	10.00
Bowl, 8½", 2 hdld.	35.00	25.00	Plate, 9½", dinner	60.00	35.00
Bowl, 8½", w/cover, 3 pt.	95.00	45.00	Plate, 11", 2 hdld.	30.00	20.00
Bowl, 10"	45.00	30.00	Platter, 12"	75.00	45.00
Bowl, 10", 2 hdld.	50.00	30.00	Platter, 15"	125.00	80.00
Bowl, 11"	55.00	30.00	Relish, 9", 2 pt.	25.00	15.00
Bowl, 11", basket, 2 hdld.	55.00	40.00	Relish, 11", 2 pt.	35.00	20.00
Bowl, 11½"	75.00	50.00	Salt dip, 1½", ftd.	60.00	40.00
Bowl, 12", decagon	110.00	80.00	Saucer	5.00	4.00
Bowl, 13", console	75.00		Stem, 1 oz., cordial, #3077	95.00	60.00
Bowl, 14", decagon	235.00	175.00	Stem, 3½ oz., cocktail, #3077	20.00	15.00
Bowl, 15", oval console	95.00	70.00	Stem, 6 oz., low sherbet, #3077	15.00	12.00
Bowl, 15", oval, flanged	95.00	70.00	Stem, 6 oz., high sherbet, #3077	18.00	14.00
Bowl, 15½", oval	110.00	75.00	Stem, 9 oz., water goblet, #3077	25.00	20.00
Candlestick, 4", 2 styles	30.00	20.00	Stem, 10 oz., goblet, #801	30.00	20.00
Candlestick, 5", keyhole	35.00	25.00	Sugar, ftd.	16.00	13.00
Candlestick, 6", 3-lite keyhole	55.00	35.00	Sugar shaker	295.00	210.00
Candy and cover, 6"	125.00	70.00	Tray for sugar shaker/creamer	30.00	20.00
Celery, 11"	35.00	20.00	Tray, ctr. hdld., for sugar/creamer	20.00	14.00
Cheese & cracker, 11", plate	65.00	40.00	Tray, 11", ctr. hdld.	30.00	20.00
Comport, 5½", 2 hdld.	30.00	15.00	Tumbler, 2½ oz., ftd., #3077	35.00	25.00
Comport, 5¾"	30.00	15.00	Tumbler, 5 oz., ftd., #3077	25.00	20.00
Comport, 6", ftd., almond	40.00	25.00	Tumbler, 8 oz., ftd., #3077	25.00	16.00
Comport, 6½", low ft.	40.00	25.00	Tumbler, 10 oz., ftd., #3077	27.00	20.00
Comport, 6½", high ft.	40.00	25.00	Tumbler, 12 oz., ftd., #3077	35.00	25.00
Comport, 6¾"	45.00	30.00	Vase, 5½", ftd.	50.00	30.00
Creamer, ftd.	17.00	12.00	Vase, 6"	65.00	45.00
Creamer, ftd., tall, ewer	55.00	30.00	Vase, 6½", ftd.	85.00	50.00
Cup	35.00	25.00	Wafer tray	110.00	75.00

Colors: crystal

Heisey Rose oyster cocktails and clarets are rare; buy them when you can! Low sherbets are harder to find than high and the tray for the individual sugar and creamer is harder to find than they are! The 10½" dinner plate has a large center with a small border, while the 10½" service plate has a small center and large border. Those 6" epernettes on the triple candle have turned out to be some of the rarest pieces in Rose.

	Crystal
Ash tray, 3"	37.50
Bell, dinner, #5072	150.00
Bottle, 8 oz., French dressing, blown, #5031	210.00
Bowl, finger, #3309	100.00
Bowl, 5½", ftd., mint	37.50
Bowl, 5¾", ftd., mint, CABOCHON	80.00
Bowl, 6", ftd., mint, QUEEN ANN	50.00
Bowl, 6", jelly, 2 hdld., ftd., QUEEN ANN	55.00
Bowl, 6", oval, lemon, w/cover, WAVERLY	895.00
Bowl, 6½", 2 pt., oval, dressing, WAVERLY	70.00
Bowl, 6½", ftd., honey/cheese, WAVERLY	60.00
Bowl, 6½", ftd., jelly, WAVERLY	45.00
Bowl, 6½", lemon, w/cover, QUEEN ANN	250.00
Bowl, 7", ftd., honey, WAVERLY	60.00
Bowl, 7", ftd., jelly, WAVERLY	45.00
Bowl, 7", lily, QUEEN ANN	125.00
Bowl, 7", relish, 3 pt., round, WAVERLY	67.50
Bowl, 7", salad, WAVERLY	60.00
Bowl, 7", salad dressings, QUEEN ANN	60.00
Bowl, 9", ftd., fruit or salad, WAVERLY	195.00
Bowl, 9", salad, WAVERLY	135.00
Bowl, 9", 4 pt., rnd, relish, WAVERLY	90.00
Bowl, 9½", crimped, floral, WAVERLY	75.00
Bowl, 10", gardenia, WAVERLY	75.00
Bowl, 10", crimped, floral, WAVERLY	75.00
Bowl, 11", 3 pt., relish, WAVERLY	77.50
Bowl, 11", 3 ftd., floral, WAVERLY	165.00
Bowl, 11", floral, WAVERLY	70.00
Bowl, 11", oval, 4 ftd., WAVERLY	150.00
Bowl, 12", crimped, floral, WAVERLY	70.00
Bowl, 13", crimped, floral, WAVERLY	110.00
Bowl, 13", floral, WAVERLY	100.00
Bowl, 13", gardenia, WAVERLY	80.00
Butter, w/cover, 6", WAVERLY	195.00
Butter, w/cover, ¼ lb., CABOCHON	325.00
Candlestick, 1-lite, #112	45.00
Candlestick, 2-lite, FLAME	100.00
Candlestick, 3-lite, #142, CASCADE	85.00
Candlestick, 3-lite, WAVERLY	100.00
Candlestick, 5", 2-lite, #134, TRIDENT	75.00
Candlestick, 6", epergnette, deep, WAVERLY	1,250.00
Candy, w/cover, 5", ftd., WAVERLY	195.00
Candy, w/cover, 6", low, bowknot cover	175.00
Candy, w/cover, 6¼", #1951, CABOCHON	175.00
Celery tray, 12", WAVERLY	65.00
Celery tray, 13", WAVERLY	70.00
Cheese compote, 4½" & cracker (11" plate), WAVERLY	145.00
Cheese compote, 5½" & cracker (12" plate), QUEEN ANNE	145.00
Chocolate, w/cover, 5", WAVERLY	195.00
Cigarette holder, #4035	125.00

	Crystal
Cocktail icer, w/liner, #3304, UNIVERSAL	285.00
Cocktail shaker, #4225, COBEL	195.00
Comport, 6½", low ft., WAVERLY	65.00
Comport, 7", oval, ftd., WAVERLY	145.00
Creamer, ftd., WAVERLY	35.00
Creamer, indiv., WAVERLY	40.00
Cup, WAVERLY	55.00
Decanter, 1 pt., #4036½, #101 stopper	225.00
Hurricane lamp, w/12" globe, #5080	375.00
Hurricane lamp, w/12" globe, PLANTATION	495.00
Ice bucket, dolphin ft., QUEEN ANN	325.00
Ice tub, 2 hdld., WAVERLY	450.00
Mayonnaise, 5½", 2 hdld., WAVERLY	55.00
Mayonnaise, 5½", div., 1 hdld., WAVERLY	55.00
Mayonnaise, 5½", ftd., WAVERLY	60.00
Oil, 3 oz., ftd., WAVERLY	185.00
Pitcher, 73 oz., #4164	575.00
Plate, 7", salad, WAVERLY	20.00
Plate, 7", mayonnaise, WAVERLY	20.00
Plate, 8", salad, WAVERLY	30.00
Plate, 10½", dinner WAVERLY	175.00
Plate, 10½", service, WAVERLY	75.00
Plate, 11", sandwich, WAVERLY	60.00
Plate, 11", demi-torte, WAVERLY	70.00
Plate, 12", ftd., salver, WAVERLY	250.00
Plate, 15", ftd., cake, WAVERLY	325.00
Plate, 14", torte, WAVERLY	90.00
Plate, 14", sandwich, WAVERLY	110.00
Plate, 14", ctr. hdld., sandwich, WAVERLY	215.00
Salt & pepper, ftd., pr., WAVERLY	65.00
Saucer, WAVERLY	10.00
Stem, #5072, 1 oz., cordial	150.00
Stem, #5072, 3 oz., wine	115.00
Stem, #5072, 3½ oz., oyster cocktail, ftd.	60.00
Stem, #5072, 4 oz., claret	135.00
Stem, #5072, 4 oz., cocktail	45.00
Stem, #5072, 6 oz., sherbet	30.00
Stem, #5072, 6 oz., saucer champagne	33.00
Stem, #5072, 9 oz., water	42.00
Sugar, indiv., WAVERLY	40.00
Sugar, ftd., WAVERLY	35.00
Tumbler, #5072, 5 oz., ftd., juice	55.00
Tumbler, #5072, 12 oz., ftd., tea	65.00
Tray, indiv. creamer/sugar, QUEEN ANN	65.00
Vase, 3½", ftd., violet, WAVERLY	110.00
Vase, 4", ftd., violet, WAVERLY	120.00
Vase, 7", ftd., fan, WAVERLY	120.00
Vase, 8", #4198	175.00
Vase, 8", sq., ftd., urn	185.00
Vase, 10", #4198	245.00
Vase, 10", sq., ftd, urn	250.00
Vase, 12", sq., ftd., urn	295.00

Colors: crystal; some crystal with gold

Without a doubt, Rose Point is the most known pattern in Cambridge. There were so many divergent mould lines used to make the pattern that individual collectors can choose what they prefer; consequently, not all are always looking for same pieces! Variety is a good thing! Throughout the photographs on the following pages are many unusual and rare pieces; but in order to show them, I have limited room to comment. Look carefully, and admire!

A primary uncertainty confronting new collectors is identifying different blanks on which Rose Point is found. With the photos on page 169, I am trying to clarify both blank and stemware items. All of the stems pictured are #3121 or #3500, but it is the shape that is the valuable information! For example in row 4 (itemized below) be sure to notice the difference between the juice tumbler and the parfait. Many mistakes have been made in identifying them. There is a $40.00 difference in pricing; so, it pays to know which is which!

Row 1: #3400 cup and saucer, #3900 plate, #3400 plate, #3900 cup and saucer
Row 2: #3500 cup and saucer, plate, cereal, individual sugar and creamer
Row 3: water goblet, ftd. iced tea, ftd. water tumbler, tall sherbet, cocktail, low sherbet, oyster cocktail
Row 4: cocktail icer, claret, parfait, ftd. juice, wine, cordial, short wine, brandy

	Crystal		Crystal
Ash tray, stack set on metal pole, #1715	235.00	Bowl, 9", 4 ftd. (#3400/135)	210.00
Ash tray, 2½", sq., #721	32.50	Bowl, 9", ram's head (#3500/25)	365.00
Ash tray, 3¼" (#3500/124)	32.50	Bowl, 9½", pickle (like corn), #477	50.00
Ash tray, 3¼", sq. (#3500/129)	55.00	Bowl, 9½", ftd., w/hdl. (#3500/115)	125.00
Ash tray, 3½" (#3500/125)	35.00	Bowl, 9½", 2 hdld. (#3400/34)	70.00
Ash tray, 4" (#3500/126)	40.00	Bowl, 9½", 2 part, blown (#225)	425.00
Ash tray, 4", oval (#3500/130)	85.00	Bowl, 2 hdld. (#3400/1185)	70.00
Ash tray, 4¼" (#3500/127)	45.00	Bowl, 10", 2 hdld. (#3500/28)	77.50
Ash tray, 4½" (#3500/128)	50.00	Bowl, 10", 4 tab ftd., flared (#3900/54)	70.00
Ash tray, 4½", oval (#3500/131)	65.00	Bowl, 10½", crimp edge, #1351	85.00
Basket, 3", favor (#3500/79)	325.00	Bowl, 10½", flared (#3400/168)	67.50
Basket, 5", 1 hdld. (#3500/51)	250.00	Bowl, 10½", 3 part, #222	325.00
Basket, 6", 1 hdld. (#3500/52)	295.00	Bowl, 10½", 3 part (#1401/122)	325.00
Basket, 6", 2 hdld. (#3400/1182)	37.50	Bowl, 11", ftd. (#3500/16)	115.00
Basket, 6", sq., ftd., 2 hdld (#3500/55)	40.00	Bowl, 11", ftd., fancy edge (#3500/19)	135.00
Basket, 7", 1 hdld., #119	425.00	Bowl, 11", 4 ftd., oval (#3500/109)	325.00
Basket, 7", wide (#3500/56)	55.00	Bowl, 11", 4 ftd., shallow, fancy edge (#3400/48)	110.00
Basket, sugar, w/handle and tongs (#3500/13)	295.00	Bowl, 11", fruit (#3400/1188)	105.00
Bell, dinner, #3121	150.00	Bowl, 11", low foot (#3400/3)	160.00
Bowl, 3", 4 ftd., nut (#3400/71)	70.00	Bowl, 11", tab hdld. (#3900/34)	77.50
Bowl, 3½", bonbon, cupped, deep (#3400/204)	80.00	Bowl, 11½", ftd., w/tab hdl. (#3900/28)	80.00
Bowl, 3½", cranberry (#3400/70)	85.00	Bowl, 12", crimped, pan (Pristine #136)	310.00
Bowl, 5", hdld. (#3500/49)	35.00	Bowl, 10", salad (Pristine #427)	150.00
Bowl, 5", fruit (#3500/10)	75.00	Bowl, 12", 4 ftd., oval (#3400/1240)	120.00
Bowl, 5", fruit, blown #1534	80.00	Bowl, 12", 4 ftd., oval, w/"ears" hdl. (#3900/65)	90.00
Bowl, 5¼", fruit (#3400/56)	75.00	Bowl, 12", 4 ftd., fancy rim oblong (#3400/160)	90.00
Bowl, 5½", nappy (#3400/56)	65.00	Bowl, 12", 4 ftd., flared (#3400/4)	75.00
Bowl, 5½", 2 hdld., bonbon (#3400/1179)	35.00	Bowl, 12", 4 tab ftd., flared (#3900/62)	77.50
Bowl, 5½", 2 hdld., bonbon (#3400/1180)	35.00	Bowl, 12", ftd., (#3500/17)	120.00
Bowl, 6", bonbon, crimped (#3400/203)	85.00	Bowl, 12", ftd., oblong (#3500/118)	160.00
Bowl, 6", bonbon, cupped, shallow (#3400/205)	80.00	Bowl, 12", ftd., oval w/hdl. (#3500/21)	210.00
Bowl, 6", cereal (#3400/53)	95.00	Bowl, 12½", flared, rolled edge (#3400/2)	155.00
Bowl, 6", cereal (#3400/10)	95.00	Bowl, 12½", 4 ftd., #993	90.00
Bowl, 6", cereal (#3500/11)	95.00	Bowl, 13", #1398	120.00
Bowl, 6", hdld. (#3500/50)	47.50	Bowl, 13", 4 ftd., narrow, crimped (#3400/47)	125.00
Bowl, 6", 2 hdld. (#1402/89)	45.00	Bowl, 13", flared (#3400/1)	75.00
Bowl, 6", 2 hdld., ftd., bonbon (#3500/54)	37.50	Bowl, 14", 4 ftd., crimp edge, oblong, #1247	150.00
Bowl, 6", 4 ftd., fancy rim (#3400/136)	150.00	Bowl, 18", crimped, pan (Pristine #136)	650.00
Bowl, 6½", bonbon, crimped (#3400/202)	85.00	Bowl, cream soup, w/liner (#3400)	165.00
Bowl, 7", bonbon, crimped, shallow (#3400/201)	115.00	Bowl, cream soup, w/liner (#3500/2)	175.00
Bowl, 7", tab hdld., ftd., bonbon (#3900/130)	38.00	Bowl, finger, w/liner, #3106	100.00
Bowl, 8", ram's head, squared (#3500/27)	350.00	Bowl, finger, w/liner, #3121	100.00
Bowl, 8½", rimmed soup, #361	275.00	Butter, w/cover, round, #506	185.00
Bowl, 8½", 3 part, #221	215.00	Butter, w/cover, 5" (#3400/52)	175.00

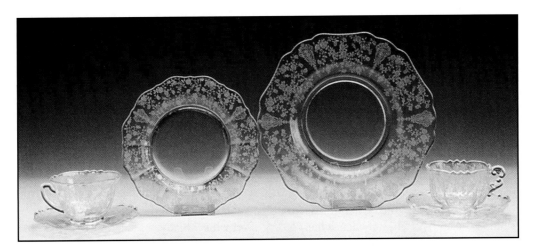

	Crystal		Crystal
Butter dish, ¼ lb. (#3900/52)	375.00	Cocktail shaker, 46 oz., metal top, #98	185.00
Candelabrum, 2-lite w/bobeches & prisms, #1268.	150.00	Cocktail shaker, 48 oz., glass stopper, #102.........	185.00
Candelabrum, 2-lite (#3500/94)	100.00	Comport, 5" (#3900/135)	47.50
Candelabrum, 3-lite, #1338	65.00	Comport, 5", 4 ftd. (#3400/74).......................	70.00
Candelabrum, 5½", 3-lite w/#19 bobeche & #1 prisms, #1545.......................................	135.00	Comport, 5½", scalloped edge (#3900/136)........	60.00
		Comport, 5⅜", blown (#3500/101)	65.00
Candelabrum, 6½", 2-lite, w/bobeches & prisms (Martha #496)...	175.00	Comport, 5⅜", blown, 3121 stem	60.00
		Comport, 5⅜", blown, 1066 stem	70.00
Candle, torchere, cup ft. (#3500/90)	195.00	Comport, 6" (#3500/36)	125.00
Candle, torchere, flat ft. (#3500/88)	185.00	Comport, 6" (#3500/111)	150.00
Candlestick (Pristine #500)	135.00	Comport, 6", 4 ftd. (#3400/13)	40.00
Candlestick, sq. base & lites (#1700/501)	185.00	Comport, 7", 2 hdld. (#3500/37)	125.00
Candlestick, 2½" (#3500/108)	33.00	Comport, 7", keyhole (#3400/29)	135.00
Candlestick, 3½", #628	38.00	Comport, 7", keyhole, low (#3400/28)	87.50
Candlestick, 4", #627	55.00	Creamer (#3400/68)	20.00
Candlestick, 4", ram's head (#3500/74).............	110.00	Creamer (#3500/14)	22.00
Candlestick, 5", 1-lite keyhole (#3400/646)........	35.00	Creamer, flat, #137	125.00
Candlestick, 5", inverts to comport (#3900/68)...	95.00	Creamer, flat, #944	150.00
Candlestick, 5½", 2-lite (Martha #495)	70.00	Creamer, ftd., (#3400/16)	90.00
Candlestick, 6" (#3500/31)	90.00	Creamer, ftd., (#3900/41)	20.00
Candlestick, 6", 2-lite keyhole (#3400/647)........	42.50	Creamer, indiv. (#3500/15) pie crust edge..........	25.00
Candlestick, 6", 2-lite (#3900/72)	47.50	Creamer, indiv. (#3900/40) scalloped edge.........	20.00
Candlestick, 6", 3-lite (#3900/74)	52.50	Cup, 3 styles (#3400/54, #3500/1, #3900/17)	32.50
Candlestick, 6", 3-lite keyhole (#3400/638)........	52.50	Cup, 5 oz., punch, #488	37.50
Candlestick, 6", 3-tiered lite, #1338	75.00	Cup, after dinner (#3400/69)	275.00
Candlestick, 6½", Calla Lily, #499	100.00	Decanter, 12 oz., ball, w/stopper (#3400/119).....	265.00
Candlestick, 7", #3121	75.00	Decanter, 14 oz., ftd., #1320	425.00
Candlestick, 7½", w/prism (Martha #497)..........	135.00	Decanter, 26 oz., sq., #1380	425.00
Candy box, w/cover, 5", apple shape, #316........	995.00	Decanter, 28 oz., tall, #1372	695.00
Candy box, w/cover, 5⅜", #1066 stem	155.00	Decanter, 28 oz., w/stopper, #1321	325.00
Candy box, w/cover, 5⅜", tall stem (3121/3).....	150.00	Decanter, 32 oz., ball, w/stopper (#3400/92)	395.00
Candy box, w/cover, 5⅜", short stem (3121/4)..	160.00	Dressing bottle, flat, #1263	300.00
Candy box, w/cover, blown, 5⅜" (#3500/103).....	165.00	Dressing bottle, ftd., #1261	325.00
Candy box, w/cover, 6", ram's head (#3500/78) ..	275.00	Epergne (candle w/vases) (#3900/75)	250.00
Candy box, w/rose finial, 6", 3 ftd., #300	295.00	Grapefruit, w/liner, #187	115.00
Candy box, w/cover, 7" (#3400/9)	145.00	Hat, 5", #1704	435.00
Candy box, w/cover, 7", round, 3 pt., #103	165.00	Hat, 6", #1703	435.00
Candy box, w/cover, 8", 3 pt. (#3500/57)...........	90.00	Hat, 8", #1702	495.00
Candy box, w/cover, rnd. (#3900/165)	120.00	Hat, 9", #1701	595.00
Celery, 12" (#3400/652)	47.50	Honey dish, w/cover (#3500/139)	300.00
Celery, 12" (#3500/652)	50.00	Hot plate or trivet	95.00
Celery, 12", 5 pt. (#3400/67)	80.00	Hurricane lamp, w/prisms, #1613	350.00
Celery, 14", 4 pt., 2 hdld. (#3500/97)	155.00	Hurricane lamp, candlestick base, #1617	250.00
Celery & relish, 9", 3 pt. (#3900/125)	55.00	Hurricane lamp, keyhole base, w/prisms, #1603 .	250.00
Celery & relish, 12", 3 pt. (#3900/126).............	65.00	Hurricane lamp, 8", etched chimney, #1601	275.00
Celery & relish, 12", 5 pt. (#3900/120).............	70.00	Hurricane lamp, 10", etched chimney & base, #1604	325.00
Cheese (5" comport) & cracker (13" plate) (#3900/135)	120.00		
		Ice bucket (#1402/52)	210.00
Cheese (5½" comport) & cracker (11½" plate) (#3400/6)	120.00	Ice bucket, w/chrome hand. (#3900/671)	155.00
		Ice pail, #1705..	225.00
Cheese (6" comport) & cracker (12" plate) (#3500/162)	145.00	Ice pail (#3400/851).....................................	135.00
		Ice tub (Pristine), #671	235.00
Cheese dish, w/cover, 5", #980........................	495.00	Icer, cocktail, #968 or #18	75.00
Cigarette box, w/cover, #615	125.00	Marmalade, 8 oz., #147	175.00
Cigarette box, w/cover, #747	155.00	Marmalade, w/cover, 7 oz., ftd., #157	195.00
Cigarette holder, oval, w/ash tray ft., #1066........	170.00	Mayonnaise (sherbet type w/ladle), #19.............	55.00
Cigarette holder, round, w/ash tray ft., #1337.....	155.00	Mayonnaise, div., w/liner & 2 ladles (#3900/111) .	77.50
Coaster, 3½", #1628	55.00	Mayonnaise, 3 pc. (#3400/11)	67.50
Cocktail icer, 2 pc. (#3600)	75.00	Mayonnaise, 3 pc. (#3900/129)	65.00
Cocktail shaker, metal top (#3400/157)	175.00	Mayonnaise, w/liner & ladle (#3500/59)	75.00
Cocktail shaker, metal top (#3400/175)	150.00	Mustard, 3 oz., #151	165.00
Cocktail shaker, 12 oz., metal top, #97	325.00	Mustard, 4½ oz., ftd., #1329	335.00
Cocktail shaker, 32 oz., w/glass stopper, #101	210.00	Oil, 2 oz., ball, w/stopper (#3400/96)	95.00

	Crystal
Oil, 6 oz., ball, w/stopper (#3400/99)	135.00
Oil, 6 oz., hdld. (#3400/193)	110.00
Oil, 6 oz., loop hdld., w/stopper (#3900/100)	145.00
Oil, 6 oz., w/stopper, ftd., hdld. (#3400/161)	235.00
Pickle, 9" (#3400/59).................................	65.00
Pickle or relish, 7" (#3900/123)......................	35.00
Pitcher, 20 oz. (#3900/117)...........................	295.00
Pitcher, 20 oz. w/ice lip, #70.......................	295.00
Pitcher, 32 oz. (#3900/118)...........................	325.00
Pitcher, 32 oz. martini (slender), w/metal insert (#3900/114).......................	465.00
Pitcher, 60 oz., martini, #1408.....................	1,995.00
Pitcher, 76 oz. (#3900/115)..........................	195.00
Pitcher, 76 oz., ice lip (#3400/100)	200.00
Pitcher, 76 oz., ice lip (#3400/152)	285.00
Pitcher, 80 oz., ball (#3400/38)	195.00
Pitcher, 80 oz., ball (#3900/116)	210.00
Pitcher, 80 oz., Doulton (#3400/141)	325.00
Pitcher, nite set, 2 pc., w/tumbler insert top, #103	750.00
Plate, 6", bread/butter (#3400/60)	13.50
Plate, 6", bread/butter (#3500/3)	15.00
Plate, 6", 2 hdld. (#3400/1181)	20.00
Plate, 6⅛", canape, #693...........................	165.00
Plate, 6½", bread/butter (#3900/20)	13.50
Plate, 7½" (#3500/4)................................	15.00
Plate, 7½", salad (#3400/176)......................	15.00
Plate, 8", salad (#3900/22)........................	20.00
Plate, 8", 2 hdld., ftd. (#3500/161)...............	42.50
Plate, 8", tab hdld., ftd., bonbon (#3900/131)......	40.00
Plate, 8½", breakfast (#3400/62)...................	24.00
Plate, 8½", salad (#3500/5)........................	24.00
Plate, 9½", crescent salad, #485	250.00
Plate, 9½", luncheon (#3400/63)....................	40.00
Plate, 10½", dinner (#3400/64).....................	135.00
Plate, 10½", dinner (#3900/24).....................	135.00
Plate, 11", 2 hdld. (#3400/35).....................	50.00
Plate, 12", 4 ftd., service (#3900/26)	70.00
Plate, 12", ftd. (#3500/39)........................	90.00
Plate, 12½", 2 hdld. (#3400/1186)..................	70.00
Plate, 13", rolled edge, ftd. (#3900/33)..........	70.00
Plate, 13", 4 ftd., torte (#3500/110)	125.00
Plate, 13", ftd., cake (Martha #170)	250.00
Plate, 13", torte (#3500/38)	185.00
Plate, 13½", #242	150.00
Plate, 13½", rolled edge, #1397	70.00
Plate, 13½", tab hdld., cake (#3900/35)	70.00
Plate, 14", rolled edge (#3900/166)	65.00
Plate, 14", service (#3900/167)....................	75.00
Plate, 14", torte (#3400/65).......................	150.00
Plate, 18", punch bowl liner (Martha #129)........	565.00
Punch bowl, 15", Martha #478	3,635.00
Punch set, 15-pc. (Martha)	4,750.00
Relish, 5½", 2 pt. (#3500/68)......................	25.00
Relish, 5½", 2 pt., hdld. (#3500/60)...............	30.00
Relish, 6", 2 pt. (#3400/90).......................	32.50
Relish, 6", 2 pt., 1 hdl. (#3400/1093)	85.00
Relish, 6½", 3 pt. (#3500/69)......................	32.50
Relish, 6½", 3 pt., hdld. (#3500/61)...............	37.50
Relish, 7", 2 pt. (#3900/124)......................	37.50
Relish, 7½", 3 pt., center hdld. (#3500/71)........	140.00

	Crystal
Relish, 7½", 4 pt. (#3500/70)......................	37.50
Relish, 7½", 4 pt., 2 hdld. (#3500/62)	55.00
Relish, 8", 3 pt., 3 hdld. (#3400/91)	37.50
Relish, 10", 2 hdld. (#3500/85)....................	70.00
Relish, 10", 3 pt., 2 hdld. (#3500/86)	52.50
Relish, 10", 3 pt., 4 ftd., 2 hdld. (#3500/64)........	52.50
Relish, 10", 4 pt., 4 ftd. (#3500/65)	62.50
Relish, 10", 4 pt., 2 hdld. (#3500/87)	60.00
Relish, 11", 2 pt., 2 hdld. (#3400/89)	80.00
Relish, 11", 3 pt. (#3400/200)	57.50
Relish, 12", 5 pt. (#3400/67)	75.00
Relish, 12", 5 pt. (Pristine #419)................	250.00
Relish, 12", 6 pc. (#3500/67)	250.00
Relish, 14", w/cover, 4 pt., 2 hdld. (#3500/142)....	750.00
Relish, 15", 4 pt., hdld. (#3500/113)	195.00
Salt & pepper, egg shape, pr., #1468	90.00
Salt & pepper, individual, rnd., glass base, pr., #1470......................	85.00
Salt & pepper, individual, w/chrome tops, pr., #360......................	70.00
Salt & pepper, lg., rnd., glass base, pr., #1471	85.00
Salt & pepper, w/chrome tops, pr., #395	175.00
Salt & pepper, w/chrome tops, pr. (#3400/37)......	175.00
Salt & pepper, w/chrome tops, pr., ftd. (#3400/77)......................	55.00
Salt & pepper w/chrome tops, pr., flat (#3900/1177)......................	45.00
Sandwich tray, 11", center handled (#3400/10) ..	140.00
Saucer, after dinner (#3400/69)...................	55.00
Saucer, 3 styles (#3400, #3500, #3900)	5.00
Stem, #3104, 3½ oz., cocktail.....................	275.00
Stem, #3106, ¾ oz., brandy	125.00
Stem, #3106, 1 oz., cordial	125.00
Stem, #3106, 1 oz., pousse cafe	135.00
Stem, #3106, 2 oz., sherry	50.00
Stem, #3106, 2½ oz., wine	50.00
Stem, #3106, 3 oz., cocktail......................	35.00
Stem, #3106, 4½ oz., claret	50.00
Stem, #3106, 5 oz., oyster cocktail	32.50
Stem, #3106, 7 oz., high sherbet	30.00
Stem, #3106, 7 oz., low sherbet	25.00
Stem, #3106, 10 oz., water goblet	35.00
Stem, #3121, 1 oz., brandy........................	130.00
Stem, #3121, 1 oz., cordial	70.00
Stem, #3121, 3 oz., cocktail......................	32.50
Stem, #3121, 3½ oz., wine	65.00
Stem, #3121, 4½ oz., claret	92.50
Stem, #3121, 4½ oz., low oyster cocktail	37.50
Stem, #3121, 5 oz., low ft. parfait	95.00
Stem, #3121, 6 oz., low sherbet	20.00
Stem, #3121, 6 oz., tall sherbet	22.00
Stem, #3121, 10 oz., water	35.00
Stem, #3500, 1 oz., cordial	70.00
Stem, #3500, 2½ oz., wine	57.50
Stem, #3500, 3 oz., cocktail	35.00
Stem, #3500, 4½ oz., claret	82.50
Stem, #3500, 4½ oz., low oyster cocktail	37.50
Stem, #3500, 5 oz., low ft. parfait	115.00
Stem, #3500, 7 oz., low ft. sherbet	20.00
Stem, #3500, 7 oz., tall sherbet	25.00
Stem, #3500, 10 oz. water	35.00

	Crystal
Stem, #37801, 4 oz., cocktail	45.00
Stem, #7801, 4 oz. cocktail, plain stem	40.00
Stem, #7966, 1 oz., cordial, plain ft.	135.00
Stem, #7966, 2 oz., sherry, plain ft.	100.00
Sugar (#3400/68)	20.00
Sugar (#3500/14)	20.00
Sugar, flat, #137	115.00
Sugar, flat, #944	140.00
Sugar, ftd. (#3400/16)	85.00
Sugar, ftd. (#3900/41)	20.00
Sugar, indiv. (#3500/15), pie crust edge	22.50
Sugar, indiv. (#3900/40), scalloped edge	21.50
Syrup, w/drip stop top, #1670	395.00
Tray, 6", 2 hdld., sq. (#3500/91)	170.00
Tray, 12", 2 hdld., oval, service (#3500/99)	235.00
Tray, 12", rnd. (#3500/67)	175.00
Tray, 13", 2 hdld., rnd. (#3500/72)	175.00
Tray, sugar/creamer (#3900/37)	25.00
Tumbler, #498, 2 oz., straight side	115.00
Tumbler, #498, 5 oz., straight side	50.00
Tumbler, #498, 8 oz., straight side	50.00
Tumbler, #498, 10 oz., straight side	50.00
Tumbler, #498, 12 oz., straight side	55.00
Tumbler, #3000, 3½ oz., cone, ftd.	100.00
Tumbler, #3000, 5 oz., cone, ftd.	125.00
Tumbler, #3106, 3 oz., ftd.	35.00
Tumbler, #3106, 5 oz., ftd.	35.00
Tumbler, #3106, 9 oz., ftd.	35.00
Tumbler, #3106, 12 oz., ftd.	40.00
Tumbler, #3121, 2½ oz., ftd.	70.00

	Crystal
Tumbler, #3121, 5 oz., low ft., juice	37.50
Tumbler, #3121, 10 oz., low ft., water	30.00
Tumbler, #3121, 12 oz., low ft., ice tea	35.00
Tumbler, #3400/1341, 1 oz., cordial	110.00
Tumbler, #3400/92, 2½ oz.	115.00
Tumbler, #3400/38, 5 oz.	100.00
Tumbler, #3400/38, 12 oz.	60.00
Tumbler, #3900/115, 13 oz.	50.00
Tumbler, #3500, 2½ oz., ftd.	65.00
Tumbler, #3500, 5 oz., low ft., juice	40.00
Tumbler, #3500, 10 oz., low ft., water	30.00
Tumbler, #3500, 13 oz., low ftd.	35.00
Tumbler, #3500, 12 oz., tall ft., ice tea	35.00
Tumbler, #7801, 5 oz., ftd.	40.00
Tumbler, #7801, 12 oz., ftd., ice tea	55.00
Tumbler, #3900/117, 5 oz.	50.00
Tumbler, #3400/115, 13 oz.	50.00
Urn, 10", w/cover (#3500/41)	550.00
Urn, 12", w/cover (#3500/42)	695.00
Vase, 5", #1309	70.00
Vase, 5", globe (#3400/102)	75.00
Vase, 5", ftd., #6004	50.00
Vase, 6", high ftd., flower, 6004	55.00
Vase, 6", #572	150.00
Vase, 6½", globe (#3400/103)	85.00
Vase, 7", ivy, ftd., ball, #1066	265.00
Vase, 8", #1430	160.00
Vase, 8", flat, flared, #797	135.00
Vase, 8", ftd. (#3500/44)	125.00
Vase, 8", high ftd., flower, 6004	60.00
Vase, 9", ftd., keyhole, #1237	95.00
Vase, 9", ftd., #1620	130.00
Vase, 9½" ftd., keyhole, #1233	85.00
Vase, 10", ball bottom, #400	195.00
Vase, 10", bud, #1528	80.00
Vase, 10", cornucopia (#3900/575)	210.00
Vase, 10", flat, #1242	145.00
Vase, 10", ftd., #1301	75.00
Vase, 10", ftd., #6004	75.00
Vase, 10", ftd. (#3500/45)	185.00
Vase, 10", slender, #274	55.00
Vase, 11", ftd., flower, #278	135.00
Vase, 11", ped. ftd., flower, #1299	165.00
Vase, 12", ftd., #6004	95.00
Vase, 12", ftd., keyhole, #1234	95.00
Vase, 12", ftd., keyhole, #1238	165.00
Vase, 13", ftd., flower, #279	245.00
Vase 18", #1336	2,100.00
Vase, sweet pea, #629	295.00

Colors: amber, Ebony, Blue, green

Royal is a Fostoria pattern that is sometimes erroneously labeled Vesper since both etchings are comparable, both are found on the #2350 blank and both were made in the same colors! There are fewer collectors for Royal than for Vesper, possibly due to a more limited distribution of Royal. New collectors should find Royal priced more to their liking.

Royal has several seldom found pieces including the covered cheese, cologne bottle, and both styles of pitchers. Enough amber or green can be found to complete a set; but only a smattering of pieces can be found in blue and black. Fostoria's blue color found with Royal etching was called "Blue" as opposed to the "Azure" blue which is a lighter color found with etchings of June, Kashmir, and Versailles. It is a shame that there is so little obtainable of this very beautiful blue color!

According to previously published material, production of Royal continued until 1934 although the January 1, 1933, Fostoria catalogs no longer listed Royal as being for sale. I have adapted my cutoff date of production to 1932. If you can find a May 1928 copy of *House and Garden*, there is a fascinating Fostoria Royal advertisement included!

	*Amber, Green		*Amber, Green
Ash tray, #2350, 3½"	22.50	Ice bucket, #2378	60.00
Bowl, #2350, bouillon, flat	15.00	Mayonnaise, #2315	25.00
Bowl, #2350½, bouillon, ftd.	15.00	Pickle, 8", #2350	20.00
Bowl, #2350, cream soup, flat	16.00	Pitcher, #1236	365.00
Bowl, #2350½, cream soup, ftd.	18.00	Pitcher, #5000, 48 oz.	265.00
Bowl, #869, 4½", finger	20.00	Plate, 8½", deep soup/underplate	37.50
Bowl, #2350, 5½", fruit	13.00	Plate, #2350, 6", bread/butter	3.00
Bowl, #2350, 6½", cereal	22.00	Plate, #2350, 7½", salad	4.00
Bowl, #2267, 7", ftd.	35.00	Plate, #2350, 8½", luncheon	8.00
Bowl, #2350, 7¾", soup	25.00	Plate, #2321, 8¾, Maj Jongg (canape)	37.50
Bowl, #2350, 8", nappy	30.00	Plate, #2350, 9½", small dinner	13.00
Bowl, #2350, 9", nappy	32.00	Plate, #2350, 10½", dinner	30.00
Bowl, #2350, 9", oval, baker	37.50	Plate, #2350, 13", chop	30.00
Bowl, #2324, 10", ftd.	45.00	Plate, #2350, 15", chop	40.00
Bowl, #2350, 10", salad	35.00	Platter, #2350, 10½"	30.00
Bowl, #2350, 10½", oval, baker	45.00	Platter, #2350, 12"	45.00
Bowl, #2315, 10½", ftd.	45.00	Platter, #2350, 15½"	90.00
Bowl, #2329, 11", console	22.00	Salt and pepper, #5100, pr.	60.00
Bowl, #2297, 12", deep	22.00	Sauce boat, w/liner	135.00
Bowl, #2329, 13", console	30.00	Saucer, #2350/#2350½	3.00
Bowl, #2324, 13", ftd.	50.00	Saucer, #2350, demi	5.00
Bowl, #2371, 13", oval, w/flower frog	125.00	Server, #2287, 11", center hdld.	25.00
Butter, w/cover, #2350	265.00	Stem, #869, ¾ oz., cordial	67.50
Candlestick, #2324, 4"	15.00	Stem, #869, 2¾ oz., wine	32.50
Candlestick, #2324, 9"	50.00	Stem, #869, 3 oz., cocktail	22.50
Candy, w/cover, #2331, 3 part	75.00	Stem, #869, 5½ oz., oyster cocktail	15.00
Candy, w/cover, ftd., ½ lb.	175.00	Stem, #869, 5½ oz., parfait	32.50
Celery, #2350, 11"	25.00	Stem, #869, 6 oz., low sherbet	12.50
Cheese, w/cover/plate, #2276 (plate 11")	125.00	Stem, #869, 6 oz., high sherbet	16.00
Cologne, #2322, tall	50.00	Stem, #869, 9 oz., water	20.00
Cologne, #2323, short	45.00	Sugar, flat, w/lid	165.00
Cologne/powder jar combination	225.00	Sugar, #2315, ftd., flat	17.00
Comport, #1861½, 6", jelly	25.00	Sugar, #2350½, ftd.	12.00
Comport, #2327, 7"	28.00	Sugar lid, #2350½	115.00
Comport, #2358, 8" wide	30.00	Tumbler, #869, 5 oz., flat	22.50
Creamer, flat	14.00	Tumbler, #859, 9 oz., flat	25.00
Creamer, #2315½, ftd., fat	18.00	Tumbler, #859, 12 oz., flat	30.00
Creamer, #2350½, ftd.	13.00	Tumbler, #5000, 2½ oz., ftd.	35.00
Cup, #2350, flat	12.00	Tumbler, #5000, 5 oz., ftd.	14.00
Cup, #2350½, ftd.	13.00	Tumbler, #5000, 9 oz., ftd.	16.00
Cup, #2350, demi	25.00	Tumbler, #5000, 12 oz., ftd.	27.50
Egg cup, #2350	27.50	Vase, #2324, urn, ftd.	85.00
Grapefruit, w/insert	80.00	Vase, #2292, flared	100.00

* Add up to 50% more for blue or black.   176

Colors: Smokey Topaz, Jungle Green, French Crystal, Silver Gray, Lilac, Sunshine, Jade; some milk glass, Apple Green, black, French Opalescent

If you look up rombic in the dictionary, you will find that it means irregular in shape, a fitting name! I've discovered that collectors either love or abhor it. There appear to be no feelings in between!

Prices for several pieces of Ruba Rombic have fallen rather dramatically in some instances. Several large collections have recently been sold and softened the demand for this rarely seen pattern! Ruba Rombic has always belonged to a specialized market that evades many dealers who do not have an outlet where they can sell this at prices once attained.

In the past, this pattern was displayed occasionally at Depression glass shows; but in the last few years, upper echelon Art Deco collectors and museums started displaying Ruba Rombic, and prices soared out of the reach of the average collector.

Collectors of Consolidated glass do not presently number in the thousands as do collectors of other glass company products. Little demand at the already high prices gives few reasons at the moment for these glassware prices to increase.

The predominate color shown here is Smokey Topaz, priced below with the Jungle Green. Smokey Topaz will be the color you are most likely to find; make note of its color.

The cased color column in the prices below includes three colors. They are Lilac (lavender), Sunshine (yellow), and Jade (green). French crystal is a white, applied color except that the raised edges are crystal with no white coloring at all. Silver is sometimes referred to as Gray Silver.

	Smokey Topaz/ Jungle Green	Cased Colors	French Opal/ French Crystal/ Silver
Ash tray, 3½"	600.00	750.00	850.00
Bonbon, flat, 3 part	250.00	350.00	400.00
Bottle, decanter, 9"	1,800.00	2,200.00	2,500.00
Bottle, perfume, 4¾"	1,200.00	1,500.00	1,800.00
Bottle, toilet, 7½"	1,200.00	1,500.00	1,800.00
Bowl, 3", almond	225.00	250.00	300.00
Bowl, 8", cupped	950.00	1,200.00	1,300.00
Bowl, 9", flared	950.00	1,200.00	1,300.00
Bowl, 12", oval	1,500.00	1,800.00	1,800.00
Bowl, bouillon	175.00	250.00	275.00
Bowl, finger	95.00	125.00	140.00
Box, cigarette, 3½" x 4¼"	850.00	1,250.00	1,500.00
Box, powder, 5", round	850.00	1,250.00	1,500.00
Candlestick, 2½" high, pr.	500.00	650.00	750.00
Celery, 10", 3 part	850.00	950.00	1,000.00
Comport, 7", wide	850.00	950.00	1,000.00
Creamer	200.00	250.00	300.00
Light, ceiling fixture, 10"		1,500.00	1,500.00
Light, ceiling fixture, 16"		2,500.00	2,500.00
Light, table light		1,200.00	1,200.00

	Smokey Topaz/ Jungle Green	Cased Colors	French Opal/ French Crystal/ Silver
Light, wall sconce		1,500.00	1,500.00
Pitcher, 8¼"	2,500.00	3,000.00	4,000.00
Plate, 7"	75.00	100.00	150.00
Plate, 8"	75.00	100.00	150.00
Plate, 10"	250.00	275.00	300.00
Plate, 15"	1,200.00	1,400.00	1,400.00
Relish, 2 part	350.00	450.00	500.00
Sugar	200.00	250.00	300.00
Sundae	100.00	135.00	150.00
Tray for decanter set	2,000.00	2,250.00	2,500.00
Tumbler, 2 oz., flat, 2¾"	100.00	125.00	150.00
Tumbler, 3 oz., ftd	125.00	150.00	175.00
Tumbler, 9 oz., flat	125.00	175.00	200.00
Tumbler, 10 oz., ftd.	175.00	300.00	350.00
Tumbler, 12 oz., flat	175.00	300.00	350.00
Tumbler, 15 oz., ftd., 7"	350.00	450.00	500.00
Vase, 6"	850.00	1,000.00	1,500.00
Vase, 9½"	1,500.00	2,500.00	3,000.00
Vase, 16"	10,000.00	12,000.00	12,000.00

Colors: crystal, amber, pink, green, red, cobalt blue

Lancaster Colony continues to produce some Sandwich pieces in their lines today. Those bright blue, green, and amberina color combinations are from Duncan moulds (made by Indiana) and were sold by Montgomery Ward in the early 1970s. The cobalt blue and red pieces pictured here seem to loosen the purse strings of a few Duncan collectors!

Tiffin also made a few Sandwich pieces in milk glass out of Duncan moulds.

An overabundance of Sandwich stemware makes it as economical to use as nearly all currently made stemware. I have included some Duncan catalog reprints on pages 183 – 185. I hope these will add to your viewing pleasure!

	Crystal
Ash tray, 2½" x 3¾", rect.	10.00
Ash tray, 2¾", sq.	8.00
Basket, 6½", w/loop hdld.	125.00
Basket, 10", crimped, w/loop hdl.	175.00
Basket, 10", oval, w/loop hdl.	175.00
Basket, 11½", w/loop hdl.	235.00
Bonbon, 5", heart shape, w/ring hdl.	15.00
Bonbon, 5½", heart shape, hdld.	15.00
Bonbon, 6", heart shape, w/ring hdl.	20.00
Bonbon, 7½", ftd., w/cover	42.50
Bowl, 2½", salted almond	11.00
Bowl, 3½", nut	10.00
Bowl, 4", finger	12.50
Bowl, 5½", hdld.	15.00
Bowl, 5½", ftd., grapefruit, w/rim liner	17.50
Bowl, 5½", ftd., grapefruit, w/fruit cup liner	17.50
Bowl, 5", 2 pt., nappy	12.00
Bowl, 5", ftd., crimped ivy	30.00
Bowl, 5", fruit	10.00
Bowl, 5", nappy, w/ring hdl.	12.00
Bowl, 6", 2 pt., nappy	15.00
Bowl, 6", fruit salad	12.00
Bowl, 6", grapefruit, rimmed edge	17.50

	Crystal
Bowl, 6", nappy, w/ring hdl.	18.00
Bowl, 10", salad, deep	72.50
Bowl, 10", 3 pt., fruit	82.50
Bowl, 10", lily, vertical edge	52.50
Bowl, 11", cupped nut	55.00
Bowl, 11½", crimped flower	57.50
Bowl, 11½", gardenia	45.00
Bowl, 11½", ftd., crimped fruit	62.50
Bowl, 12", fruit, flared edge	45.00
Bowl, 12", shallow salad	40.00
Bowl, 12", oblong console	40.00
Bowl, 12", epergne, w/ctr. hole	100.00
Butter, w/cover, ¼ lb.	37.50
Cake stand, 11½", ftd., rolled edge	90.00
Cake stand, 12", ftd., rolled edge, plain pedestal	75.00
Cake stand, 13", ftd., plain pedestal	75.00
Candelabra, 10", 1-lite, w/bobeche & prisms	75.00
Candelabra, 10", 3-lite, w/bobeche & prisms	195.00
Candelabra, 16", 3-lite, w/bobeche & prisms	250.00
Candlestick, 4", 1-lite	14.00
Candlestick, 4", 1-lite, w/bobeche & stub. prisms	32.50

	Crystal
Candlestick, 5", 3-lite	45.00
Candlestick, 5", 3-lite, w/bobeche & stub. prisms	125.00
Candlestick, 5", 2-lite, w/bobeche & stub. prisms	95.00
Candlestick, 5", 2-lite	30.00
Candy, 6" square	375.00
Candy box, w/cover, 5", flat	40.00
Candy jar, w/cover, 8½", ftd.	55.00
Cheese, w/cover (cover 4¾", plate 8")	115.00
Cheese/cracker (3" compote, 13" plate)	55.00
Cigarette box, w/cover, 3½"	22.00
Cigarette holder, 3", ftd.	27.50
Coaster, 5"	12.00
Comport, 2¼"	15.00
Comport, 3¼", low ft., crimped candy	20.00
Comport, 3¼", low ft., flared candy	17.50
Comport, 4¼", ftd.	20.00
Comport, 5", low ft.	20.00
Comport, 5½", ftd., low crimped	25.00
Comport, 6", low ft., flared	22.50
Condiment set (2 cruets, 3¾" salt & pepper, 4 pt. tray)	105.00
Creamer, 4", 7 oz., ftd.	9.00
Cup, 6 oz., tea	10.00
Epergne, 9", garden	125.00
Epergne, 12", 3 pt., fruit or flower	250.00
Jelly, 3", indiv.	7.00
Mayonnaise set, 3 pc.: ladle, 5" bowl, 7" plate	32.00
Oil bottle, 5¾"	35.00
Pan, 6¾" x 10½", oblong, camelia	65.00
Pitcher, 13 oz., metal top	65.00
Pitcher, w/ice lip, 8", 64 oz.	130.00
Plate, 3", indiv. jelly	6.00
Plate, 6", bread/butter	6.00
Plate, 6½", finger bowl liner	8.00
Plate, 7", dessert	7.50
Plate, 8", mayonnaise liner, w/ring	8.00
Plate, 8", salad	10.00
Plate, 9½", dinner	37.50
Plate, 11½", hdld., service	37.50
Plate, 12", torte	45.00
Plate, 12", ice cream, rolled edge	55.00
Plate, 12", deviled egg	65.00
Plate, 13", salad dressing, w/ring	32.00
Plate, 13", service	50.00
Plate, 13", service, rolled edge	55.00
Plate, 13", cracker, w/ring	30.00
Plate, 16", lazy susan, w/turntable	110.00
Plate, 16", hostess	105.00
Relish, 5½", 2 pt., rnd., ring hdl.	15.00

	Crystal
Relish, 6", 2 pt., rnd., ring hdl.	17.00
Relish, 7", 2 pt., oval	20.00
Relish, 10", 4 pt., hdld.	25.00
Relish, 10", 3 pt., oblong	27.50
Relish, 10½", 3 pt., oblong	27.50
Relish, 12", 3 pt.	37.50
Salad dressing set: (2 ladles, 5" ftd. mayonnaise, 13" plate w/ring)	80.00
Salad dressing set: (2 ladles, 6" ftd. div. bowl, 8" plate w/ring)	65.00
Salt & pepper, 2½", w/glass tops, pr.	18.00
Salt & pepper, 2½", w/metal tops, pr.	18.00
Salt & pepper, 3¾", w/metal top (on 6" tray), 3 pc.	30.00
Saucer, 6", w/ring	4.00
Stem, 2½", 6 oz., ftd., fruit cup/jello	11.00
Stem, 2¾", 5 oz., ftd., oyster cocktail	15.00
Stem, 3½", 5 oz., sundae (flared rim)	12.00
Stem, 4¼", 3 oz., cocktail	15.00
Stem, 4¼", 5 oz., ice cream	12.50
Stem, 4¼", 3 oz., wine	20.00
Stem, 5¼", 4 oz., ftd., parfait	30.00
Stem, 5¼", 5 oz., champagne	20.00
Stem, 6", 9 oz., goblet	18.50
Sugar, 3¼", ftd., 9 oz.	8.00
Sugar, 5 oz.	7.50
Sugar (cheese) shaker, 13 oz., metal top	70.00
Tray, oval (for sugar/creamer)	10.00
Tray, 6" mint, rolled edge, w/ring hdl.	17.50
Tray, 7", oval, pickle	15.00
Tray, 7", mint, rolled edge, w/ring hdl.	22.00
Tray, 8", oval	18.00
Tray, 8", for oil/vinegar	20.00
Tray, 10", oval, celery	18.00
Tray, 12", fruit epergne	52.00
Tray, 12", ice cream, rolled edge	45.00
Tumbler, 3¾", 5 oz., ftd., juice	12.00
Tumbler, 4¾", 9 oz., ftd., water	14.00
Tumbler, 5¼", 13 oz., flat, iced tea	20.00
Tumbler, 5¼", 12 oz., ftd., iced tea	17.50
Urn, w/cover, 12", ftd.	150.00
Vase, 3", ftd., crimped	17.50
Vase, 3", ftd., flared rim	15.00
Vase, 4", hat shape	20.00
Vase, 4½", flat base, crimped	25.00
Vase, 5", ftd., flared rim	22.50
Vase, 5", ftd., crimped	25.00
Vase, 5", ftd., fan	45.00
Vase, 7½", epergne, threaded base	60.00
Vase, 10", ftd.	70.00

DUNCAN

EARLY AMERICAN SANDWICH

No. 41 PATTERN

Washington, Pa.   1-1-43

THE DUNCAN & MILLER GLASS CO.

No. 41
9 oz. Goblet
Height—6"

No. 41
5 oz. Saucer
Champagne
Height—5¼"

No. 41
3 oz. Wine
Height—4½"

No. 41
3 oz. Cocktail
Height—4¼"

No. 41
5 oz. Ice Cream
Height—4¼"

No. 41
5 oz. Flared Sundae
Height—3½"

No. 41
3 in. Ind. Jelly

No. 41
½ gal. Ice Lip Jug
Height—8"

No. 41
6 oz. Fruit Cup or Jello
Height—2½"

No. 41
5 oz. Oyster Cocktail
Height—2¾"

No. 41
13 oz. Ice Tea
Tumbler—Straight
Height—5¼"

No. 41
12 oz. Ftd. Ice Tea
Height—5½"

No. 41
9 oz. Ftd. Tumbler
Height—4¼"

No. 41
5 oz. Ftd. Orange Juice
Height—3¼"

No. 41
4 oz. Parfait
Height—5¼"

DUNCAN

**EARLY AMERICAN
SANDWICH**

No. 41 PATTERN

Duncan

Washington, Pa.   1-1-43

THE DUNCAN & MILLER GLASS CO.

No. 41
6 in. Tall Hld.
Basket

No. 41
5 in. Ftd. Ivy Bowl

No. 41
4½ in. Crimped Vase

No. 41
5 in. Ftd. Vase Crimped
Also made 3 in. size

No. 41
11½ in. Crimped Flower Bowl
Height—3½"

No. 41
10 in. Ftd. Vase

No. 41
10 in. Lily Bowl
Height—2"

No. 41
12 in. Urn and Cover

DUNCAN

EARLY AMERICAN SANDWICH
No. 41 PATTERN

Washington, Pa. 1-1-43

THE DUNCAN & MILLER GLASS CO.

No. 1-B-41—3 Light
Candelabrum W/U Prisms
Height—10"   Width—13"
2 Bobeches

No. 1-41—1 Light
Candelabrum W/U Prisms
Height—10"

No. 1-41—1 Light
Hurricane Lamp Candelabrum
W/Prisms
Height—15"

No. 1-C-41—3 Light
Candelabrum W/U Prisms
Height—16"   Width—13"
3 Bobeches

Colors: amber, green

Seville is a Fostoria pattern that has generally been overlooked by the collecting realm. Seville would be a cheaper Elegant pattern to collect despite there not being a great deal of it to go around. Green would be simpler to acquire than amber as you may note by the lack of amber in my photos. The butter dish, pitcher, grapefruit and liner, and sugar lid are all exasperating to find, but oh, so gratifying when you do run across them!

To distinguish between the bouillon and the cream soup with liners, the bouillon is shown in the right corner of the top picture. The stemmed piece at the bottom of the page is a grapefruit liner. Most Fostoria patterns have the design on both the grapefruit and the liner. The ice bowl liners are usually plain (no etched pattern).

	Amber	Green		Amber	Green
Ash tray, #2350, 4"	17.50	22.50	Comport, #2327, 7½", (twisted stem)	20.00	25.00
Bowl, #2350, fruit, 5½"	10.00	12.00	Comport, #2350, 8"	27.50	35.00
Bowl, #2350, cereal, 6½"	18.00	22.00	Creamer, #2315½, flat, ftd.	13.50	15.00
Bowl, #2350, soup, 7¾"	20.00	27.50	Creamer, #2350½, ftd.	12.50	13.50
Bowl, #2315, low foot, 7"	16.00	20.00	Cup, #2350, after dinner	25.00	30.00
Bowl, #2350, vegetable	22.00	27.50	Cup, #2350, flat	10.00	12.50
Bowl, #2350, nappy, 9"	30.00	37.50	Cup, #2350½, ftd.	10.00	12.50
Bowl, #2350, oval, baker, 9"	25.00	30.00	Egg cup, #2350	30.00	35.00
Bowl, #2315, flared, 10½", ftd.	25.00	30.00	Grapefruit, #945½, blown	40.00	45.00
Bowl, #2350, oval, baker, 10½"	35.00	40.00	Grapefruit, #945½, liner, blown	30.00	35.00
Bowl, 10", ftd.	35.00	42.50	Grapefruit, #2315, molded	25.00	32.00
Bowl, #2350, salad, 10"	30.00	35.00	Ice bucket, #2378	50.00	55.00
Bowl, #2329, rolled edge, console, 11"	27.50	32.50	Pickle, #2350, 8"	13.50	15.00
Bowl, #2297, deep, flared, 12"	30.00	32.50	Pitcher, #5084, ftd.	235.00	265.00
Bowl, #2371, oval, console, 13"	35.00	40.00	Plate, #2350, bread and butter, 6"	3.50	4.00
Bowl, #2329, rolled edge, console, 13"	30.00	32.50	Plate, #2350, salad, 7½"	5.00	5.50
Bowl, #2350, bouillon, flat	13.50	16.00	Plate, #2350, luncheon, 8½"	6.00	6.50
Bowl, #2350½, bouillon, ftd.	14.00	16.00	Plate, #2321, Maj Jongg (canape), 8¾".	35.00	40.00
Bowl, #2350, cream soup, flat	14.50	17.50	Plate, #2350, sm. dinner, 9½"	12.00	13.50
Bowl, #2350½, cream soup, ftd.	15.50	17.50	Plate, #2350, dinner, 10½"	32.50	42.50
Bowl, #869/2283, finger, w/6" liner	20.00	22.00	Plate, #2350, chop, 13¾"	30.00	35.00
Butter, w/cover, #2350, round	185.00	235.00	Plate, #2350, round, 15"	35.00	40.00
Candlestick, #2324, 2"	18.00	22.00	Plate, #2350, cream soup liner	5.00	6.00
Candlestick, #2324, 4"	15.00	20.00	Platter, #2350, 10½"	22.50	25.00
Candlestick, #2324, 9"	30.00	35.00	Platter, #2350, 12"	35.00	40.00
Candy jar, w/cover, #2250, ½ lb., ftd.	95.00	120.00	Platter, #2350, 15"	70.00	80.00
Candy jar, w/cover, #2331, 3 pt., flat	65.00	85.00	Salt and pepper shaker, #5100, pr.	60.00	65.00
Celery, #2350, 11"	15.00	17.50	Sauce boat liner, #2350	25.00	30.00
Cheese and cracker, #2368 (11" plate)	40.00	45.00	Sauce boat, #2350	55.00	75.00
			Saucer, #2350	3.00	3.00
			Saucer, after dinner, #2350	5.00	5.00
			Stem, #870, cocktail	15.00	16.00
			Stem, #870, cordial	65.00	70.00
			Stem, #870, high sherbet	15.00	16.00
			Stem, #870, low sherbet	12.50	13.50
			Stem, #870, oyster cocktail	16.50	17.50
			Stem, #870, parfait	30.00	35.00
			Stem, #870, water	20.00	22.50
			Stem, #870, wine	22.50	25.00
			Sugar cover, #2350½	80.00	110.00
			Sugar, fat, ftd., #2315	13.50	14.50
			Sugar, ftd., #2350½	12.50	13.50
			Tray, 11", center handled, #2287	27.50	30.00
			Tumbler, #5084, ftd., 2 oz.	35.00	40.00
			Tumbler, #5084, ftd., 5 oz.	13.50	15.00
			Tumbler, #5084, ftd., 9 oz.	15.00	16.50
			Tumbler, #5084, ftd., 12 oz.	18.00	20.00
			Urn, small, #2324	75.00	100.00
			Vase, #2292, 8"	55.00	65.00

Colors: amber, green, pink, crystal

   "Spiral Flutes" is a Duncan & Miller pattern that has been essentially ignored by collectors. Only a few pieces are easily found; namely the 6¾" flanged bowls, 7 oz. footed tumblers, and 7½" plates; after that, there is little found effortlessly. Green can be gathered more readily than any other color. Amber and crystal sets may be rounded up, but few are trying either!

	Amber, Green, Pink		Amber, Green, Pink
Bowl, 2", almond	13.00	Ice tub, handled	50.00
Bowl, 3¾", bouillon	15.00	Lamp, 10½", countess	265.00
Bowl, 4⅜", finger	7.00	Mug, 6½", 9 oz., handled	27.50
Bowl, 4¾", ftd., cream soup	15.00	Mug, 7", 9 oz., handled	35.00
Bowl, 4" w., mayonnaise	17.50	Oil, w/stopper, 6 oz.	175.00
Bowl, 5", nappy	6.00	Pickle, 8⅝"	12.00
Bowl, 6½", cereal, sm. flange	32.50	Pitcher, ½ gal.	175.00
Bowl, 6¾", grapefruit	7.50	Plate, 6", pie	3.00
Bowl, 6", handled nappy	22.00	Plate, 7½", salad	4.00
Bowl, 6", handled nappy, w/cover	85.00	Plate, 8⅜", luncheon	4.00
Bowl, 7", nappy	15.00	Plate, 10⅜", dinner	22.50
Bowl, 7½", flanged (baked apple)	22.50	Plate, 13⅝", torte	27.50
Bowl, 8", nappy	17.50	Plate, w/star, 6" (fingerbowl item)	6.00
Bowl, 8½", flanged (oyster plate)	22.50	Platter, 11"	35.00
Bowl, 9", nappy	27.50	Platter, 13"	50.00
Bowl, 10", oval, veg., two styles.	45.00	Relish, 10" x 7⅜", oval, 3 pc. (2 inserts)	90.00
Bowl, 10½", lily pond	40.00	Saucer	3.00
Bowl, 11¾" w. x 3¾" t., console, flared	30.00	Saucer, demi	5.00
Bowl, 11", nappy	30.00	Seafood sauce cup, 3" w. x 2½" h.	25.00
Bowl, 12", cupped console	30.00	Stem, 3¾", 3½ oz., wine	17.50
Candle, 3½"	15.00	Stem, 3¾", 5 oz., low sherbet	8.00
Candle, 7½"	55.00	Stem, 4¾", 6 oz., tall sherbet	12.00
Candle, 9½"	75.00	Stem, 5⅝", 4½ oz., parfait	17.50
Candle, 11½"	110.00	Stem, 6¼", 7 oz., water	17.50
Celery, 10¾" x 4¾"	17.50	Sugar, oval	8.00
* Chocolate jar, w/cover	265.00	Sweetmeat, w/cover, 7½"	115.00
Cigarette holder, 4"	32.00	Tumbler, 3⅜", ftd., 2½ oz., cocktail (no stem)	7.00
Comport, 4⅜"	15.00		
Comport, 6⅝"	17.50	Tumbler, 4¼", 8 oz., flat	30.00
Comport, 9", low ft., flared	55.00	Tumbler, 4⅜", ftd., 5½ oz., juice (no stem)	14.00
Console stand, 1½" h. x 4⅝" w.	12.00	Tumbler, 4¾", 7 oz., flat, soda	35.00
Creamer, oval	8.00	Tumbler, 5⅛", ftd., 7 oz., water (1 knob)	8.00
Cup	9.00	Tumbler, 5⅛", ftd., 9 oz., water (no stem)	20.00
Cup, demi	25.00	Tumbler, 5½", 11 oz., ginger ale	70.00
* Fernery, 10" x 5½", 4 ftd., flower box	375.00	Vase, 6½"	15.00
Grapefruit, ftd.	20.00	Vase, 8½"	20.00
		Vase, 10½"	30.00

*Crystal, $135.00

Colors: crystal, some blown stemware in Zircon

Heisey's Stanhope is another pattern kept alive by Deco collectors! As with New Era, there continues to be heightened rivalry for this! Notice that prices have inflated in almost all areas except stemware!

For those who asked what I mean by T knobs, they are insert handles (black and red, round, wooden knobs) which are like wooden dowel rods that act as horizontal handles. The insert handles are capricious to some; but others think them magnificent!

Some people mistake the salad bowl shown at the bottom for a punch bowl; it would not hold much punch!

	Crystal
Ash tray, indiv.	25.00
Bottle, oil, 3 oz. w or w/o rd. knob	325.00
Bowl, 6" mint, 2 hdld., w or w/o rd. knobs	35.00
Bowl, 6" mint, 2 pt., 2 hdld., w or w/o rd. knobs	35.00
Bowl, 11", salad	90.00
Bowl, finger, #4080 (blown, plain)	10.00
Bowl, floral, 11", 2 hdld., w or w/o "T" knobs	80.00
Candelabra, 2-lite, w bobeche & prisms	180.00
Candy box & lid, rnd., w or w/o rd. knob	180.00
Cigarette box & lid, w or w/o rd. knob	65.00
Creamer, 2 hdld., w or w/o rd. knobs	45.00
Cup, w or w/o rd. knob	25.00
Ice tub, 2 hdld., w or w/o "T" knobs	70.00
Jelly, 6", 1 hdld., w or w/o rd. knobs	25.00
Jelly, 6", 3 pt., 1 hdld., w or w/o rd. knobs	25.00
Nappy, 4½", 1 hdld., w or w/o rd. knob	25.00
Nut, indiv., 1 hdld., w or w/o rd. knob	40.00
Plate, 7"	20.00
Plate, 12" torte, 2 hdld., w or w/o "T" knobs	35.00
Plate, 15" torte, rnd. or salad liner	45.00
Relish, 11" triplex buffet, 2 hdld., w or w/o "T" knobs	35.00
Relish, 12", 4 pt., 2 hdld., w or w/o "T" knobs	55.00
Relish, 12", 5 pt., 2 hdld., w or w/o "T" knobs	55.00
Salt & pepper, #60 top	90.00
Saucer	10.00
Stem, 1 oz., cordial, #4083 (blown)	70.00
Stem, 2½ oz., pressed wine	35.00
Stem, 2½ oz., wine, #4083	25.00
Stem, 3½ oz., cocktail, #4083	20.00
Stem, 3½ oz., pressed cocktail	25.00
Stem, 4 oz., claret, #4083	25.00
Stem, 4 oz., oyster cocktail, #4083	10.00
Stem, 5½ oz., pressed saucer champagne	20.00
Stem, 5½ oz., saucer champagne, #4083	15.00
Stem, 9 oz., pressed goblet	45.00
Stem, 10 oz., goblet, #4083	22.50
Stem, 12 oz., pressed soda	45.00
Sugar, 2 hdld., w or w/o rd. knobs	45.00
Tray, 12" celery, 2 hdld., w or w/o "T" knobs	55.00
Tumbler, 5 oz., soda, #4083	20.00
Tumbler, 8 oz., soda, #4083	22.50
Tumbler, 12 oz., soda, #4083	25.00
Vase, 7", ball	90.00
Vase, 9", 2 hdld., w or w/o "T" knobs	85.00

Colors: crystal, red, blue, green, yellow

There are additional listings for Fostoria's Sun Ray recorded since several readers have been kind enough to send them! Pricing has been difficult because of the disparity I have seen. I price crystal; but be aware there are pieces to be found in red, blue, green, and yellow. I recently bought a red Sun Ray item to show in the next book.

The cream soup is tab handled (bottom photo). By putting a lid on the cream soup (top photo), it becomes an onion soup according to Fostoria's catalogs. The condiment tray is shaped similar to the one in American. It is probably rarer than the American one, but not as many collectors are seeking it!

Notice the two tumblers on the right in the upper photograph. One has frosted panels and the other is clear. Pieces with frosted panels were considered a separate pattern named Glacier by Fostoria. Some Sun Ray enthusiasts are willing to mix the two, but most gather one or the other. As I see it, the frosting adds to the overall design. Both patterns sell in the same price range.

	Crystal		Crystal
Almond, ftd., ind.	12.00	Pitcher, 64 oz., ice lip	185.00
Ash tray, ind., 2510½	8.00	Plate, 6"	5.00
Ash tray, square	10.00	Plate, 7½"	8.00
Bonbon, hdld.	16.00	Plate, 8½"	12.00
Bonbon. 3 toed	17.50	Plate, 9½"	28.00
Bowl, 5", fruit	8.00	Plate, 11", torte	35.00
Bowl, 9½", flared	30.00	Plate, 12", sandwich	35.00
Bowl, 12", salad	35.00	Plate, 15", torte	65.00
Bowl, 13", rolled edge	40.00	Plate, 16"	70.00
Bowl, custard, 2¼", high	12.00	Relish, 2 part	16.00
Bowl, hdld.	35.00	Relish, 3 part	20.00
Butter, w/lid, ¼ lb.	25.00	Relish, 4 part	22.00
Candelabra, 2-lite	45.00	Salt dip	9.00
Candlestick, 3"	18.00	Saucer	3.00
Candlestick, 5½"	25.00	Shaker, 4", pr.	45.00
Candlestick, duo	37.50	Shaker, individual, 2¼", #2510½	15.00
Candy jar, w/cover	45.00	Stem, 3½", 5½ oz., sherbet, low	9.00
Celery, hdld.	22.00	Stem, 3¼", 3½ oz., fruit cocktail	12.00
Cigarette and cover	22.00	Stem, 3", 4 oz., cocktail, ftd.	12.00
Cigarette box, oblong	25.00	Stem, 4⅞", 4½ oz., claret	25.00
Coaster, 4"	6.00	Stem, 5¾", 9 oz., goblet	16.00
Comport	18.00	Sugar, ftd.	12.00
Cream soup	25.00	Sugar, individual	12.00
Cream soup liner	8.00	Sweetmeat, hdld., divided	30.00
Cream, ftd.	12.00	Tray, 6½", ind sug/cream	10.00
Cream, individual	12.00	Tray, 10½", oblong	25.00
Cup	12.00	Tray, 10", square	35.00
Decanter, w/stopper, 18 oz.	45.00	Tray, condiment, 8½"	40.00
Decanter, w/stopper, oblong, 26 oz.	60.00	Tray, oval hdld.	25.00
Ice bucket, no handle	45.00	Tumbler, 2¼", 2 oz., whiskey, #2510½	12.00
Ice bucket, w/handle	50.00	Tumbler, 3½", 5 oz., juice, #2510½	12.50
Jelly	16.00	Tumbler, 3½", 6 oz., old fashion, #2510½	14.00
Jelly, w/cover	28.00	Tumbler, 4⅛", 9 oz., table, #2510½	13.00
Mayonnaise, w/liner, ladle	35.00	Tumbler, 4¾", 9 oz., ftd. table	14.00
Mustard, w/cover, spoon	30.00	Tumbler, 4⅝", 5 oz., ftd. juice	15.00
Nappy, hdld., flared	13.00	Tumbler, 5¼", 13 oz., ftd. tea	18.00
Nappy, hdld., reg.	12.00	Tumbler, 5⅛", 13 oz., tea, #2510½	22.00
Nappy, hdld., square	14.00	Vase, 3½", rose bowl	22.00
Nappy, hdld., tri-corner	15.00	Vase, 5", rose bowl	30.00
Oil bottle, w/stopper, 3 oz.	32.00	Vase, 6", crimped	37.50
Onion soup, w/cover	40.00	Vase, 7"	50.00
Pickle, hdld.	22.00	Vase, 9", sq. ftd.	55.00
Pitcher, 16 oz., cereal	40.00	Vase, sweet pea	65.00
Pitcher, 64 oz.	150.00		

late 1920s – early 1930s

Colors: pink, green, blue, crystal

Sunrise Medallion (Morgantown's etching #758) previously has been christened "Dancing Girl" by collectors. Old names are hard to overcome; however, more new collectors are adopting the Sunrise Medallion name.

Blue is the most sought color, but pink and crystal can be found. Few pieces of green have been seen, and I have never heard of any green stemware. Have you? I have only owned a green sugar and 10" vase, and I have reports of a creamer.

Catalog measurements were usually recorded in ounces, not heights. Those twisted stem items (#7642½) are slightly taller than the plain stem (#7630) counterparts. Measurements below are mainly from the #7630 line that I seem to find more often. Twisted stemware champagne and waters are the only #7642½ stems I have. If you find others, I would appreciate having measurements.

Two different styled oyster cocktails, which look more like juice or bar tumblers to me, are pictured in the foreground of the lower photo. These measure 2⁷⁄₁₆" to 2⁹⁄₁₆" tall and hold four ounces, (shown center bottom page 197).

Collecting Sunrise Medallion will take a deep pocketbook, no matter what color you strive to attain. Serving pieces do not seem to exist, this may have only been a luncheon set with some stems and a vase or two.

	Crystal	Blue	Pink/ Green
Bowl, finger, ftd.		75.00	
Creamer		325.00	275.00
Cup	40.00	100.00	80.00
Parfait, 5 oz.	55.00	110.00	80.00
Pitcher		550.00	
Plate, 5⅞", sherbet	6.00	12.50	10.00
Plate, 7½", salad	10.00	25.00	20.00
Plate, 8⅜"	12.50	30.00	22.50
Saucer	15.00	22.50	17.50
Sherbet, cone	20.00		
Stem, 1½ oz., cordial	110.00	265.00	185.00
Stem, 2½ oz., wine	45.00	85.00	55.00
Stem, 6¼", 7 oz., champagne (twist stem, 6¾")	25.00	40.00	30.00
Stem, 6⅛", cocktail	30.00	55.00	40.00
Stem, 7¾", 9 oz., water (twist stem, 8¼")	35.00	65.00	45.00
Sugar		300.00	250.00
Tumbler, 2½", 4 oz, ftd.	25.00	150.00	
Tumbler, 3½", 4 oz., ftd.			35.00
Tumbler, 4¼", 5 oz., ftd.	45.00	50.00	35.00
Tumbler, 4¼", flat	20.00		
Tumbler, 4¾", 9 oz., ftd.	20.00	55.00	40.00
Tumbler, 5½", 11 oz., ftd.	35.00	85.00	65.00
Tumbler, 5½", flat	25.00		
Vase, 6" tall, 5" wide			350.00
Vase, 10", slender, bud	65.00	400.00	250.00
Vase, 10", bulbous bottom			325.00

DUNCAN
TEAR DROPS
No. 5301 STEMWARE
No. 5300 TUMBLERS
(Lead Blown)

No. 5301—4½ oz. Ftd.
Orange Juice
Height—4"

No. 5301—3 oz. Ftd.
Whiskey or Cocktail
Height—3"

No. 5301—2 oz.
Ftd. Whiskey
Height—2¾"

No. 5301
½ Gal. Pitcher with Ice Guard Lip
Height—8½"

No. 5301
No. 5301—14 oz. Ftd.
Ice Tea or Hiball
Height—6"
Also made 12 oz.
Height—5½"

No. 5301
8 oz. Ftd. Split
or Party Glass
Height—5"

No. 5301—9 oz.
Ftd. Tumbler
Height—4½"

No. 5300—2 oz.
Whiskey
Height—2¼"

No. 5300—3½ oz.
Orange Juice
Height—3¼"

No. 5300—5 oz.
Orange Juice
Height—3½"

No. 5300
9 oz. Tumbler
Height—4¼"

No. 5300
10 oz. Hiball
Height—4¼"

No. 5300
14 oz. Hiball
Height—5¼"

No. 5300
12 oz. Ice Tea
Height—5¼"

No. 5300
8 oz. Split
Height—4½"

No. 5300
7 oz. Old Fashioned
Height—3¼"

Washington, Pa.   1-1-43

THE DUNCAN & MILLER GLASS CO.

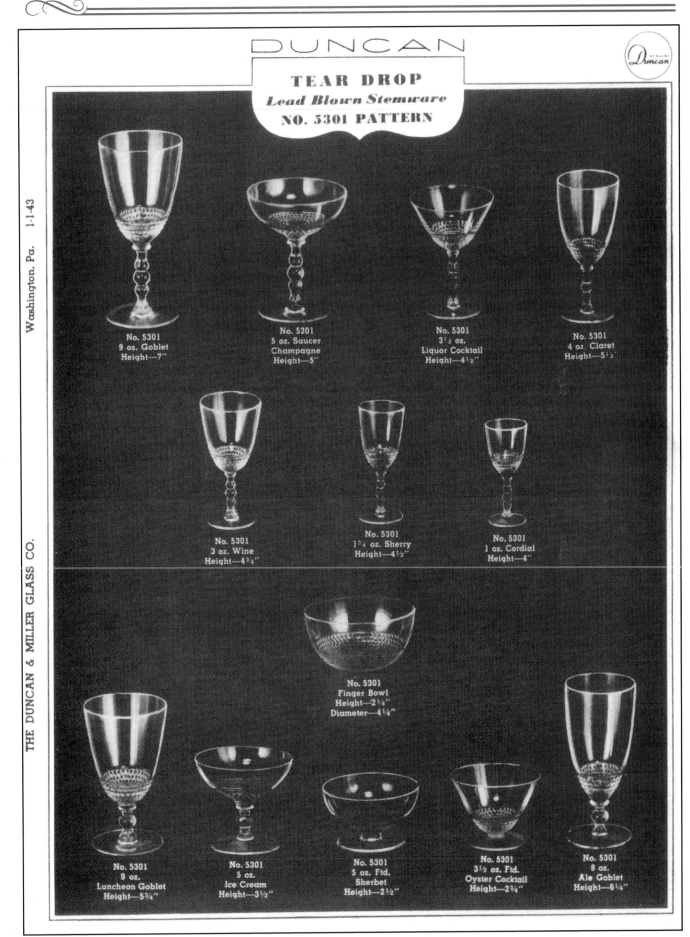

DUNCAN

TEAR DROP
Lead Blown Stemware
NO. 5301 PATTERN

Duncan

No. 5301
9 oz. Goblet
Height—7"

No. 5301
5 oz. Saucer
Champagne
Height—5"

No. 5301
3½ oz.
Liquor Cocktail
Height—4½"

No. 5301
4 oz. Claret
Height—5½"

No. 5301
3 oz. Wine
Height—4¾"

No. 5301
1¾ oz. Sherry
Height—4½"

No. 5301
1 oz. Cordial
Height—4"

No. 5301
Finger Bowl
Height—2¼"
Diameter—4¼"

No. 5301
9 oz.
Luncheon Goblet
Height—5¾"

No. 5301
5 oz.
Ice Cream
Height—3½"

No. 5301
5 oz. Ftd.
Sherbet
Height—2½"

No. 5301
3½ oz. Ftd.
Oyster Cocktail
Height—2¾"

No. 5301
8 oz.
Ale Goblet
Height—6¼"

Color: crystal, amber, cobalt, red

Terrace is one Duncan pattern that collectors seek for the rich red and cobalt blue colors. Few buy amber or crystal. Crystal Terrace is readily recognized as the blank on which First Love is etched. Finding enough colored Terrace to photograph has been difficult, but I have slowly accumulated what you see.

Terrace collectors are generally not very fond of decorated ware as illustrated by the gold decorated amber sugar and creamer. Keep that in mind if you are collecting with future selling in mind!

Note the crystal bowls with cobalt bases. Learn to recognize that base pattern so you do not pass one of these!

	Crystal/ Amber	Cobalt/ Red		Crystal/ Amber	Cobalt/ Red
Ash tray, 3½", sq.	17.50	30.00	Plate, 11", hdld.	40.00	
Ash tray, 4¾", sq.	22.00	95.00	Plate, 11", hdld., cracker w/ring	40.00	95.00
Bowl, 4¼", finger, #5111½	35.00	35.00	Plate, 11", hdld., sandwich	40.00	
Bowl, 6¾" x 4¼", ftd., flared rim	30.00		Plate, 12", torte, rolled edge	40.00	
Bowl, 8" sq. x 2½", hdld.	55.00		Plate, 13", cake, ftd.	75.00	195.00
Bowl, 9" x 4½", ftd.	42.00		*Plate, 13", torte, flat edge	50.00	
Bowl, 9½" x 2½", hdld.	45.00		Plate, 13", torte, rolled edge	57.50	
Bowl, 10" x 3¾", ftd., flared rim	55.00		Plate, 13¼", torte	57.50	185.00
* Bowl, 10¼" x 4¾", ftd.	75.00	125.00	Relish, 6" x 1¾", hdld., 2 pt.	20.00	45.00
Bowl, 11" x 3¼", flared rim	32.50		Relish, 9", 4 pt.	35.00	95.00
Butter or cheese, 7" sq. x 1¼"	115.00		Relish, 10½" x 1½", hdld., 5 pt.	75.00	
Candle, 3", 1-lite	25.00	65.00	Relish, 12", 4 pt., hdld.	40.00	
Candle, 4", low	25.00		Relish, 12", 5 pt., hdld.	50.00	
Candlesticks, 1-lite, bobeche & prisms	175.00		Relish, 12", 5 pt., w/lid	150.00	275.00
Candlesticks, 2-lite, 7" x 9¼", bobeche & prisms.	225.00		Salad dressing bowl, 2 pt., 5½" x 4¼"	45.00	95.00
Candy urn, w/lid	135.00	395.00	Saucer, sq	6.00	12.00
Cheese stand, 3" x 5¼"	25.00	40.00	Saucer, demi	5.00	
Cocktail shaker, metal lid	85.00	185.00	Stem, 3¾", 1 oz., cordial, #5111½	42.50	
Comport, w/lid, 8¾" x 5½"	135.00	395.00	Stem, 3¾", 4½ oz., oyster cocktail,		
Comport, 3½" x 4¾" w	30.00	75.00	#5111½	22.50	
Creamer, 3", 10 oz.	18.00	40.00	Stem, 4", 5 oz., ice cream, #5111½	14.00	
Cup	15.00	35.00	Stem, 4½", 3½ oz., cocktail, #5111½	22.50	
Cup, demi	20.00		Stem, 5", 5 oz., saucer champagne,		
Mayonnaise, 5½" x 2½", ftd., hdld.,			#5111½	18.00	
#111	35.00		Stem, 5¼", 3 oz., wine, #5111½	32.50	
Mayonnaise, 5½" x 3½", crimped,	32.00		Stem, 5¼", 5 oz., ftd. juice, #5111½	24.00	
Mayonnaise, 5¾" x 3", w/dish hdld.			Stem, 5¾", 10 oz., low luncheon		
tray	35.00	75.00	goblet, #5111½	17.50	
Mayonnaise, w/7" tray, hdld	35.00		Stem, 6", 4½ oz., claret, #5111½	45.00	
Nappy, 5½" x 2", div., hdld.	18.00		Stem, 6½", 12 oz., ftd. ice tea, #5111½	35.00	
Nappy, 6" x 1¾", hdld.	22.00	35.00	Stem, 6¾", 10 oz., tall water goblet,		
Pitcher	295.00	825.00	#5111½	24.00	
Plate, 6"	12.00	25.00	Stem, 6¾", 14 oz., ftd. ice tea, #5111½	35.00	
Plate, 6", hdld., lemon	14.00	30.00	Stem, cordial	17.50	
Plate, 6", sq.	14.00	30.00	Sugar, 3", 10 oz.	15.00	40.00
Plate, 7"	17.50	35.00	Sugar lid	12.50	60.00
Plate, 7½"	18.00	35.00	Tumbler	17.50	45.00
Plate, 7½", sq.	19.00	38.00	Tray, 8" x 2", hdld., celery	17.50	
Plate, 8½"	20.00	25.00	Urn, 4½" x 4½"	27.50	
Plate, 9", sq.	35.00	75.00	Urn, 10½" x 4½"	135.00	395.00
Plate, 11"	47.50	90.00	Vase, 10, ftd.	115.00	

*Colored foot

Colors: Rose pink, Topaz yellow; some green

Pink Trojan is a rapid seller and yellow has picked up of late. Until recently, there was an overabundance of yellow being marketed due to the dispersal of several large sets. New collectors are once again having difficulty finding serving pieces at prices they are hoping to pay.

Trojan stemware can be found except for cordials and clarets in both colors. Clarets are nearly unattainable in most Fostoria patterns. If you need them, you had better buy them whenever you find them!

Price increases for soup and cereal bowls have surpassed those for all other Trojan pieces. If you find either one, be pleased and pull out the checkbook.

	Rose	Topaz
Ash tray, #2350, lg.	50.00	40.00
Ash tray, #2350, sm.	30.00	25.00
Bottle, salad dressing, #2983	525.00	350.00
Bowl, baker, #2375, 9"		65.00
Bowl, bonbon, #2375		15.00
Bowl, bouillon, #2375, ftd.		18.00
Bowl, cream soup, #2375, ftd.	27.50	22.50
Bowl, finger, #869/2283, w/6¼" liner	45.00	40.00
Bowl, lemon, #2375	18.00	16.00
Bowl, #2394, 3 ftd., 4½", mint	25.00	22.00
Bowl, #2375, fruit, 5"	20.00	18.00
Bowl, #2354, 3 ftd., 6"	30.00	35.00
Bowl, cereal, #2375, 6½"	47.50	37.50
Bowl, soup, #2375, 7"	100.00	95.00
Bowl, lg. dessert, #2375, 2 hdld	85.00	75.00
Bowl, #2395, 10"	110.00	75.00
Bowl, #2395, scroll, 10"	75.00	65.00
Bowl, combination #2415, w/candleholder handles	210.00	175.00
Bowl, #2375, centerpiece, flared optic, 12"	50.00	45.00
Bowl, #2394, centerpiece, ftd., 12"	50.00	45.00
Bowl, #2375, centerpiece, mushroom, 12"	55.00	50.00
Candlestick, #2394, 2"	22.00	20.00
Candlestick, #2375, flared, 3"	25.00	22.00
Candlestick, #2395½, scroll, 5"	65.00	60.00
Candy, w/cover, #2394, ¼ lb.	275.00	250.00
Candy, w/cover, #2394, ½ lb.	200.00	175.00
Celery, #2375, 11½"	40.00	30.00
Cheese & cracker, set, #2375, #2368	75.00	65.00
Comport, #5299 or #2400, 6"	35.00	30.00
Comport, #2375, 7"	50.00	45.00
Creamer, #2375, ftd.	22.50	20.00
Creamer, tea, #2375½	60.00	50.00
Cup, after dinner, #2375	50.00	40.00
Cup, #2375½, ftd.	20.00	18.00
Decanter, #2439, 9"	1,000.00	850.00
Goblet, claret, #5099, 4 oz., 6"	135.00	90.00
Goblet, cocktail, #5099, 3 oz., 5¼"	32.00	30.00
Goblet, cordial, #5099, ¾ oz., 4"	100.00	70.00
Goblet, water, #5299, 10 oz., 8¼"	37.50	27.50
Goblet, wine, #5099, 3 oz., 5½"	60.00	45.00
Grapefruit, #5282½	60.00	50.00
Grapefruit liner, #945½	50.00	40.00
Ice bucket, #2375	75.00	65.00
Ice dish, #2451, #2455	45.00	35.00

	Rose	Topaz
Ice dish liner (tomato, crab, fruit), #2451	20.00	10.00
Mayonnaise ladle	30.00	30.00
Mayonnaise, w/liner, #2375	60.00	50.00
Oil, ftd., #2375	350.00	235.00
Oyster, cocktail, #5099, ftd.	30.00	27.50
Parfait, #5099	70.00	50.00
Pitcher, #5000	375.00	295.00
Plate, #2375, canape	30.00	20.00
Plate, #2375, bread/butter, 6"	6.00	5.00
Plate, #2375, salad, 7½"	9.00	8.00
Plate, 2375, cream soup or mayo liner, 7½",	9.00	8.00
Plate, #2375, luncheon, 8¾"	17.50	15.00
Plate, #2375, sm., dinner, 9½"	22.50	20.00
Plate, #2375, cake, handled, 10"	35.00	32.50
Plate, #2375, grill, rare, 10¼"	100.00	90.00
Plate, #2375, dinner, 10¼"	75.00	60.00
Plate, #2375, chop, 13"	50.00	50.00
Plate, #2375, round, 14"	55.00	50.00
Platter, #2375, 12"	70.00	60.00
Platter, #2375, 15"	150.00	120.00
Relish, #2375, 8½"		35.00
Relish, #2350, 3 pt., rnd., 8¾"	45.00	40.00
Sauce boat, #2375	125.00	100.00
Sauce plate, #2375	45.00	40.00
Saucer, #2375, after dinner	10.00	10.00
Saucer, #2375	6.00	5.00
Shaker, #2375, pr., ftd.	100.00	80.00
Sherbet, #5099, high, 6"	25.00	20.00
Sherbet, #5099, low, 4¼"	20.00	16.00
Sugar, #2375½, ftd.	22.50	20.00
Sugar cover, #2375½	135.00	110.00
Sugar pail, #2378	185.00	125.00
Sugar, tea, #2375½	55.00	45.00
Sweetmeat, #2375	18.00	18.00
Tray, 11", ctr. hdld, #2375	35.00	32.50
Tray, #2429, service & lemon insert		250.00
Tumbler, #5099, ftd., 2½ oz.	55.00	40.00
Tumbler, #5099, ftd., 5 oz., 4½"	30.00	25.00
Tumbler, #5099, ftd., 9 oz., 5¼"	22.50	17.50
Tumbler, #5099, ftd., 12 oz., 6"	37.50	30.00
Vase, #2417, 8"	145.00	120.00
Vase, #4105, 8"	225.00	160.00
Vase, #2369, 9"		225.00
Whipped cream bowl, #2375	15.00	12.00
Whipped cream pail, #2378	135.00	115.00

Note: See page 89 for stem identification.

On the bottom of page 205, the two-handled plate in the top row served as a cake plate, and also, as the cracker plate for the cheese pictured in the bottom row. They became separated in the photos. Speaking of separation, the grapefruit liner is shown next to the mayonnaise in row 2 on page 206, but the grapefruit itself is in row 2 on page 207. The liner sits inside the grapefruit with ice packed around the liner to keep its contents cold!

Additionally, in row three of page 207 are two ice dishes. There are three different inserts for these which work on the same principle as the grapefruits. The first insert is a crab and the other is a fruit. The missing style was known as a tomato liner. Often there is confusion between the two sizes of candy jars shown in the bottom row. The taller candy on the end is the one-half pound and the shorter is the one-quarter pound size.

If you order or ship via ads, you need to know the following Fostoria facts: liners for cream soups and mayonnaise liners are the same piece; two-handled cake plates come with and without an indent in the center. The indented version also serves as a plate for one of two styles of cheese comports; bonbon, lemon dish, sweetmeat, and whipped cream bowls all come with loop or bow handles; and sugars come with a straight and ruffled edge. Strangely enough, it is the ruffled top sugar that takes a lid.

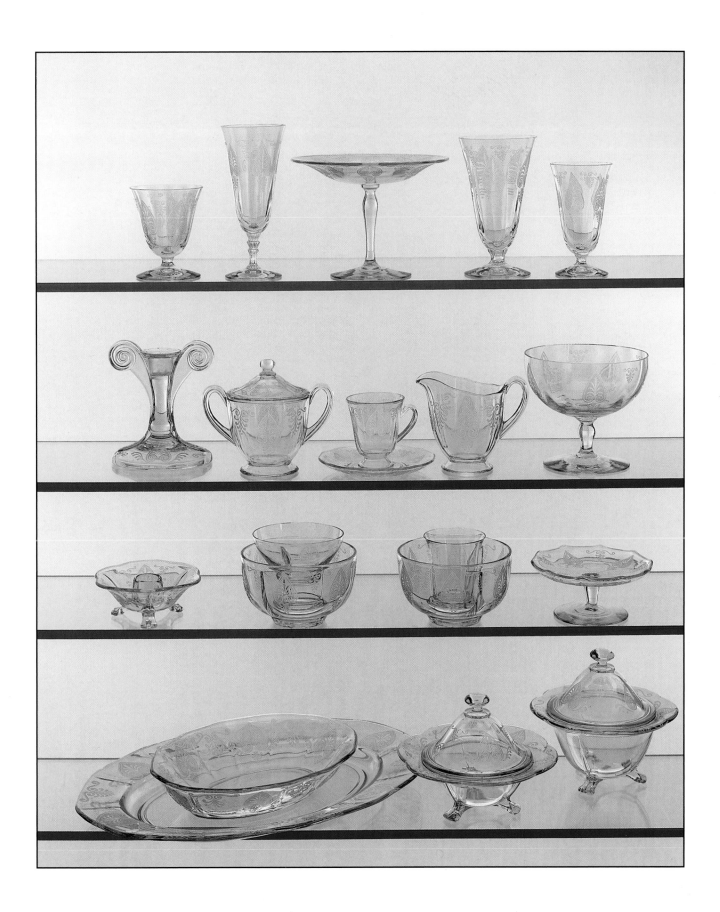

Colors: crystal, Flamingo pink, Moongleam green, Marigold amber/yellow; Sahara yellow; some Alexandrite (rare)

Prices for Twist have made increases in all colors of stemware and tumblers. Few collectors search for crystal. Twist pieces are marked with the H in diamond on the stem of the piece if you have difficulty finding it.

	Crystal	Flamingo	Moongleam	Marigold	Alexandrite	Sahara
Baker, 9", oval	25.00	35.00	45.00	60.00		
Bonbon, individual	15.00	35.00	40.00	40.00		
Bonbon, 6", 2 hdld.	10.00	20.00	25.00	30.00		
Bottle, French dressing	50.00	90.00	110.00	135.00		
Bowl, cream soup/bouillon	15.00	25.00	32.00	50.00		
Bowl, ftd., almond/indiv. sugar	35.00	45.00	55.00	65.00		
Bowl, indiv. nut	10.00	25.00	40.00	45.00		
Bowl, 4", nappy	10.00	20.00	25.00	30.00		
Bowl, 6", 2 hdld.	7.00	15.00	18.00	20.00		
Bowl, 6", 2 hdld., jelly	10.00	20.00	28.00	30.00		
Bowl, 6", 2 hdld., mint	7.00	20.00	35.00	30.00		20.00
Bowl, 8", low ftd.		55.00	60.00	75.00		
Bowl, 8", nappy, ground bottom	20.00	40.00	45.00	50.00		
Bowl, 8", nasturtium, rnd.	45.00	70.00	90.00	80.00	450.00	80.00
Bowl, 8", nasturtium, oval	45.00	70.00	90.00	80.00		
Bowl, 9", floral	25.00	40.00	50.00	65.00		
Bowl, 9", floral, rolled edge	30.00	40.00	45.00	65.00		
Bowl, 12", floral, oval, 4 ft.	45.00	100.00	110.00	90.00	550.00	85.00
Bowl, 12", floral, rnd., 4 ft.	30.00	40.00	50.00	65.00		
Candlestick, 2", 1-lite		40.00	50.00	85.00		
Cheese dish, 6", 2 hdld.	10.00	20.00	25.00	30.00		
Claret, 4 oz.	15.00	30.00	40.00	50.00		
Cocktail shaker, metal top			400.00			
Comport, 7", tall	40.00	60.00	100.00	150.00		
Creamer, hotel, oval	25.00	40.00	45.00	50.00		
Creamer, individual (unusual)	18.00	35.00	60.00	65.00		
Creamer, zigzag handles, ftd.	20.00	40.00	50.00	70.00		
Cup, zigzag handles	10.00	25.00	32.00	35.00		
Grapefruit, ftd.	15.00	25.00	35.00	60.00		
Ice tub	50.00	125.00	110.00	125.00		125.00
Ice bucket					425.00	
Pitcher, 3 pint	95.00	175.00	230.00			
Mayonnaise	35.00	65.00	80.00	80.00		
Mayonnaise, #1252½	20.00	35.00	45.00	50.00		
Mustard, w/cover, spoon	40.00	90.00	100.00	100.00		
Oil bottle, 2½ oz., w/#78 stopper	50.00	100.00	120.00	120.00		
Oil bottle, 4 oz., w/#78 stopper	50.00	110.00	120.00	120.00		
Plate, cream soup liner	5.00	7.00	10.00	15.00		
Plate, 8", Kraft cheese	20.00	40.00	60.00	50.00		
Plate, 8", ground bottom	7.00	14.00	20.00	30.00		20.00
Plate, 10", utility, 3 ft.	30.00	50.00	60.00			
Plate, 12", 2 hdld., sandwich	30.00	60.00	90.00	80.00		
Plate, 12", muffin, 2 hdld., turned sides	40.00	80.00	90.00	80.00		
Plate, 13", 3 part, relish	10.00	17.00	22.00	35.00		
Platter, 12"	15.00	50.00	60.00	75.00		
Salt & pepper, ftd.	100.00	140.00	160.00	200.00		140.00
Saucer	3.00	5.00	7.00	10.00		
Stem, 2½ oz., wine, 2 block stem	30.00	35.00	40.00	45.00		
Stem, 3 oz., oyster cocktail, ftd.	10.00	30.00	40.00	50.00		
Stem, 3 oz., cocktail, 2 block stem	10.00	30.00	40.00	50.00		
Stem, 5 oz., saucer champagne, 2 block stem	10.00	35.00	25.00	30.00		
Stem, 5 oz., sherbet, 2 block stem	10.00	18.00	40.00	28.00		
Stem, 9 oz., luncheon (1 block in stem) *	40.00	60.00	70.00	70.00		
Sugar, ftd.	20.00	30.00	37.50	60.00		
Sugar, hotel, oval	25.00	35.00	40.00	50.00		
Sugar, individual (unusual)	18.00	35.00	60.00	65.00		
Sugar, w/cover, zigzag handles	25.00	40.00	60.00	80.00		
Tray, 7", pickle, ground bottom	7.00	15.00	22.00	25.00		
Tray, 10", celery	30.00	50.00	50.00	40.00		40.00
Tray, 13", celery	25.00	35.00	60.00	50.00		
Tumbler, 5 oz., soda, flat bottom	10.00	22.00	32.00	36.00		
Tumbler, 6 oz., ftd., soda	10.00	22.00	32.00	36.00		
Tumbler, 8 oz., flat, ground bottom	15.00	35.00	70.00	40.00		
Tumbler, 8 oz., soda, straight & flared	12.00	25.00	30.00	40.00		
Tumbler, 9 oz., ftd. soda	20.00	40.00	50.00	60.00		
Tumbler, 12 oz., iced tea, flat bottom	20.00	45.00	60.00	70.00		
Tumbler, 12 oz., ftd. iced tea	20.00	40.00	50.00	60.00		

*also made 2 block stem, 9 oz.

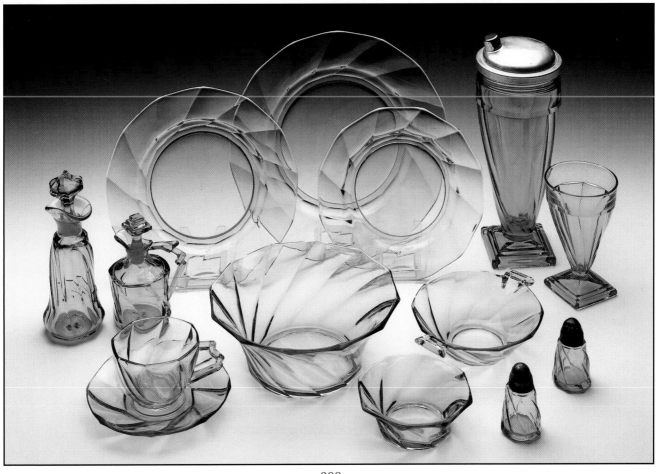

Colors: crystal, pink

Valencia is frequently confused with another Cambridge pattern, Minerva. Notice in the photo of Valencia that the lines in the pattern are perpendicular to each other (think of a volleyball net). On Minerva, the lines in the pattern meet on a diagonal forming diamonds instead of squares. I've explained that in every book, but had to settle a dispute between a couple of longtime dealers at a recent show in Chicago. Valencia is found so infrequently that dealers have to look it up when they do find it.

Every time I write about Valencia, I have to logically imagine how much more expensive the pieces pictured would be if they were only Rose Point! Most pieces shown are acutely desired in Rose Point, but are only just being noticed in Valencia. Valencia items are, without a doubt, rarer than the enormously popular Rose Point. Yet, there are legions of collectors searching for Rose Point and only a small number buying Valencia.

Some of the more exceptional pieces pictured include the covered honey dish, six-piece relish on #3500 12" plate, and the 15" long, three-part, two-handled relish. That metal-handled piece on the left of the photo behind the squared honey dish was called a sugar basket by Cambridge. This is similar to Fostoria's sugar pail, but closer in size to Fostoria's whipped cream pail. Different terminology used by glass companies causes problems for collectors.

	Crystal		Crystal
Ash tray, #3500/124, 3¼", round	10.00	Relish, #1402/91, 8", 3 comp.	30.00
Ash tray, #3500/126, 4", round	14.00	Relish, #3500/64, 10", 3 comp.	32.00
Ash tray, #3500/128, 4½", round	18.00	Relish, #3500/65, 10", 4 comp.	35.00
Basket, #3500/55, 6", 2 hdld., ftd.	22.00	Relish, #3500/67, 12", 6 pc.	135.00
Bowl, #3500/49, 5", hdld.	18.00	Relish, #3500/112, 15", 3 pt., 2 hdld.	90.00
Bowl, #3500/37, 6", cereal	25.00	Relish, #3500/13, 15", 4 pt., 2 hdld.	90.00
Bowl, #1402/89, 6", 2 hdld.	18.00	Salt and pepper, #3400/18	65.00
Bowl, #1402/88, 6", 2 hdld., div.	20.00	Saucer, #3500/1	3.00
Bowl, #3500/115, 9½", 2 hdld., ftd.	38.00	Stem, #1402, cordial	70.00
Bowl, #1402/82, 10"	35.00	Stem, #1402, wine	35.00
Bowl, #1402/88, 11"	40.00	Stem, #1402, cocktail	22.00
Bowl, #1402/95, salad dressing, div.	45.00	Stem, #1402, claret	45.00
Bowl, #1402/100, finger, w/liner	35.00	Stem, #1402, oyster cocktail	20.00
Bowl, #3500, ftd., finger	30.00	Stem, #1402, low sherbet	14.00
Candy dish, w/cover, #3500/103	125.00	Stem, #1402, tall sherbet	17.00
Celery, #1402/94, 12"	32.00	Stem, #1402, goblet	25.00
Cigarette holder, #1066, ftd.	45.00	Stem, #3500, cordial	70.00
Comport, #3500/36, 6"	30.00	Stem, #3500, wine, 2½ oz.	32.00
Comport, #3500/37, 7"	45.00	Stem, #3500, cocktail, 3 oz	20.00
Creamer, #3500/14	17.00	Stem, #3500, claret, 4½ oz.	45.00
Creamer, #3500/15, individual	20.00	Stem, #3500, oyster cocktail, 4½ oz.	18.00
Cup, #3500/1	20.00	Stem, #3500, low sherbet, 7 oz.	14.00
Decanter, #3400/92, 32 oz., ball	175.00	Stem, #3500, tall sherbet, 7 oz.	16.00
Decanter, #3400/119, 12 oz., ball	135.00	Stem, #3500, goblet, long bowl	25.00
Honey dish, w/cover, #3500/139	135.00	Stem, #3500, goblet, short bowl	22.00
Ice pail, #1402/52	75.00	Sugar, #3500/14	15.00
Mayonnaise, #3500/59, 3 pc.	45.00	Sugar, #3500/15, individual	20.00
Nut, #3400/71, 3", 4 ftd.	60.00	Sugar basket, #3500/13	110.00
Perfume, #3400/97, 2 oz., perfume	125.00	Tumbler, #3400/92, 2½ oz.	25.00
Plate, #3500/167, 7½", salad	10.00	Tumbler, #3400/100, 13 oz.	25.00
Plate, #3500/5, 8½", breakfast	12.00	Tumbler, #3400/115, 14 oz.	27.00
Plate, #1402, 11½", sandwich, hdld.	25.00	Tumbler, #3500, 2½ oz., ftd.	20.00
Plate, #3500/39, 12", ftd.	35.00	Tumbler, #3500, 3 oz., ftd.	16.00
Plate, #3500/67, 12"	30.00	Tumbler, #3500, 5 oz., ftd.	15.00
Plate, #3500/38, 13", torte	35.00	Tumbler, #3500, 10 oz., ftd.	16.00
Pitcher, 80oz., Doulton, #3400/141	295.00	Tumbler, #3500, 12 oz., ftd.	20.00
Relish, #3500/68, 5½", 2 comp.	20.00	Tumbler, #3500, 13 oz., ftd.	20.00
Relish, #3500/69, 6½", 3 comp.	25.00	Tumbler, #3500, 16 oz., ftd.	22.00

Colors: blue, yellow, pink, green

Fostoria line numbers which can also be correlated into June and Fairfax listings are listed for each piece of Versailles. The sugar and creamer are sitting on the rarely seen lemon/service tray in the bottom photo. The plain, six-sided insert that belongs in the center is usually missing. The 7" soup bowl shown behind the finger bowl in the top photo is the nemesis of most collectors. There is a liner for the finger bowl, missing from my inventory. In front is the hard to find canapé set which has an indent for the 2½ ounce footed bar tumbler.

Be sure to see page 89 for Fostoria stemware identification. Confusion reigns because stem heights are so analogous. Here, shapes and capacities are more important. Clarets and cordials are the most troublesome stems to find.

	Pink, Green	Blue	Yellow
Ash tray, #2350	24.00	30.00	25.00
Bottle, #2083, salad dressing, crystal glass top	425.00	750.00	395.00
Bottle, #2375, salad dressing, w/ sterling top or colored top	425.00	750.00	395.00
Bowl, #2375, baker, 9"	55.00	125.00	55.00
Bowl, #2375, bonbon	15.00	25.00	17.50
Bowl, #2375, bouillon, ftd.	20.00	35.00	20.00
Bowl, #2375, cream soup, ftd.	22.00	30.00	22.00
Bowl, #869/2283, finger, w/6" liner	40.00	65.00	40.00
Bowl, lemon	15.00	22.00	17.50
Bowl, 4½", mint, 3 ftd.	27.50	40.00	27.50
Bowl, #2375, fruit, 5"	22.00	35.00	25.00
Bowl, #2394, 3 ftd., 6"			30.00
Bowl, #2375, cereal, 6½"	35.00	65.00	35.00
Bowl, #2375, soup, 7"	70.00	110.00	70.00
Bowl, #2375, lg., dessert, 2 hdld.	30.00	110.00	50.00
Bowl, #2375, baker, 10"	50.00	95.00	50.00
Bowl, #2395, centerpiece, scroll, 10"	55.00	75.00	55.00
Bowl, #2375, centerpiece, flared top, 12"	40.00	60.00	45.00
Bowl, #2394, ftd., 12"	35.00	60.00	45.00
Bowl, #2375½, oval, centerpiece 13"	55.00	110.00	
Candlestick, #2394, 2"	20.00	27.50	20.00
Candlestick, #2395, 3"	17.50	35.00	22.00
Candlestick, #2395½, scroll, 5"	35.00	55.00	35.00
Candy, w/cover, #2331, 3 pt.	155.00	250.00	
Candy, w/cover, #2394, ¼ lb.			195.00
Candy, w/cover, #2394, ½ lb.			175.00
Celery, #2375, 11½"	40.00	95.00	45.00
Cheese & cracker, #2375 or #2368, set	85.00	125.00	85.00
Comport, #5098, 3"	25.00	40.00	25.00
Comport, #5099/2400, 6"	30.00	50.00	30.00
Comport, #2375, 7"	32.50	65.00	
Comport, #2400, 8"	65.00	110.00	
Creamer, #2375½, ftd.	17.50	22.50	15.00
Creamer, #2375½, tea	45.00	60.00	45.00
Cup, #2375, after dinner	40.00	60.00	40.00
Cup, #2375½, ftd.	17.50	21.00	19.00
Decanter, #2439, 9"	1,200.00	2,000.00	750.00
Goblet, cordial, #5098 or #5099, ¾ oz., 4"	85.00	110.00	70.00
Goblet, #5098 or #5099, claret, 4 oz., 6"	85.00	135.00	85.00
Goblet, cocktail, #5098 or #5099, 3 oz., 5¼"	25.00	37.50	28.00
Goblet, water, #5098 or #5099, 10 oz., 8¼"	27.50	40.00	30.00
Goblet, wine, #5098 or #5099, 3 oz., 5½"	40.00	75.00	45.00
Grapefruit, #5082½	50.00	75.00	45.00
Grapefruit liner, #945½	40.00	75.00	40.00
Ice bucket, #2375	65.00	95.00	80.00
Ice dish, #2451	35.00	55.00	35.00
Ice dish liner (tomato, crab, fruit), #2451	20.00	20.00	10.00
Mayonnaise, w/liner, #2375	35.00	50.00	40.00
Mayonnaise ladle	30.00	40.00	30.00
Oil, #2375, ftd.	395.00	595.00	350.00
Oyster cocktail, #5098 or #5099	22.50	32.50	25.00
Parfait, #5098 or #5099	35.00	45.00	35.00
Pitcher, #5000	350.00	550.00	375.00
Plate, #2375, bread/butter, 6"	4.00	5.00	4.00
Plate, #2375, canape, 6"	25.00	40.00	32.00
Plate, #2375, salad, 7½"	6.00	12.00	8.00
Plate, #2375, cream soup or mayo liner, 7½"	8.00	16.00	9.00
Plate, #2375, luncheon, 8¾"	8.00	20.00	10.00
Plate, #2375, sm., dinner, 9½"	22.00	35.00	25.00
Plate, #2375, cake, 2 hdld., 10"	26.00	45.00	30.00
Plate, #2375, dinner, 10¼"	70.00	100.00	65.00
Plate, #2375, chop, 13"	50.00	85.00	45.00
Platter, #2375, 12"	75.00	100.00	75.00
Platter, #2375, 15"	110.00	175.00	110.00
Relish, #2375, 8½"	30.00		35.00
Sauce boat, #2375	80.00	145.00	80.00
Sauce boat plate, #2375	25.00	55.00	25.00
Saucer, #2375, after dinner	7.50	10.00	7.50
Saucer, #2375	4.00	6.00	5.00
Shaker, #2375, pr., ftd.	95.00	150.00	95.00
Sherbet, #5098/5099, high, 6"	20.00	27.50	22.50
Sherbet, #5098/5099, low, 4¼"	20.00	25.00	22.00
Sugar, #2375½, ftd.	15.00	20.00	15.00
Sugar cover, #2375½	140.00	200.00	125.00
Sugar pail, #2378	155.00	235.00	145.00
Sugar, #2375½, tea	42.50	55.00	42.50
Sweetmeat, #2375	14.00	20.00	15.00
Tray, #2375, ctr. hdld., 11"	30.00	45.00	35.00
Tray, service & lemon	325.00	450.00	250.00
Tumbler, flat, old-fashioned (pink only)	100.00		
Tumbler, flat, tea (pink only)	110.00		
Tumbler, #5098 or #5099 2½ oz., ftd.	45.00	65.00	45.00
Tumbler, #5098 or #5099, 5 oz., ftd., 4½"	20.00	35.00	22.00
Tumbler, #5098 or #5099, 9 oz., ftd., 5¼"	20.00	37.50	21.50
Tumbler, #5098 or #5099 12 oz., ftd., 6"	35.00	55.00	32.00
Vase, #2417, 8"			165.00
Vase, #4100, 8"	150.00	275.00	
Vase, #2385, fan, ftd., 8½"	135.00	250.00	
Whipped cream bowl, #2375	15.00	18.00	13.00
Whipped cream pail, #2378	135.00	175.00	125.00

Note: See page 89 for stem identification.

Colors: amber, green; some blue

A blown style of Vesper grapefruit with an etched liner is shown in the top row. Both pieces are etched; do not accept a plain liner for the price listed as Vesper. There is a moulded style grapefruit that doubled as a mayonnaise. There is no inside liner and it is similar in shape to the footed bowl pictured first in row 3. Other companies called these shrimp dishes. You filled the inside compote with shrimp or fruit and put ice in the larger container to keep it chilled. Since ice was a valuable commodity in those days, only the well-to-do had these items and consequently they are in short supply.

Vesper comes on stem line #5093 and tumbler line #5100. An example of each stem and tumbler is shown on row 2. The shapes are slightly different from those Fostoria etches found on the Fairfax blank (page 89). The #5093 stems are left to right: cordial, low sherbet, cocktail, wine, high sherbet, claret, parfait, and water goblet. The #5100 footed tumblers left to right are as follows: ice tea, water, juice, oyster cocktail, and bar glass. I hope this will help eliminate confusion.

Row 3 shows the flat creamer, footed bouillon with liner, footed cream soup with liner, flat cream soup with liner, and the finger bowl with liner.

Row 5 shows shallow soup, fruit, cereal, deep soup, and 8" vegetable bowls.

All other pieces should be easily recognized. Hopefully, this display on shelves will make it simpler. I hope you like the way it turned out.

Amber Vesper is not as collected as some other Fostoria colors; but as you can see here, amber has a multitude of pieces! Many are easily found; others will take some patience and searching. Etched amber Fostoria patterns might possibly be the "sleepers" in the glass collecting field. I've seen gorgeous table settings made with amber glass and the appropriate accoutrements.

Photos of blue and green Vesper have been deficient in my earlier books. I have tried to remedy that on page 217! There is little blue Vesper to be found on the market at a price collectors are willing to pay! Rarely found, attractive, colored glassware often gets priced "out of this world" as one collector put it! Green Vesper is more easily found than blue, but has captivated few collectors at the present time.

	Green	Amber	Blue
Ash tray, #2350, 4"	25.00	30.00	
Bowl, #2350, bouillon, ftd.	12.00	17.50	30.00
Bowl, #2350, cream soup, flat.................................	25.00	30.00	
Bowl, #2350, cream soup, ftd.................................	20.00	20.00	35.00
Bowl, #2350, fruit, 5½"	10.00	12.50	25.00
Bowl, #2350, cereal, sq. or rnd., 6½"	25.00	30.00	45.00
Bowl, #2267, low, ftd., 7"	20.00	25.00	
Bowl, #2350, soup, shallow, 7¾"........................	25.00	40.00	60.00
Bowl, soup, deep, 8¼"		40.00	
Bowl, 8⅞"...	30.00	40.00	
Bowl, #2350, baker, oval, 9"................................	60.00	70.00	90.00
Bowl, #2350, rd.	40.00	50.00	
Bowl, #2350, baker, oval, 10½"	75.00	85.00	125.00
Bowl, #2375, flared bowl, 10½"..........................	35.00	35.00	
Bowl, #2350, ped., ftd., 10½".............................	40.00	55.00	
Bowl, #2329, console, rolled edge, 11".................	35.00	37.50	
Bowl, #2375, 3 ftd., 12½".................................	40.00	47.50	
Bowl, #2371, oval, 13"......................................	40.00	50.00	
Bowl, #2329, rolled edge, 13".............................	40.00	45.00	
Bowl, #2329, rolled edge, 14".............................	45.00	50.00	
Butter dish, #2350..	300.00	800.00	
Candlestick, #2324, 2"......................................	17.50	25.00	
Candlestick, #2394, 3"......................................	15.00	17.50	40.00
Candlestick, #2324, 4"......................................	15.00	20.00	
Candlestick, #2394, 9"......................................	55.00	90.00	100.00
Candy jar, w/cover, #2331, 3 pt.	110.00	110.00	250.00
Candy jar, w/cover, #2250, ftd., ½ lb......................	225.00	195.00	
Celery, #2350	17.00	22.00	45.00
Cheese, #2368, ftd.	18.00	20.00	
Comport, 6"...	22.50	25.00	50.00

	Green	Amber	Blue
Comport, #2327 (twisted stem), 7½"	27.50	30.00	55.00
Comport, 8"	40.00	50.00	65.00
Creamer, #2350½, ftd.	14.00	20.00	
Creamer, #2315½, fat, ftd.	18.00	22.00	35.00
Creamer, #2350½, flat		22.00	
Cup, #2350	14.00	15.00	35.00
Cup, #2350, after dinner	40.00	40.00	85.00
Cup, #2350½, ftd.	14.00	15.00	35.00
Egg cup, #2350		40.00	
Finger bowl and liner, #869/2283, 6"	27.50	30.00	55.00
Grapefruit, #5082½, blown	50.00	50.00	90.00
Grapefruit liner, #945½, blown	45.00	45.00	55.00
Grapefruit, #2315, molded	50.00	55.00	
Ice bucket, #2378	60.00	70.00	
Oyster cocktail, #5100	16.00	20.00	40.00
Pickle, #2350	22.00	25.00	40.00
Pitcher, #5100, ftd.	300.00	335.00	500.00
Plate, #2350, bread/butter, 6"	4.50	5.00	10.00
Plate, #2350, salad, 7½"	6.00	6.50	15.00
Plate, #2350, luncheon, 8½"	7.50	8.50	20.00
Plate, #2321, Maj Jongg (canape), 8¾"		50.00	
Plate, #2350, sm., dinner, 9½"	18.00	22.50	35.00
Plate, dinner, 10½"	35.00	45.00	
Plate, #2287, ctr. hand., 11"	22.50	30.00	55.00
Plate, chop, 13¾"	32.00	37.50	75.00
Plate, #2350, server, 14"	55.00	65.00	100.00
Plate, w/indent for cheese, 11"	20.00	25.00	
Platter, #2350, 10½"	35.00	40.00	
Platter, #2350, 12"	50.00	60.00	110.00
Platter, #2350, 15",	85.00	95.00	150.00
Salt & pepper, #5100, pr.	70.00	80.00	
Sauce boat, w/liner, #2350	135.00	150.00	
Saucer, #2350, after dinner	10.00	10.00	25.00
Saucer, #2350	4.00	4.50	5.00
Stem, #5093, high sherbet	16.00	17.50	32.00
Stem, #5093, water goblet	25.00	27.50	45.00
Stem, #5093, low sherbet	15.00	17.00	25.00
Stem, #5093, parfait	35.00	40.00	60.00
Stem, #5093, cordial, ¾ oz.	70.00	75.00	135.00
Stem, #5093, wine, 2¾ oz.	35.00	37.50	60.00
Stem, #5093, cocktail, 3 oz.	25.00	27.50	45.00
Sugar, #2350½, flat		20.00	
Sugar, #2315, fat ftd.	18.00	20.00	32.00
Sugar, #2350½, ftd.	14.00	16.00	
Sugar, lid	185.00	175.00	
Tumbler, #5100, ftd., 2 oz.	35.00	45.00	65.00
Tumbler, #5100, ftd., 5 oz.	15.00	20.00	40.00
Tumbler, #5100, ftd., 9 oz.	16.00	20.00	45.00
Tumbler, #5100, ftd., 12 oz.	25.00	35.00	60.00
Urn, #2324, small	65.00	90.00	
Urn, large	75.00	100.00	
Vase, #2292, 8"	85.00	95.00	150.00
Vanity set, combination cologne/ powder & stopper	225.00	250.00	365.00

Note: See stemware identification on page 89.

VICTORIAN, #1425 A.H. Heisey Co., 1933 – 1953

Colors: crystal, Sahara, Cobalt, rare in pale Zircon

I have seen more Victorian for sale in the last year than I have ever seen before. Most of the pieces that were fairly priced sold quickly. Those items that were priced high because it was Heisey did not sell even though there were some rarely found pieces in the sets. I might point out that sets are more difficult to sell than individual pieces because of cost and the make up of the set. Collectors rarely buy sets of anything. Few collectors are willing to buy a set containing pieces they already have just to get a piece or two that they want. A display of any set will attract more collectors than only having a few pieces offered. Similarly, offering those pieces individually and giving several people the chance to buy is the way to go rather than pricing the whole as a set which eliminates most of the market except for other dealers. Besides, most collectors do not have the finances to buy a set all at once plus the fun of pursuit is gone!

Heisey Victorian was only made in the colors listed. If you find pink, green, or amber Victorian in your travels, then you have Imperial's legacy to this pattern made from 1964 and 1965. These colors are usually marked with the H in diamond trademark; they were made from Heisey moulds after the company was no longer in business. Amber Victorian is striking, but it is Imperial and not Heisey.

Imperial also made about ten pieces in crystal, but they can not be distinguished from the original Heisey... and they are not as strictly scorned by Heisey collectors as are the colored pieces!

	Crystal		Crystal
Bottle, 3 oz., oil	65.00	Plate, 21", buffet or punch bowl liner	200.00
Bottle, 27 oz., rye	180.00	Relish, 11", 3 pt.	50.00
Bottle, French dressing	80.00	Salt & pepper	65.00
Bowl, 10½", floral	40.00	Stem, 2½ oz., wine	30.00
Bowl, finger	25.00	Stem, 3 oz., claret	28.00
Bowl, punch	250.00	Stem, 5 oz., oyster cocktail	20.00
Bowl, rose	90.00	Stem, 5 oz., saucer champagne	20.00
Bowl, triplex, w/flared or cupped rim	125.00	Stem, 5 oz., sherbet	18.00
Butter dish, ¼ lb.	70.00	Stem, 9 oz., goblet (one ball)	26.00
Candlestick, 2-lite	110.00	Stem, 9 oz., high goblet (two ball)	30.00
Cigarette box, 4"	80.00	Sugar	30.00
Cigarette box, 6"	100.00	Tray, 12", celery	40.00
Cigarette holder & ash tray, ind.	30.00	Tray, condiment (s/p & mustard)	170.00
Comport, 5"	60.00	Tumbler, 2 oz., bar	40.00
Comport, 6", 3 ball stem	140.00	Tumbler, 5 oz., soda (straight or	
Compote, cheese (for center sandwich)	40.00	curved edge)	25.00
Creamer	30.00	Tumbler, 8 oz., old fashioned	35.00
Cup, punch, 5 oz.	10.00	Tumbler, 10 oz., w/rim foot	40.00
Decanter and stopper, 32 oz.	70.00	Tumbler, 12 oz., ftd. soda	30.00
Jug, 54 oz.	350.00	Tumbler, 12 oz., soda (straight or	
Nappy, 8"	40.00	curved edge)	28.00
Plate, 6", liner for finger bowl	10.00	Vase, 4"	50.00
Plate, 7"	20.00	Vase, 5½"	60.00
Plate, 8"	35.00	Vase, 6", ftd.	100.00
Plate, 12", cracker	75.00	Vase, 9", ftd., w/flared rim	140.00
Plate, 13", sandwich	90.00		

Colors: crystal; rare in amber

This Heisey blank is known more for the Orchid and Rose etchings appearing on it than for itself.

	Crystal
Bowl, 6", oval, lemon, w/cover	40.00
Bowl, 6½", 2 hdld., ice	60.00
Bowl, 7", 3 part, relish, oblong	25.00
Bowl, 7", salad	20.00
Bowl, 9", 4 part, relish, round	25.00
Bowl, 9", fruit	30.00
Bowl, 9", vegetable	35.00
Bowl, 10", crimped edge	25.00
Bowl, 10", gardenia	20.00
Bowl, 11", seahorse foot, floral	70.00
Bowl, 12", crimped edge	35.00
Bowl, 13", gardenia	30.00
Box, 5", chocolate, w/cover	80.00
Box, 5" tall, ftd., w/cover, seahorse hand.	90.00
Box, 6", candy, w/bow tie knob	45.00
Box, trinket, lion cover (rare)	600.00
Butter dish, w/cover, 6", square	65.00
Candleholder, 1-lite, block (rare)	100.00
Candleholder, 2-lite	40.00
Candleholder, 2-lite, "flame" center	65.00
Candleholder, 3-lite	70.00
Candle epergnette, 5"	15.00
Candle epergnette, 6", deep	20.00
Candle epergnette, 6½"	15.00
Cheese dish, 5½", ftd.	20.00
Cigarette holder	60.00
Comport, 6", low ftd.	20.00
Comport, 6½", jelly	35.00
Comport, 7", low ftd., oval	50.00
Creamer, ftd.	25.00
Creamer & sugar, individual, w/tray	50.00
Cruet, 3 oz., w/#122 stopper	75.00
Cup	14.00
Honey dish, 6½", ftd.	50.00
Mayonnaise, w/liner & ladle, 5½"	50.00
Plate, 7", salad	8.00
Plate, 8", luncheon	10.00
Plate, 10½", dinner	50.00
Plate, 11", sandwich	20.00
Plate, 13½", ftd., cake salver	70.00
Plate, 14", center handle, sandwich	65.00
Plate, 14", sandwich	35.00
Salt & pepper, pr.	60.00
Saucer	4.00
Stem, #5019, 1 oz., cordial	60.00
Stem, #5019, 3 oz., wine, blown	20.00
Stem, #5019, 3½ oz., cocktail	15.00
Stem, #5019, 5½ oz., sherbet/champagne	9.00
Stem, #5019, 10 oz., blown	20.00
Sugar, ftd.	25.00
Tray, 12", celery	20.00
Tumbler, #5019, 5 oz., ftd., juice, blown	20.00
Tumbler, #5019, 13 oz., ftd., tea, blown	22.00
Vase, 3½", violet	60.00
Vase, 7", ftd.	35.00
Vase, 7", ftd., fan shape	45.00

Colors: crystal, mainly; some pieces in color

Wildflower can be found on additional Cambridge blanks. I have tried to price a significant portion of the pattern, but (as with other Cambridge patterns shown in this book) there seems to be a never ending list! You can figure that, like Rose Point, almost any Cambridge blank may have been used to etch this pattern. I have given you the basics. Price yellow, green, or gold encrusted items up to 25% higher. Most collectors are searching for crystal. Possibly the most desirable piece pictured is the hat in the bottom photograph. There are collectors of glass hats searching for these as well as Wildflower collectors.

	Crystal		Crystal
Basket, #3400/1182, 2 hdld., ftd., 6"	30.00	Plate, #3900/20, bread/butter, 6½"	7.50
Bowl, #3400/1180, bonbon, 2 hdld., 5¼"	20.00	Plate, #3900/130, bonbon, 2 hdld., 7"	17.50
Bowl, bonbon, 2 hdld., ftd., 6"	17.50	Plate, #3400/176, 7½"	10.00
Bowl, #3400/90, 2 pt., relish, 6"	17.50	Plate, #3900/161, 2 hdld., ftd., 8"	22.50
Bowl, 3 pt., relish, 6½"	25.00	Plate, #3900/22, salad, 8"	17.50
Bowl, #3900/123, relish, 7"	20.00	Plate, #3400/62, 8½"	15.00
Bowl, #3900/130, bonbon, 2 hdld., 7"	22.00	Plate, #3900/24, dinner, 10½"	67.50
Bowl, #3900/124, 2 pt., relish, 7"	25.00	Plate, #3900/26, service, 4 ftd., 12"	40.00
Bowl, #3400/91, 3 pt., relish, 3 hdld., 8"	25.00	Plate, #3900/35, cake, 2 hdld., 13½"	45.00
Bowl, #3900/125, 3 pt., celery & relish, 9"	25.00	Plate, #3900/167, torte, 14"	45.00
Bowl, #477, pickle (corn), ftd., 9½"	25.00	Plate, #3900/65, torte, 14"	45.00
Bowl, #3900/54, 4 ft., flared, 10"	37.50	Salt & pepper, #3400/77, pr.	40.00
Bowl, #3900/34, 2 hdld., 11"	45.00	Salt & pepper, #3900/1177	37.50
Bowl, #3900/28, w/tab hand., ftd., 11½"	47.50	Saucer, #3900/17 or #3400/54	3.50
Bowl, #3900/126, 3 pt., celery & relish, 12"	40.00	Set: 2 pc. Mayonnaise, #3900/19	
Bowl, #3400/4, 4 ft., flared, 12"	40.00	(ftd. sherbet w/ladle)	32.50
Bowl, #3400/1240, 4 ft., oval,		Set: 3 pc. Mayonnaise, #3900/129	
"ears" hand., 12"	45.00	(bowl, liner, ladle)	40.00
Bowl, 5 pt., celery & relish, 12"	40.00	Set: 4 pc. Mayonnaise #3900/111	
Butter dish, #3900/52, ¼ lb.	185.00	(div. bowl, liner, 2 ladles)	45.00
Butter dish, #3400/52, 5"	135.00	Stem, #3121, cordial, 1 oz.	57.50
Candlestick, #3400/638, 3-lite, ea.	35.00	Stem, #3121, cocktail, 3 oz.	22.50
Candlestick, #3400/646, 5"	27.50	Stem, #3121, wine, 3½ oz.	35.00
Candlestick, #3400/647, 2-lite,		Stem, #3121, claret, 4½ oz.	45.00
"fleur-de-lis," 6"	32.50	Stem, #3121, 4½ oz., low oyster cocktail	18.00
Candy box, w/cover, #3900/165	75.00	Stem, #3121, 5 oz., low parfait	37.50
Candy box, w/cover, #3900/165, rnd.	75.00	Stem, #3121, 6 oz., low sherbet	15.00
Cocktail icer, #968, 2 pc.	65.00	Stem, #3121, 6 oz., tall sherbet	17.50
Cocktail shaker, #3400/175	95.00	Stem, #3121, 10 oz., water	27.50
Comport, #3900/136, 5½"	35.00	Sugar, 3900/41	14.00
Comport, #3121, blown, 5⅜"	45.00	Sugar, indiv., 3900/40	20.00
Creamer, #3900/41	15.00	Tray, creamer & sugar, 3900/37	15.00
Creamer, #3900/40, individual	20.00	Tumbler, #3121, 5 oz., juice	18.00
Cup, #3900/17 or #3400/54	17.50	Tumbler, #3121, 10 oz., water	22.00
Hat, #1704, 5"	195.00	Tumbler, #3121, 12 oz., tea	27.00
Hat, #1703, 6"	250.00	Tumbler, #3900/115, 13 oz.	32.00
Hurricane lamp, #1617, candlestick base	160.00	Vase, #3400/102, globe, 5"	40.00
Hurricane lamp, #1603,		Vase, #6004, flower, ftd., 6"	40.00
keyhole base & prisms	225.00	Vase, #6004, flower, ftd., 8"	60.00
Ice bucket, w/chrome hand., #3900/671	70.00	Vase, #1237, keyhole ft., 9"	75.00
Oil, w/stopper, #3900/100, 6 oz.	85.00	Vase, #1528, bud, 10"	40.00
Pitcher, ball, #3400/38, 80 oz.	165.00	Vase, #278, flower, ftd., 11"	60.00
Pitcher, #3900/115, 76 oz.	175.00	Vase, #1299, ped. ft., 11"	75.00
Pitcher, Doulton, #3400/141	325.00	Vase, #1238, keyhole ft., 12"	110.00
Plate, crescent salad	175.00	Vase, #279, ftd., flower, 13"	125.00

Note: See pages 228 – 229 for stem identification.

Colors: crystal, Flamingo pink, Sahara yellow, Moongleam green, Hawthorne orchid/pink, Marigold deep, amber/yellow; some cobalt

Etched patterns on Yeoman blank #1184 will bring 10% to 25% more than the prices listed below. Empress etch is the most commonly found pattern on Yeoman blanks and the most collectible. Notice some tremendous price increases on the covered lemon bowls, cologne bottles, and pitchers. The main reason this pattern is so collectible is due to the colors in which it was made!

	Crystal	Flamingo	Sahara	Moongleam	Hawth.	Marigold
Ash tray, 4", hdld. (bow tie)	10.00	20.00	22.00	25.00	30.00	35.00
Bowl, 2 hdld., cream soup	12.00	20.00	25.00	30.00	35.00	40.00
Bowl, finger	5.00	11.00	17.00	20.00	27.50	30.00
Bowl, ftd., banana split	7.00	23.00	30.00	35.00	40.00	45.00
Bowl, ftd., 2 hdld., bouillon	10.00	20.00	25.00	30.00	35.00	40.00
Bowl, 4½", nappy	4.00	7.50	10.00	12.50	15.00	17.00
Bowl, 5", low, ftd., jelly	12.00	20.00	25.00	27.00	30.00	40.00
Bowl, 5", oval, lemon and cover	30.00	60.00	65.00	75.00	90.00	90.00
Bowl, 5", rnd., lemon and cover	30.00	60.00	65.00	75.00	90.00	90.00
Bowl, 5", rnd., lemon, w/cover	15.00	20.00	25.00	30.00	40.00	50.00
Bowl, 6", oval, preserve	7.00	12.00	17.00	22.00	27.00	30.00
Bowl, 6", vegetable	5.00	10.00	14.00	16.00	20.00	24.00
Bowl, 6½", hdld., bonbon	5.00	10.00	14.00	16.00	20.00	24.00
Bowl, 8", rect., pickle/olive	12.00	15.00	20.00	25.00	30.00	35.00
Bowl, 8½", berry, 2 hdld.	14.00	22.00	25.00	30.00	35.00	50.00
Bowl, 9", 2 hdld., veg., w/cover	35.00	60.00	60.00	70.00	95.00	175.00
Bowl, 9", oval, fruit	20.00	25.00	35.00	45.00	55.00	55.00
Bowl, 9", baker	20.00	25.00	35.00	45.00	55.00	55.00
Bowl, 12", low, floral	15.00	25.00	35.00	45.00	60.00	55.00
Candle Vase, single, w/short prisms & inserts	90.00			150.00		
Cigarette box (ashtray)	25.00	60.00	65.00	70.00	80.00	100.00
Cologne bottle, w/stopper	100.00	160.00	160.00	160.00	170.00	180.00
Comport, 5", high ftd., shallow	15.00	25.00	37.00	45.00	55.00	70.00
Comport, 6", low ftd., deep	20.00	30.00	34.00	40.00	42.00	48.00
Creamer	10.00	20.00	20.00	22.00	50.00	28.00
Cruet, 2 oz., oil	20.00	70.00	80.00	85.00	90.00	85.00
Cruet, 4 oz., oil	30.00	70.00	80.00	85.00		
Cup	5.00	20.00	20.00	25.00	50.00	
Cup, after dinner	20.00	40.00	40.00	45.00	50.00	60.00
Egg cup	20.00	35.00	40.00	45.00	60.00	60.00
Grapefruit, ftd.	10.00	17.00	24.00	31.00	38.00	45.00
Gravy (or dressing) boat, w/underliner	13.00	25.00	30.00	45.00	50.00	45.00
Marmalade jar, w/cover	25.00	35.00	40.00	45.00	55.00	65.00
Parfait, 5 oz.	10.00	15.00	20.00	25.00	30.00	35.00
Pitcher, quart	70.00	130.00	130.00	140.00	160.00	180.00
Plate, 2 hdld., cheese	5.00	10.00	13.00	15.00	17.00	25.00
Plate, cream soup underliner	5.00	7.00	9.00	12.00	14.00	16.00
Plate, finger bowl underliner	3.00	5.00	7.00	9.00	11.00	13.00
Plate, 4½", coaster	3.00	5.00	10.00	12.00		
Plate, 6"	3.00	6.00	8.00	10.00	13.00	15.00
Plate, 6", bouillon underliner	3.00	6.00	8.00	10.00	13.00	15.00

	Crystal	Flamingo	Sahara	Moongleam	Hawth.	Marigold
Plate, 6½", grapefruit bowl	7.00	12.00	15.00	19.00	27.00	32.00
Plate, 7"	5.00	8.00	10.00	14.00	17.00	22.00
Plate, 8", oyster cocktail	9.00					
Plate, 8", soup	9.00					
Plate, 9", oyster cocktail	10.00					
Plate, 10½"	20.00	50.00		50.00	60.00	
Plate, 10½", ctr. hand., oval, div.	15.00	26.00		32.00		
Plate, 11", 4 pt., relish	20.00	27.00		32.00		
Plate, 14"	20.00					
Platter, 12", oval	10.00	17.00	19.00	26.00	33.00	
Salt, ind. tub (cobalt: $30.00)	10.00	20.00		30.00		
Salver, 10", low ftd.	15.00	50.00		70.00		
Salver, 12", low ftd.	10.00	50.00		70.00		
Saucer	3.00	5.00	7.00	7.00	10.00	10.00
Saucer, after dinner	3.00	5.00	7.00	8.00	10.00	10.00
Stem, 2¾ oz., ftd., oyster cocktail	4.00	8.00	10.00	12.00	14.00	
Stem, 3 oz., cocktail	10.00	12.00	17.00	20.00		
Stem, 3½ oz., sherbet	5.00	8.00	11.00	12.00		
Stem, 4 oz., fruit cocktail	3.00	10.00	10.00	12.00		
Stem, 4½ oz., sherbet	3.00	10.00	10.00	12.00		
Stem, 5 oz., soda	9.00	8.00	30.00	20.00		
Stem, 5 oz., sherbet	5.00	5.00	7.00	9.00		
Stem, 6 oz., champagne	6.00	16.00	18.00	22.00		
Stem, 8 oz.	5.00	12.00	18.00	20.00		
Stem, 10 oz., goblet	10.00	15.00	35.00	25.00		
Sugar, w/cover	15.00	45.00	45.00	50.00	70.00	40.00
Sugar shaker, ftd.	50.00	95.00		110.00		
Syrup, 7 oz., saucer ftd.	30.00	75.00				
Tray, 7" x 10", rect.	26.00	30.00	40.00	35.00		
Tray, 9", celery	10.00	14.00	16.00	15.00		
Tray, 11", ctr. hand., 3 pt.	15.00	35.00	40.00			
Tray, 12", oblong	16.00	60.00	65.00			
Tray, 13", 3 pt., relish	20.00	27.00	32.00			
Tray, 13", celery	20.00	27.00	32.00			
Tray, 13", hors d'oeuvre, w/cov. ctr.	32.00	42.00	52.00	75.00		
Tray insert, 3½" x 4½"	4.00	6.00	7.00	8.00		
Tumbler, 2½ oz., whiskey	3.00	20.00	25.00	40.00		
Tumbler, 4½ oz., soda	4.00	6.00	10.00	15.00		
Tumbler, 8 oz.	4.00	15.00	20.00	20.00		
Tumbler, 10 oz., cupped rim	4.00	15.00	20.00	22.50		
Tumbler, 10 oz., straight side	5.00	15.00	20.00	22.50		
Tumbler, 12 oz., tea	5.00	20.00	25.00	30.00		
Tumbler cover (unusual)	35.00					

1066
11 oz. Goblet

1402
Brandy Inhaler (Tall)

3025
10 oz. Goblet

3035
3 oz. Cocktail

3077
6 oz. Tall Sherbet

3104
1 oz. Cordial

3106
9 oz. Goblet Tall Bowl

3115
3½ oz. Cocktail

3120
6 oz. Tall Sherbet

3121
10 oz. Goblet

3122
9 oz. Goblet

3124
3 oz. Wine

3126
11 oz. Tall Sherbet

3130
6 oz. Tall Sherbet

3135
6 oz. Tall Sherbet

3400
11 oz. Lunch Goblet

3500
10 oz. Goblet

3600
2½ oz. Wine

3775
4½ oz. Claret

3625
4½ oz. Claret

3779
1 oz. Cordial

Row 1:
Ball vase, 9" (4045) 800.00
Ball vase, 6" (4045) 525.00
Ball vase, 4" (4045) 440.00
Row 2:
Tumbler, 2½ oz., bar, Glenford (3481) 200.00
Tumbler, 5 oz., ftd., soda, Creole (3381) 100.00
Tumbler, 8½ oz., ftd., soda, Creole (3381) 110.00
Tumbler, 12 oz., ftd., soda, Creole (3381) 120.00

Row 3:
Candlesticks, Trident, pr. (134) 780.00
Plate, Yeoman (1184) 40.00
Row 4:
Vase, Cathedral (1413) 825.00
Plate, Colonial Star (1150) 325.00
Stem, 2½ oz., wine, Creole (3381) 170.00
Stem, 11 oz., water goblet, Creole (3381) 220.00

Row 1:

Iced Tea, footed, 12 oz., Old Williamsburg (341) ... 400.00
Tumbler, 2½ oz., wine, Gascony (3397).................. 190.00
Tumbler, 11 oz., low footed goblet, Gascony (3397) . 400.00
Decanter, Gascony (3397) 740.00
Tumbler, 14 oz., footed soda, New Era (4044) 175.00
Stem, 10 oz., goblet, New Era (4044) 200.00

Row 2:

Plate, Cactus (1432) 250.00
Candleholder, single, Old Sandwich (1404)........... 325.00
Beer mug, Old Sandwich (1404) 380.00
Cream pitcher, Old Sandwich (1404)...................... 575.00

Row 3:

Stem, water, Plymouth (3409) 600.00
Floral bowl, Empress (1401)................................... 400.00
Ash tray, Empress (1401).. 300.00
Candy, w/cover, Empress (1401) 450.00

Row 4:

Tumbler, Arch (1417)... 100.00
Vase, favor (4230)... 200.00
Vase, favor (4229)... 200.00
Vase, favor (4228)... 200.00
Vase, ivy ball (4224)... 250.00
Salt & pepper (25) pr 255.00
Ash tray, individual, Old Sandwich (1404)........... 60.00
Tub, salt, Revere (1183) 100.00

Row 5:

Vase, 6", ball (4045) 360.00
Vase, 2", ball (4045) 475.00
Vase, 9", ball (4045) 700.00
Vase, 12", ball (4045) 2,500.00

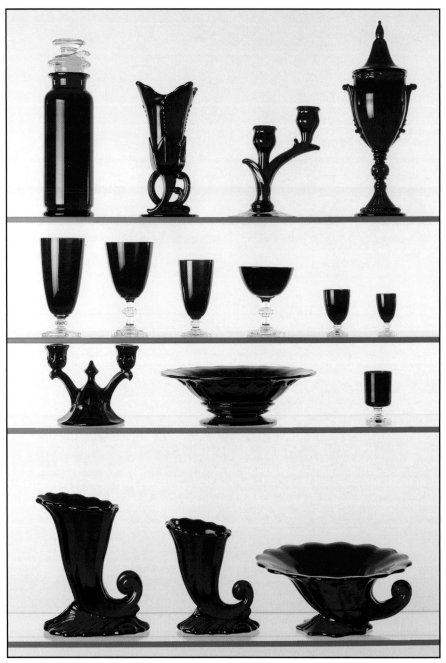

Row 1:
Cocktail shaker, Cobel (4225) 450.00
Vase, 9", Tulip (1420) 500.00
Candleholder, 2-lite, Crocus (140) 400.00
Candy, w/cover, tall, Aristocrat (1430) 1,000.00

Row 2:
Tumbler, 12 oz., soda, ftd., Carcassonne
 (3390) 70.00
Stem, 11 oz., tall stem, Carcassonne (3390) ... 100.00
Tumbler, 8 oz., soda, ftd., Carcassonne (3390). 65.00
Stem, 6 oz., saucer champagne, Carcassonne
 (3390) 55.00
Tumbler, 2½ oz., wine, ftd., Carcassonne
 (3390) 110.00
Tumbler, 1 oz., cordial, Carcassonne (3390) ... 150.00

Row 3:
Candleholder, 2-lite, Thumbprint
 and Panel (1433)... 150.00
Bowl, 12", floral, Thumbprint and Panel
 (1433) 250.00
Cigarette holder, Carcassonne (3390) 110.00

Row 4:
Vase, 9", Warwick (1428)................................ 300.00
Vase, 7", Warwick (1428)................................ 240.00
Bowl, 11", floral, Warwick (1428)................... 400.00

Row 1:
Tumbler, 5¼", 13 oz., iced tea, Coleport (1487).. 50.00
Tumbler, 4", water, Coleport (1487)............... 40.00
Sherbet, 20th Century (1415)......................... 40.00
Oil, 3 oz., Saturn (1485) 350.00
Plate, 10", dinner, Town & Country (1637)..... 175.00
Cocktail shaker, Roundelay (6009) 3,000.00
Ash tray, 6", square, Prism Square................. 125.00

Page 234, Row 1:
Sugar, Cabochon (1951)....................................... 65.00
Butter dish, ¼ lb., Cabochon (1951) 180.00
Creamer, Cabochon (1951) 65.00
Row 2:
Relish, 3 part, Cabochon (1951)..................... 75.00
Candy and cover, 6¼", Cabochon (1951)....... 280.00
Row 3:
Bowl, 12½", Town & Country (1637)............. 140.00
Bowl, 5", Town & Country (1637)................... 55.00
Bowl, 8", Town & Country (1637)................... 75.00

Row 2:
Bowl, 13", handled fruit, Fern (1495)............ 220.00
Bowl, 6¾", jelly, Leaf (1565) 50.00
Tray, 12", 4-part relish, Octagon (500)........... 350.00
Salt & pepper, Saturn (1485).......................... 340.00

Row 4:
Plate, 10", Dinner, Town & Country (1637) 175.00
Tumbler, 5¼", 13 oz., iced tea, Town &
   Country 50.00
Tumbler, 4⅜", 9 oz., Town & Country (1637) . 35.00
Plate, 8⅝", luncheon, Town & Country (1637).. 75.00

Tumbler, 5 oz., ftd. soda, Kohinoor (4085) .... $550.00+ ea.

Notice the top soda has a blue top and foot with a crystal stem while the bottom left one has a blue top and crystal stem and foot. The bottom right soda is all blue.

Row 1:

Stem, 5 oz., champagne, Duquesne
blank (3389) 165.00

Stem, 5 oz., parfait, Duquesne blank (3389)... 170.00

Stem, water, 9 oz., Duquesne blank (3389) 220.00

Tumbler, juice, ftd., 5 oz., Duquesne blank
(3389) 140.00

Row 2:

Vase, favor (4229) 700.00

Vase, favor (4232) 700.00

Plate, 8", square, Empress (1401) 150.00

Tumbler, 12 oz., ftd. soda, Spanish (3404) 360.00

Stem, 10 oz., water goblet, Spanish (3404) 430.00

Row 3:

Tumbler, 3 oz., cocktail, Gascony (3397) 180.00

Tumbler, 14 oz., ftd. soda, Gascony (3397) 160.00

Tumbler, 12 oz., ftd. soda, Gascony (3397) 150.00

Goblet, 11 oz., low ftd. Gascony (3397) 270.00

Tumbler, 10 oz., ftd. soda, Gascony
(3397) 160.00

Row 4:

Vase, ivy (4224) 225.00

Candleholder, Trident (134) 800.00

Tumbler, 14 oz., ftd. soda, Gascony (3397) 160.00

Fruit cocktail or finger side bowl, 6 oz., Gascony
(3397) 225.00

Cup, Empress blank (1401) 800.00
Saucer, Empress blank (1401) 200.00
Sugar, Empress blank (1401) 650.00
Creamer, Empress blank (1401) 650.00

There are two colors of Tiffin's Twilight; the older is represented by the last two items in the top row. This glass has the ability to look blue in artificial light and pink in natural light. It is sometimes confused with similar colors of other companies, namely Heisey's Alexandrite, Cambridge's Heatherbloom, and Fostoria's Wisteria. All the preceeding colors are enjoying a surge in collecting popularity. Tiffin's Twilight just happens to be the "new kid on the block," so to speak.

Row 1:

Bonbon, 6", ctr hdl (5480)	95.00
Horn of plenty, 13" (5508)	175.00
Juice tumbler, #17594	35.00
Candle garden (9153-110)	85.00

Row 2:

Candleholder, 7" (6554)	135.00
Cordial	65.00
Ash tray (17430)	140.00
Flower basket, Modern, 13" (6553)	150.00

Row 3:

Flower arranger, Modern (6552)	165.00
Tumbler (17430)	75.00
Lily vase, 13" (85)	275.00
Water goblet	40.00
Vase, Optic, 5-rib, 12¼"	175.00

Books By Gene Florence

Recommended Publication

DEPRESSION GLASS DAZE

P.O. Box 576F, Otisville, MI 48463

A monthly newspaper devoted to the collecting of colored glass (Depression glass & china) — features ads, articles, prices, news pertaining to this hobby (12 issues).

Club Information

National Cambridge Collectors Inc.
P.O. Box 416 GF
Cambridge, OH 43725
Dues: $17 Individual, $3 Each Associate